Spinoza and Other Heretics

THE MARRANO OF REASON

Spinoza
and
Other Heretics

THE MARRANO
OF REASON

★

YIRMIYAHU YOVEL

PRINCETON UNIVERSITY PRESS

Library of Congress Cataloging-in-Publication Data
Yovel, Yirmiahu.
Spinoza and other heretics / Yirmiyahu Yovel.
p.   cm.
Bibliography: p.
Includes index.
Contents: v. 1. The Marrano of reason.
ISBN 0-691-07344-9 (v. 1 : alk. paper)
1. Spinoza, Benedictus de, 1632–1677. 2. Marranos. 3. Immanence
(Philosophy)—History—17th century.   I. Title.
B3998.Y67 1988   88-28931
199'.492—dc19

9 8 7 6 5 4 3

Publication of this book has been aided by a grant from the
Whitney Darrow Fund of Princeton University Press
This book has been composed in Linotron Bembo

Printed in the United States of America by
Princeton University Press,
Princeton, New Jersey

49753

Acknowledgment is gratefully made to Dover Publications for per-
mission to quote from *The Chief Works of Benedict Spinoza*, tr. R. H.
Elwes (1951); and the University of California Press for quotes from
Fernando de Rojas, *The Celestina*, tr. L. B. Simpson (1971). "Baruch
Spinoza," by Jorges Luis Borges and translated from the Spanish by
Yirmiyahu Yovel, is published by arrangement with the Estate of Jorge
Luis Borges. All rights reserved.

For Jonathan

Baruch Spinoza

Like golden mist, the west lights up
The window. The diligent manuscript
Awaits, already laden with infinity.
Someone is building God in the twilight.
A man engenders God. He is a Jew
Of sad eyes and citrine skin.
Time carries him as the river carries
A leaf in the downstream water.
No matter. The enchanted one insists
And shapes God with delicate geometry.
Since his illness, since his birth,
He goes on constructing God with the word.
The mightiest love was granted him
Love that does not expect to be loved.

—Jorge Luis Borges,
translated by Yirmiyahu Yovel

Contents

Preface

Baruch Spinoza (1632–1677) is a major figure in Western intellectual history, but his role is not always fully recognized. His philosophical revolution anticipated major trends in European modernization, including secularization, biblical criticism, the rise of natural science, the Enlightenment, and the liberal-democratic state. Above all, he put forward a radically new philosophical principle that I call the philosophy of immanence. It views this-worldly existence as all there is, as the only actual being and the sole source of ethical value. God himself is identical with the totality of nature, and God's decrees are written not in the Bible but in the laws of nature and reason.

Using Spinoza as axis and a detailed documentary base, I trace the adventures of the philosophy of immanence—Spinoza's main idea—in two different paths: one preceding Spinoza and the other taking its departure from him. The result is a two-volume study, a kind of diptych. While each panel in this diptych is independent, they complement one another in an ensemble that gives a broader perspective to each.

Volume 1, *The Marrano of Reason*, identifies the origins of the idea of immanence in the undercurrents of the Marrano culture, the group from which Spinoza sprang. Marranos were former Jews in Spain and Portugal who had been forcibly converted to Christianity. For generations, however, many of them had maintained a crypto-Jewish life in secret, an experience that produced many dualities—an opposition between the inner and outer life and a mixture of the two religions that, in certain cases, led to the breakdown of both Christian and Jewish beliefs. It also made disguises, including the linguistic masks of equivocation and dual language, necessary for survival.

In the present book, I analyze this Marrano experience and identify several characteristic Marrano patterns that recur in Spinoza's case, although they are translated into a new, secular, and rationalistic context. These Marrano patterns include a this-worldly disposition; a split religious identity; a metaphysical skepticism; a quest for alternative salvation through methods that oppose the official doctrine; an opposition between the inner and the outer life, and a tendency toward dual language and equivocation. By closely examining other cases of Marrano intellectuals—both in the early phases of Marranism and among Spinoza's contemporaries—I show the recurrent nature of these patterns and how they are expressed in Spinoza while being transformed from transcendent historical religion to the domain of reason and immanence. Hence my calling Spinoza the Marrano of reason.

This book draws its evidence from diverse materials: historical documents, literary analyses, and philosophical reinterpretations of relevant Spinozistic doctrines; combined, I hope they will show in detail, and not only on the level of generalization, how Spinoza's thought was informed by his Marrano experience and acquires a new dimension when seen in this light.

The epilogue reconsiders Spinoza as a Jewish heretic. A philosopher of immanence and secularization, was he also the first secular Jew? And what, more generally, was his relation to his people, as paradigmatic for the rest of humanity?

In the second volume, *The Adventures of Immanence*, I set out to uncover traces of Spinoza's revolution at some major stations in the history of modern philosophy. Since the late eighteenth century, Spinoza's philosophy of immanence has tacitly or expressly penetrated the major currents of modern thought and has helped to shape the modern mind far beyond what is usually recognized. That thinkers from Goethe to Hegel, Heine, Marx, Nietzsche, Freud, and Einstein have seen themselves in some major sense as Spinozists is significant; it suggests that much of the history of modern thought can be retold—and illuminated—from the standpoint of Spinoza's immanent revolution. This is what I do in the second book.

The Adventures of Immanence tells a conceptual story, and thereby also draws a map of the logical possibilities of construing a philosophy of immanence, as those possibilities have actually emerged in response to Spinoza and to other attempts to reinterpret and develop his ideas. The result is a tacit dialogue in the book among some of the most important modern approaches to the philosophy of immanence. In the epilogue, I use the outline of this debate to argue that a philosophy of immanence must also be a philosophy of *finitude*, and I work out a distinction between a dogmatic and a critical philosophy of immanence.

I wrote these books for a lay audience no less than for scholars. I tried to avoid unnecessary jargon and relegated the scholarly apparatus to the endnotes, in order to let the text flow unimpeded. And although each volume can be read as an independent book, together they will show how the idea of immanence took shape in a marginal and hybrid historical group—the Marranos—and then, crystallized and powerfully systematized in Spinoza, found its way into the general European context, where it became a distinct factor of modernization.

When saying that Spinoza "transcended" Christianity and Judaism, I mean that he went beyond both, even while secularizing some of their themes. As for the word *heretics*, it should be taken with a grain of salt. I use it to designate thinkers who, when properly understood, must be deemed heretical in terms of their own orthodox tradition. Again, no derogatory undertones are intended; if anything, a reader discerning a shade of ironic sympathy in the title will not be totally mistaken.

Earlier versions of a few chapters, or parts of them, have previously appeared in the following publications: "Why Was Spinoza Excommunicated?" *Commentary*, November 1977, 46–52; "Marranisme et dissidence: Spinoza et quelques prédecesseurs," *Cahiers Spinoza* 3 (1980): 67–99; "Spinoza and His People: The First Secular Jew?" *Jerusalem Quarterly* 33 (1984): 50–63; and "Spinoza: The Psychology of the Multitude and the Uses of Language," *Studia Spinozana* 1 (1985): 305–33.

Many persons have helped me in one way or another. Most prominent among them is a man I never met, the late Professor Israel Révah. That I cannot agree with some of the conclusions he drew from the all-important documents he had discovered does not detract from my debt and admiration. His disciple Henri Méchoulan, a Spinoza scholar himself, was graciously cooperative despite my differences with the Master; so were, in France, my friends Pierre-François Moreau, Alexandre Matheron, Yvon Belaval, Pierre Macherey, Sylvain Zac, Jean Marie Beyssade, Etienne Balibar, and many others in the Association des Amis de Spinoza. Raymond Polin, Janine Chanteur, and Geneviève Rodis-Lewis have made my two-year visiting professorship at the Sorbonne even more worthwhile, as has Jean-Luc Marion. In the United States, Edwin Curley, Alan Donagan, Margaret Wilson, and George Kline have made pertinent comments on my Spinoza interpretation, as did Emilia Giancotti and Filippo Mignini in Italy, Manfred Walther in Germany, Wim Klever and the late Hubertus Hubbeling in the Netherlands. Special thanks are due to my erstwhile teacher and longtime colleague Shlomo Pines, whose vast knowledge and subdued voice have never blunted the sting of a good philosophical talk, especially about Spinoza or Maimonides. In Richard Popkin, I have long found a source of inspiration and growing debate about the Marranos. Yosef Yerushalmi, in person and through his work, provided reliable postsigns for the wanderer in Marranoland. I regret not having met the late Stephen Gilman, whose work on Rojas enriched me. In Israel, I drew on Marrano documents published by Chaim Beinart and was particularly encouraged by Maurice Kriegel's pointed comments. Yoseph Kaplan first introduced me to Révah's work. Elhanan Yakira, my former assistant and present colleague, has provided valuable help in the first years of this project. Abraham Mansbach was meticulous in rechecking many notes.

The two-volume text and the often complicated notes—many about Uriel Da Costa—were diligently typed by Florence Da Costa, perhaps a relation of the famous heretic, though she can't be certain. Above all, I am thankful to my longtime collaborator and friend, Eva Shorr, Managing Editor of the philosophical quarterly *Iyyun*, for investing as much of her competence and devotion in this work as she had in many of my earlier publications.

Thanks are due to the Hebrew University of Jerusalem and its Spinoza Research Center; to the University of Paris–IV (Paris-Sorbonne); to the *Ecole des Hautes Etudes en Sciences Sociales* and its former president François Furet; to the Israel Academy of Sciences and Humanities; and to Wolfson College, Oxford, for help and hospitality during my visits.

Last but certainly not least, my dear friend Yitzhak Torchin, a physician-philosopher in the style of Spinoza's time, and his most elegant wife Suzanne, have warmly welcomed me to their country house in Barbizon, France, with its gracious surroundings and its library well stocked in Spinozana, where I labored my way through several chapters of this book. To both of them, *merci de tout mon coeur*.

Note on Sources

Bibliographical references are given in the endnotes to each chapter. When possible, the more accessible editions were used.

Translations from non-English documents, when not otherwise indicated, were made by the author.

The standard edition of Spinoza's work to date is *Spinoza Opera*, edited by Carl Gebhardt (Heidelberg: Carl Winter, 1925). For the English version I used *The Collected Works of Spinoza*, vol. 1, edited and translated by Edwin Curley (Princeton: Princeton University Press, 1985). To quote from the *Theologico-Political Treatise* (due to appear in Curley's vol. 2), I used the translation of R. H. Elwes in *The Chief Works of Benedict de Spinoza*, 2 vols. (New York: Dover, 1951), vol. 2.

Short titles and abbreviations used include:

Treatise on the Intellect = *Treatise on the Emendation of the Intellect* (quoted by section number).

Short Treatise = *Short Treatise on God, Man and His Well-Being* (quoted by part and chapter numbers).

TTP = *Theologico-Political Treatise* (quoted by Elwes's page numbers).

Metaphysical Thoughts = *Appendix Containing Metaphysical Thoughts* (quoted by Curley's page numbers).

Ethics = *Ethics Demonstrated in Geometrical Order.*

The following abbreviations apply to the *Ethics*: pt. = part; prop. = proposition; S = scholium; dem. = demonstration; exp. = explanation; ax. = axiom; def. = definition; C = corallary.

Spinoza and Other Heretics

THE MARRANO OF REASON

CHAPTER I

Prologue: Heretic and Banned

On July 27, 1656, a sentence of excommunication was pronounced on a twenty-four-year-old Jew of the Portuguese community of Amsterdam and recorded in the communal record book:

The Gentlemen of the *Ma'amad* [i.e., the Ruling Council] make known to you, that having for some time known the evil opinions and works of Baruch de Espinoza, they have endeavored by various ways and promises to draw him back from his evil ways; and not being able to remedy him, but on the contrary, receiving every day more news about the horrible heresies he practices and taught [to others], and the awful deeds he performed, and having of this many reliable testimonies, all given in the presence of the said Espinoza, which convinced them; and all this having been examined in the presence of the Gentlemen *Hahamim* [Rabbis], they resolved with the latter's consent that the said Espinoza be put to the *herem* [ban] and banished from the nation of Israel, as indeed they proclaim the following *herem* on him:

"By the decree of the Angels and the word of the Saints we ban, cut off, curse and anathemize Baruch de Espinoza . . . with all the curses written in the Torah [*Ley*]: Cursed be he by day and cursed by night, cursed in his lying down and cursed in his waking up, cursed in his going forth and cursed in his coming in; and may the L[ord] not want his pardon, and may the L[ord]'s wrath and zeal burn upon him . . . and ye that did cleave unto the L[ord] your G[od] are all alive today."

We warn that none may contact him orally or in writing, nor do him any favor, nor stay under the same roof with him, nor read any paper he made or wrote.★

★ Folio 408 of *Livro dos Acordos da Naçam*, A[nn]o 5398–5440, as transcribed (from

The object of this excommunication, Baruch d'Espinoza, belonged to the upper crust of the Jewish community. His father, Michael, was a highly respected merchant active in civic affairs who had served several times as a *parnas* (elder), an extremely powerful office in Amsterdam. The young Baruch (Bento) received a traditional Jewish education, studying Hebrew and Scripture, Talmud and Jewish philosophy, and also read independently on secular subjects (including works in Hebrew on mathematics, physics, and astronomy), preparing himself for a life in commerce. At the age of six he lost his mother, Hana Devora, and from then on death visited the family frequently, taking his younger brother, Yitzhak, his sister, Miriam, his stepmother, Esther, and finally his father.

Spinoza was twenty-two when his father died. Together with his brother, Gabriel, he founded a commercial company—Bento et Gabriel d'Espinoza—for the import and export of fruit. The venture was only moderately successful, and on one occasion the brothers suffered losses due to a shipwreck. During this period, Spinoza continued to attend the Keter Torah yeshivah headed by Rabbi Shaul Levi Morteira, and apparently also kept up his connection with his former teacher, Rabbi Menasseh ben Israel, whose home was a center for scholars and educated Jews passing through Amsterdam. On the surface, at least, no change was as yet perceptible in Spinoza's relations with the Jewish community; for more than a year after his father's death he continued to be on good terms with the synagogue authorities, was scrupulous in the payment of his dues and the honoring of his pledges, and was not involved in any open conflicts with authority.

Nevertheless, he was apparently full of doubts and heretical thoughts. He knew the Bible by heart and found many contradictions in it. The notion of miracles, for example, seemed to him to contradict both reason and the laws of nature, and in the prophets he found evidence of great imaginative power but not of ordered rational thought. The ordinances of the Torah (written law) and the *halakah* (oral law) seemed to him arbitrary and merely historical, having nothing to do with the laws of God. If God did indeed have laws, they could only be inherent in the universe itself, in the form of the universal and immutable laws of nature. Moreover, in view of the death that awaits all, (and which Spinoza himself had already encountered from the years of his early childhood on), there was no comfort in the vain idea of a life

---

photocopy) by I. S. Révah in *Spinoza et Juan de Prado* (Paris-The Hague: Mouton, 1959), "Textes et documents," pp. 57–58 (my tr.). The *Livro dos Acordos* (also known as *Ascamot* [Hebrew for *Acordos*]) is part of the archives of the Jewish-Portuguese community, kept at the Amsterdam Municipal Archives (and in photocopied form in Jerusalem).

to come. Death was the absolute end of every living creature, of both body and soul; if there was any value or purpose in life, it had to be found in this world—in a life of inquiry and understanding and in the intellectual freedom of the individual.[1] Spinoza still clung to the idea of the eternal, the infinite, the perfect—in other words, the idea of God—but this deity was not in his view a unique and separate person existing outside the world and the nature he had created. God, the object of man's love, was rather the universe itself, insofar as it could be grasped as a single whole. Nature and God were one, and the knowledge of nature was therefore the knowledge of God.

It is not known when these ideas matured in the mind of the heterodox youth, but the process apparently began at a rather early age. About four years after his excommunication, the first part of Spinoza's most important work, the *Ethics*, which contains the essence of his pantheism, already existed in manuscript form. With these ideas Spinoza distanced himself from both Judaism and Christianity, and even from the accepted philosophical tradition; he was a heretic not only from the point of view of the established religions, but also from the point of view of the freethinkers and from the several varieties of philosophic deism they were espousing at the time. Deism rejects religion in the name of an external and remote philosophic deity that does not intervene in the affairs of this world and does not possess the attributes of particular providence, punishment and reward, commandment, or ritual. But the deistic heretics at least acknowledged the existence of a transcendent deity elevated above the world, whereas Spinoza dismissed this idea and identified God with the whole of the universe. In short, Spinoza proclaimed himself a heretic not only among the faithful, but also among representatives of the accepted heresy of his period, thus separating himself from all of the major spiritual currents of his time.

In its mature form, Spinoza's system is one of the most important in the history of philosophy. Although he had few actual disciples, it has simply not been possible, ever since the modern republication of his works, to participate in the enterprise of philosophy without taking his world view into account. In the words of Henri Bergson, "Every philosopher has two philosophies: his own and Spinoza's."[2] It is no coincidence that minds as opposed as Hegel's and Nietzsche's, for example, both saw Spinoza as their great forerunner. His doctrine is more complex and multifaceted than it might at first appear.

But Spinoza's ethics and metaphysics—the essence of his teaching— were not his first achievements. They were preceded by a profound critique of religion and a vigorous attack on its sacred texts—first and foremost the Bible. When he wrote this critique, the young Spinoza, who did not know Latin, had not yet read the new scientific and philosophical works that would change the face of the age. He had not come into contact with the students of Descartes and the scholars of the Royal Society of London, and was not acquainted with Hobbes, Machiavelli, or Galileo. He developed his reflections and criticisms of religion solely from within the world of contemporary Judaism—a world far more complex and varied than one might imagine today.

The Jews of Amsterdam in Spinoza's time have been described both in literary works and by historians (mainly those following Heinrich Graetz) as a narrow-minded and fanatical lot who deliberately shut themselves off from any spark of enlightenment from the outside world. This picture is inaccurate. The truth of the matter is that the Amsterdam community was one of the most enlightened and cosmopolitan Jewish communities of the period. The people who inhabited Amsterdam's Jewish Street—which was worlds apart from the closed ghettos of eastern Europe—were former Marranos or sons of Marranos, most of them prosperous businessmen living in relative freedom within a tolerant state. Engaged mainly in import and export and other forms of international commerce, they were accustomed to mingling with Gentiles, and were open-minded and receptive, having been educated in the schools of Spain and Portugal, or later on in the flourishing educational system developed by the Amsterdam community itself. At the same time, their experience as former Marranos was a never-ending source of perplexity to them, an experience that led to difficulties of adjustment and deep-seated problems of identity. It is against this background that one must view both Spinoza's heresy and the excommunication that was its result.

Some have seen in the Marranos the "beginning of modernization in Europe."[3] Even without going so far, however, it is clear that a person who had been educated as a Christian and who then chose to return to Judaism could not belong entirely or simply to either faith. He would of necessity be faced with enormous difficulties in reintegrating himself into the community to which he indeed belonged, but whose daily life and deepest values and symbols were not actually part of his experience. It is not hard to understand how a man who is neither a Christian nor a Jew, but who is divided between the two or who possesses memories of the one existing within the other, might be inclined to develop doubts about both, or even to question the foundations of religion altogether. As Yosef Yerushalmi has argued, the wonder is not that the return of the Marranos to Judaism gave rise to doubts and heresies, but rather that the majority should have succeeded as far as they did in reintegrating themselves into the framework of normative Judaism.[4] In any case, Spinoza did not lack predecessors in his heresy among the Marranos—the dough of the "New Jews" seems to have contained a leavening agent that gave rise to a constant intellectual ferment from within.

Uriel Da Costa had twice been excommunicated for rejecting the oral law and the rabbinical canons of Judaism and for denying the immortality of the soul. Twice he had recanted, only to commit suicide in the end, after many harassments and humiliations. Indeed, Bento Baruch d'Espinoza, who was only eight years old when Da Costa killed himself, may very well have been among the little boys whose persecutions Da Costa had complained of during his ordeal. In any case, by the time Spinoza grew up and began to think for himself, both the fate and the views of Uriel Da Costa must have provided him with food for thought, just as he must certainly have been aware of the less spectacular cases of nonconformity that were then troubling the community. It is widely claimed that Spinoza's critique of religion was influenced above all by his reading of Jewish philosophy. But why should the boy have pored over ancient Jewish texts and extracted from them elements that might have sounded heretical out of context (although in context they remain in the framework of legitimate Judaism) unless there was some incentive in his external environment? There is no doubt that Spinoza's apostasy contained an element of spontaneous awakening—that spiritual breakthrough of a solitary genius which cannot be fully explained by a set of foregoing events. Yet this breakthrough did not occur in the void but within a specific social and cultural milieu, which must be taken into account if one is to understand the phenomenon of Spinoza at all.

COMING INTO THE OPEN

The curious fact that, until a mere six months before his excommunication, Spinoza continued to conform externally to the norms of Jewish life in his community may be explained by his own rules of caution, which state that we must "speak according to the understanding of ordinary people" and "conform to the customs of the community that do not conflict with our aims."[5] Although he was one of the most independent thinkers of his generation and displayed an extreme and extraordinary boldness in his intellectual attitudes, Spinoza was not interested in making a public show of his opinions or boasting of his intellectual independence. On the contrary, a combination of spiritual elitism and personal caution (both of which he inherited from Maimonides, among others) led him to speak in a covert language and to confine his activities to a small circle of trusted friends and acquaintances. Even in his most provocative book, the *Theologico-Political Treatise*, Spinoza continued to disguise his true opinions and to speak in the "language of the multitude." The ring he wore—this freest and boldest spirit of his generation—was engraved with the warning *caute* (carefully), and Spinoza remained true to this combination of daring and caution all his life. How then can one account for the fact that one day in the autumn of 1655 he suddenly began making his opinions public and became so disruptive a presence in the synagogue that, after several warnings, he was finally excommunicated and anathematized?

Two compatible conjectures are possible here. Spinoza's first biographer, Jean M. Lucas, claims that the break with the Jewish community was a product of Spinoza's own wishes;[6] at a certain stage, Spinoza discovered that his pretended conformity was beginning to conflict with his spiritual goals, and so he discontinued it. Other sources point to the influence of Juan de Prado, an Andalusian physician who had been active for many years in the Marrano underground in Spain. By leading an underground life, Prado had succeeded in escaping the clutches of the Inquisition only to fall prey, in the very midst of his activities as a secret Jew, to profound theological doubts. By the time he finally escaped to Amsterdam (less than a year before Spinoza's excommunication), these doubts had been articulated—he began to express his deistic opinions publicly, to mock the rabbis, and to transgress openly against the commandments of Judaism. Prado was an educated man who had studied science and philosophy, but he was also vain and arrogant, and he could not resist the temptation to boast of his scholarship and enlightened views. He was about twelve years older than Spinoza, and it is reasonable to suppose that when they first met in Amsterdam, the young Baruch found in him a man with whom he could discuss his own doubts. Along with Prado, an even more famous heretic appeared in Amsterdam at this time—the Calvinist theologian Isaac La Peyrère, an early biblical critic, and a friend of Spinoza's teacher Menasseh ben Israel.

It is possible that meeting these two men accelerated processes in Spinoza that were already well under way. If nothing else, these meetings doubtless helped put an end to Spinoza's isolation—the isolation of a young man who had no one with whom he could share his doubts—and must have encouraged him to be more explicit both with himself and with others. More specifically, it is possible that these contacts helped Spinoza make up his mind to declare his independence and detach himself from the daily rituals of Judaism, even at the possible cost of cutting himself off from the community.

Once Spinoza had reached this decision, nothing could stop him. He ceased attending services at the synagogue, broke the commandments of the Torah, and began to reveal his doubts to those of his acquaintances he felt he could trust. He still did not perpetrate these offenses in public, but he did at least put an end to his former pretense. The leaders of the community did what they could to dissuade him, and there is even a conjecture that among the "various means and promises" they employed (as itemized in the writ of excommunication) was an attempt to bribe him to take part in synagogue services. Similar pressure was put on Prado, since the scandal involved them both, but the reactions of the two friends were very different. Prado preferred to continue the double life he had become accustomed to in the Marrano underground in Spain and fought doggedly to remain within the Jewish community. Spinoza, however, stood up openly for his ideas, composed a detailed defense of his actions that has unfortunately not survived (although the main points seem to be included in the *Theologico-Political Treatise*), and resigned himself to excommunication and isolation.

THE BAN (HEREM)

Drastic though it may sound to modern ears, excommunication was a fairly common sanction in the Jewish community of Amsterdam. Most cases were not prominent but part of an almost routine procedure. Even Rabbi Menasseh ben Israel himself was once banned—though only for a day—for alleged implication in some affair involving taxes and the misuse of propaganda materials. Grounds for excommunication, as laid down in the community regulations, were not confined to heresy and blasphemy, but also included such seemingly minor transgressions as speaking too loudly or carrying weapons in the synagogue, disseminating libelous literature, organizing private prayers, representing the Jewish community without the permission of the *parnasim*, and associating with people who had refused to pay taxes[7]—all of which indicates that excommunication was primarily an internal sanction used by the community as a way of enforcing and maintaining discipline and authority over its members.

Those empowered to pronounce the ban were not the rabbis but the civil authorities, represented by the council known as the *ma'amad*, which was made up of six parnasim (elders) and a *gabbai* (treasurer). The *ma'amad*, which enjoyed both executive and judicial powers, was accountable to no one and was not even elected by the community, its members (like the Amsterdam burgomasters) having been appointed by their predecessors. Among the functions of the *parnasim* were those often associated with rabbis or religious officials, such as supervision of ritual-slaughter practices. They also had authority to impose excommunication, though it was carried out in consultation with the rabbis and with their consent.

Many hypotheses have been put forward to explain Spinoza's excommunication. One school argues that the reasons were political and stemmed from the community's relations with the outside world rather than from its own internal needs. Those holding this view base their case on the circumstances in which the Jews had been permitted to settle in the United Provinces and especially in Amsterdam. In 1615 the States-General of Holland and West-Frieseland had asked two officials to propose a Jewish policy: one was the young Hugo Grotius, then *pensionaris* (a legal counsel with chief executive powers) of Rotterdam, and Adriaan Pauw, who held that office in Amsterdam. Each of them presented his proposals separately. Grotius recommended that Jews be allowed to settle "and do business and manufacture, enjoying freedom, exemptions and privileges in the same way as the other burghers and citizens" (art. 6). But Grotius was aware that the Marrano immigrants had more than their share of "atheists and impious people" who, he declared, "should not be tolerated in any good republic." So he demanded all Jews over fourteen years of age to state their faith in God, Moses, the prophets, and the afterlife.[8] Grotius's *Remonstrantie*, as it is known, has never been written into law (neither was Pauw's, which some say was more restrictive, others say more liberal). The actual regulations passed in 1619 concerning the Amsterdam Jews did not adopt either resolution but rather authorized each city to make its own regulations. However—so the argument goes—the Jews had to take seriously the concerns of a person such as Grotius. They could not afford to be branded as sympathetic to atheism.

Plausible though it may sound, this hypothesis has its weaknesses. It is true that in 1619 the Jewish community was still in its infancy and fighting to secure its position in the Dutch republic. It is also true that at the time of the *Remonstrantie*, Calvinist orthodoxy was at the height of its powers, calling for the subjection of the state to the laws of religion and persecuting its opponents within the Christian faith. But Spinoza's excommunication took place about forty years later and in completely different circumstances. Calvinist orthodoxy was in retreat by this time, and the republican party, much more tolerant in its views, was in power. About six months after Spinoza's excommunication, the Netherlands States-General approved a resolution stating that theology and philosophy must be kept apart, thereby providing a basic legal safeguard for the freedom of philosophical inquiry. Moreover, the statesman Johan de Witt, the strong man of the republic (who later befriended Spinoza) was himself a cautious defender of the freedom of philosophical inquiry at the universities. In addition, the Amsterdam Jews had demonstrated their political influence and confidence in 1654 by successfully lobbying for the right of their co-religionists to settle in New Amsterdam (as New York was then called), against the stubborn opposition of the Dutch governor, Peter Stuyvesant. By 1656 the Amsterdam Jews were fairly secure, and it is difficult to imagine that Spinoza's excommunication took place simply in the name of the ancient regulations, which had never been enforced anyway, and had by then lost much of their force as a statement of principle as well. Indeed, there is room to suppose that Spinoza's excommunication was if anything opposed to the new religious policy then taking shape within the circles in power in the Netherlands.

This being the case, some scholars have argued that the political reason for Spinoza's excommunication had nothing to do with the position of the Jews in the Netherlands, but hinged rather on the possibility of their return to England.[9] On the very day of the excommunication, Spinoza's former teacher Menasseh ben Israel was in London, where he was attempting to persuade Oliver Cromwell to allow Jews (who had been expelled in the thirteenth century) to resettle in England. Scholars have argued, accordingly, that Spinoza's excommunication was a means of facilitating this scheme. To mollify opponents of Jewish resettlement and dispel their fears that the Jews might bring heretical ideas and religious apostasy to Puritan England, it was necessary to suppress any manifestations of apostasy in Amsterdam. This is an intriguing theory, but there is no evidence to support it. In the first place, Rabbi Menasseh did not have much influence in Amsterdam; in the second place, the notion of the return of the Jews to England was probably Menasseh's own personal (and essentially messianic) idea rather than the official policy of the Amsterdam Jewish community.

There is another variation of the political explanation of Spinoza's excommunication—one that has a peculiarly contemporary ring. This is the argument that blame for the excommunication rests not on the Jewish community of Amsterdam, but rather on the burgomasters of the city, who had intimated to the parnasim that Spinoza should be excommunicated. This theory, however, completely distorts the significance of the excommunication in its own time and prevents one from seeing its justification in terms of the life of the community, as well as inside the drama embodied in the whole affair.

POLITICAL REASONS ARE SECONDARY

Even if the decision to excommunicate Spinoza was influenced by political considerations, this should not blind one to the fact that the inside life of the Amsterdam Jewish community and its unique situation provide sufficient reason for the excommunication. The need to rid itself of Spinoza (as also of Da Costa and Prado) stemmed primarily from the requirements of the community's survival and the difficult task of creating a shelter for the refugees fleeing the Inquisition. The rabbis and elders of the Amsterdam community were faced with a historic responsibility: reintroducing the so-called New Jews into the religious traditions of Judaism and thereby renewing a process of historic continuity that had been cruelly disrupted. This was far from a simple task; in some respects it was an impossible one. Organic continuity could not simply be mandated, nor could the Christian-Marrano past of the New Jews be excised and replaced by an uncomplicated Jewish identity. Spinoza's apostasy stemmed in part from this problem, but so did the necessity for his excommunication.

Because the Amsterdam community was engaged in a continuous daily struggle to reintegrate the Marranos into Judaism, the issue of unity was necessarily more crucial than any other. The problem faced by the Amsterdam rabbis, and by the community's teachers and publicists, was not only to translate Jewish culture into the idiom of the Iberian peninsula, but more important to restore the daily pattern of Jewish life in accordance with the ancient customs of Israel. In light of this necessity, such acts as Spinoza's, which challenged tradition in the name of freedom of thought and sabotaged the endeavor to repair the torn fabric of Jewish life, could not be tolerated. In fact, the emphasis throughout the proceedings against Spinoza was more on his acts than on his opinions (so long as he kept those to himself); for the survival of Judaism—as Spinoza himself was later to maintain—had never depended on theory, but rather on a complex network of specific and particular actions.

The Amsterdam community, it must be remembered, was still living in the shadow of the Inquisition, whose persecutions continued unabated on the Iberian peninsula. Refugees from Spain and Portugal continued to arrive in Holland in a steady stream. In May 1655, fourteen months before Spinoza was excommunicated, one Abraham Nuñez Bernal, who had relatives and acquaintances in Amsterdam, was burned at the stake in Cordova; the community was shaken by the news. Two months earlier, amother young martyr, Yitzhak da Alameida Bernal, had been burned at the stake in Galicia; Spinoza himself speaks in his letter of a third victim of the Inquisition, Judah the Believer, whose fate must surely have shocked him deeply. The Amsterdam community was living in a state of emergency: it was fighting to crystallize its own Jewish life from within and at the same time to provide both physical security and a new social and spiritual identity to the refugees from the Inquisition. Against this background, Spinoza's challenge could be interpreted as profoundly dangerous to the community—an action that had to be countered by every possible means.

On the other hand, Spinoza's stand was also justified. Against the weight of tradition, Spinoza demanded that the tradition itself be subjected to the test of his individual judgment and reason, and he refused to accept any truth—or any practical or moral commandment—unless it was compatible with his own subjective consciousness when following the guidelines of universal reason. From the point of view of the guardians of the tradition that he was questioning, this was an act of destruction and subversion; from the point of view of his dignity and freedom as a person, it was an act of progress and emancipation. In this sense, Spinoza's break with both Judaism and Christianity was a harbinger of the modern era.

JUSTICE AGAINST JUSTICE

Spinoza's excommunication should thus be seen as a nontragic clash between two valid points of view. Hegel defined tragedy as the clash of justice with justice; in Spinoza's case the drama ended without a fall, without death or extraordinary suffering, and therefore without tragedy. Indeed, legend has greatly exaggerated his case. He was never impoverished, he was never the victim of persecution, and he was not a social outcast. Although he had cut himself off from all religious affiliations, and although he was alone in the deepest sense of the word (having no true intellectual or spiritual peers even among his colleagues), Spinoza did not lead the life of an embittered or alienated man, but remained open to social relationships and had both friends and admirers. Nor did he lack the means of a livelihood. Though his needs were modest, he did not deny himself the small pleasures of life, and he scorned the ascetic ideal both personally and on principle.

The notion that he was obliged to grind lenses for a living is also highly exaggerated. In fact, Spinoza lived on a rather adequate allowance provided by friends to enable him to pursue his studies. He ground lenses mainly to further his own research into optics, which was then a new science. In one respect, though, the legend is not entirely inaccurate: it is possible that the glass dust from the lenses may have hastened the progression of the hereditary lung disease (apparently tuberculosis) from which Spinoza suffered, a disease for which the causes were not then known, and from which Spinoza died at the age of forty-four on February 21, 1677.

Spinoza, the Marrano of Reason

THE MARRANOS

For half a millennium, Spain had been the major Jewish center of the world and the gem of the Diaspora. Having flourished under Moslem rule, Spanish Jewry retained its vitality in the early days of the reconquest, but was already past its prime as the Christians seized control over most of the peninsula. Then, in the span of one century (1391–1492), it cracked, struggled, and was extinguished.

1391 was a bitter year in the annals of Spanish Jewry. In a crisis of government, the mob, incited by the petty clergy and by a disenchanted archdeacon, was unleashed in Seville. Soon the riots spread to the rest of Andalusia and then all over Aragon and Castile. "Death or the Cross" was the cry everywhere as the mob streamed forth killing and burning. In town after town, thousands of Jews were dragged to the font or flocked there by their own choice, accepting baptism in order to save their lives. Martyrdom, though known, was rare.

In less than a year, Spanish Jewry lost a significant segment of its population—many by the sword, most to the Cross. Then, shattered and traumatized, its morale giving way, it witnessed the waves of voluntary conversions that followed the forced ones. When political order was restored, religious pressure, especially in Aragon, became official. Vicente Ferrer, a religious reformer and zealous missionary, terrorized the Jews in 1411 and 1412 as he marched through their neighborhoods at the head of a troop of barefoot flagellant monks and stormed into their synagogues in an effort to convert them by what he thought was persuasion. Antipope Benedictus XIII, meanwhile, organized a grandiose and well-orchestrated theological show—the so-called Tortosa dispute—where for about two years (1412–1414) Jewish rabbis and dignitaries were forced to argue with a renegade Jew, in an attempt to break further the Jews' morale and drive more of them to baptism.

These efforts combined to produce, in less than a quarter century, a new social phenomenon in Spain that was to evolve and mark the history of Iberia for several centuries to come: the *conversos*, or Jewish converts to Christianity, and their descendants. To distinguish them from the rest of the population, they were also called New Christians, a name that clung to their offspring from generation to generation and soon took on a pejorative connotation. The Jews called them the "forced ones" (Heb. *anussim*) and debated their legal and religious status. And, from early on, they were also known as Marranos, an originally abusive name that has become descriptive.

While many (perhaps most) of the conversos and their descendants sought integration into Catholic society, a substantial group retained Jewish rites (or a version of them) in secret. These Judaizing Marranos, as they are known, persevered in their secret Judaism for several centuries, first in Spain and later in Portugal. The Judaizing Marranos were the cause of the official worry and subsequent harassment and persecution that spread to the non-Judaizing Marranos as well.

During the first century of Marranism, Marranos and Jews lived side by side in Spain. Some socialized with one another, others kept their distance, but the two groups were separated by a rigid, one-way legal fence. While canon law disapproved of forced conversions, it considered their results as absolutely binding. Full-fledged Jews could continue practicing their own rites and religion, but for a converso to relapse into Judaism was a major crime. Baptism, even involuntary, was sacred and irreversible.

Conversion, on the other hand, removed legal barriers from the former Jews' way because it made them, at least officially, brothers in Jesus and thereby the equals of the Old Christian population. In a spurt of newfound energy, conversos penetrated into all fields of Spanish society, which was then more open and less hostile to the New Christians than it was soon to become. Conversos rose to prominence in commerce and industry, in learning and public service, and even in the ranks of the clergy and nobility. By marrying into aristocratic Old Christian families, some noble converso clans could claim a lineage back to King David, or at least to the ancestors of the Virgin Mary—a distinction no Old Christian could boast of. Conversos, however, retained not only their lineages but, more important, many of their old occupational patterns and habits as Jews, including commercial agility and a Jewish disposition to mutual help—which put them in the vanguard of the new urban bourgeoisie and, in the next century, of the protocapitalist and entrepreneurial class that was then budding in Spain and Portugal.

Yet within a few decades of the first mass conversions, envy and harsh competition from Old Christians began to be felt. Toledo in 1449 was the scene of the first serious anticonverso pogroms—again during a crisis of government and a local revolt. Since the call for discrimination against the New Christians could no longer be based upon religion, it translated itself into terms of heredity—"blood." New Christians had inferior and impure blood; they were bad Christians by birth and contaminated in their very existence, whatever their professed religion. Hence they must be barred from various public and ecclesiastical offices and honors.

A theological scandal born in political rebellion, the Statutes of the Purity of Blood were at first denounced by both the pope and the king, and were not applied until the next century. It was under Philip II that they finally triumphed and became the law of the realm in Spain and later in Portugal, spreading their rule over other races as well (black Africans, Chinese, and Moors) and into the Iberian colonies.

The Catholic Monarchs and the Inquisition

The next two stages in Marrano history were dominated by the Catholic monarchs, Fernando and Isabel, who laid the foundations of modern unified Spain and of its empire. As they ascended the thrones of Aragon and Castile, they established their own Spanish Inquisition (no longer under the pope in Rome) as a political tool in forging the new absolutist state. The primary and official reason was to purge the land of the heresies and religious contamination of the Judaizing Marranos, while other kinds of heretics and the traditional witches were not overlooked. A wave of terror, suspicion, and true and false denunciation spread over Spain from south to north. Marranos were harassed and burned at the stake in new public rituals known as "acts of faith" (*autos-de-fé*—later, in Portugal, called *autos-da-fé*). Despite its fierce methods, the Inquisition was deemed more efficient in spreading royal power everywhere than in purging Judaizers from the realm. It was argued that so long as professing Jews were allowed to live alongside the Marranos in Spain, secret Judaizing would continue. The most effective way of combating it would be to expel all the Jews—an action that would also help forge, so it was believed, the unity of Spain and its messianic mission by stressing its religious homogeneity.

As Granada, the last Moslem stronghold in Iberia, fell before Fernando and Isabel, and as Columbus, encouraged by high-placed Marranos at court, was preparing to set sail to India, the Catholic monarchs signed the decree giving all Spanish Jews the choice between expulsion and conversion to Catholicism. Many chose baptism, thus adding a new and substantial wave of conversos to the fabric of Spanish society. Of the others (whose numbers are estimated between 80,000 and 120,000), many arranged private departures by sea, frequently falling prey to greedy and corrupt captains; the others, probably the majority of those refusing baptism (that is, the religious hard core) crossed the border into Portugal, where King João II offered them temporary asylum—for a fee.

The asylum became a trap when João was succeeded by Manuel I, the Renaissance king who made Portugal a world power. Hoping that his heir would reign over a unified Iberia, Manuel sought the daughter of Fernando and Isabel in matrimony, but her parents demanded that he first expel all Jews from Portugal, as they had done in Spain. Manuel had a dilemma: he wanted the marriage, but he needed the Jews' commercial skills for the new trading empire he was building. His solution was to force all Jews to convert officially to Christianity, while granting them de facto religious liberties and immunity from the Inquisition for an entire generation.

The Marrano problem thus planted itself in Portugal with greater vigor and perseverance than in Spain. The Portuguese Marranos consisted of the more ardent segment of Spanish Jewry, those who preferred exile to voluntary conversions; they had almost half a century to establish their secret Judaizing free of persecution. The Inquisition, indeed, was not established in Portugal until 1536 and became effective only in midcentury. In addition, the share of New Christians in Portugal's population was approximately five times their share in the more populous Spain.

During the sixteenth century, the center of Marranism shifted to Portugal, where Marranos, both Judaizing and non-Judaizing, were fairly well organized, openly called Jews, or the Nation, and later simply *homens de negócios* (businessmen). Their prominence in international trade was such that the term *Portuguese* was almost synonymous with *Jew* overseas. Inside Portugal they formed a powerful political lobby, fighting against religious restrictions and for economic concessions. For almost ten years they maintained (and financed the bribing operation of) a special ambassador in Rome, to fight against their own government's intention to establish a Portuguese Inquisition.

When the Portuguese Inquisition was finally set in motion, it was even more drastic and devastating than its Spanish parent. In the 1580s hard-pressed Marranos sought refuge in Spain, where persecution was milder. Spanish Marranos by that time had been largely assimilated into Catholic society, and the Portuguese influx helped resuscitate Marranism in its original country. Meanwhile, negotiations were going on to permit the Marranos to leave the Iberian peninsula altogether. The gates were opened several times at the turn of the seventeenth century. A Marrano diaspora already existed, in Iberian colonies overseas and in the southwestern French cities of Bayonne, Bordeaux, and Toulouse, but Marranos there were not allowed to return openly to Judaism. Throughout the seventeenth century, however, Judaizing Marranos returned openly to Judaism by going to Venice and Leghorn, to Altona and Hamburg, later to London, and above all to Amsterdam—as did Baruch Spinoza's parents.

The Marrano Mixture

Although Spinoza himself was born a Jew, most of the community around him consisted of former Marranos, who brought with them from Iberia the weight and richness of the Marrano experience, including their Catholic education and symbolism. The waves of Marranos returning to Judaism—in Hamburg, in Venice and Leghorn, in Amsterdam, and later in London—were impelled by a variety of motives. Although some were prompted by social or even economic reasons,[1] probably the majority were driven by a deep religious attachment to a secret truth which they had guarded for generations from the Catholic world around them, a truth for which they had suffered persecution and humiliation, but which they deemed worthwhile because it pointed the way to salvation. Throughout their suffering, these Marranos had felt that they were superior to their oppressors, for they possessed an esoteric metaphysical key: they knew that the true way to salvation was not through Christ but through the Law of Moses, which their forefathers had received in ancient times and which Christianity pretended in vain to supersede. What this tenaciously guarded treasure consisted of, however, they knew only in a fragmentary and distorted manner. The particular rules and customs of the Law of Moses had been gradually erased from memory as the Marrano community was cut off from the official Jewish world outside Iberia. The expulsion of the Jews from Spain and Portugal, the ban on former Jews leaving the Iberian peninsula, and the network of Inquisitorial spies blocked many channels through which Judaizing Marranos could communicate about what they considered to be their true essence but which became more and more foreign to their lives. The only remaining channel was the information about Judaism contained in polemical works against it, in the Latin Vulgate and in other Christian sources.

Three processes were at work. First, because of the lack of books and instruction, the orthodox content of clandestine Judaism became ever more meager as the years passed. Second, the mortal danger of discovery by the Inquisition precluded the practice of those few laws which were committed to memory. This led to compromise—fulfilling one part of the law and neglecting another, or forfeiting the practice of major customs in favor of those which were easier to observe. Third and perhaps most important, the context in which the Marranos' residual Judaism was perceived became increasingly fraught with Christian symbols and categories. In the long run, this proved highly significant, affecting deeper layers of Marrano consciousness. Judaism itself, the hidden essence of these Marranos, existed in a world dominated by the outlook and symbols of Christianity. This was reflected in the dictum that for many generations the Inquisition attributed to Judaizing Marranos: salvation lies not in Christ but in the Law of Moses. This formula was almost definitory of Judaizing Marranos; it was like a dogma of their hidden religion and a succinct description of their faith. This is, however, basically Jewish ingredients filling a Christian formula. The mixture of religions is apparent in the secret customs and rites of the Judaizers, which have a Jewish framework but are saturated with Catholic elements and interpretations. A similar religious mixture is also found, in varying degrees, in the confessions of Inquisitorial victims, in expressions of mystical enthusiasm, and in many hymns and songs.

Salvation and the Jews   Concern with salvation as the primary religious aim sounds foreign to Judaism. Of course Jews were hoping for redemption, but this was usually understood as a collective event in the immanent world that would bring this-worldly existence to a climax. It entailed, in essence, the liberation of the Jews from gentile domination, the restoration of the temple, and the rule of God from Zion. Even Jewish mystics (in the cabalah), who thought of redemption as a cosmic event that affected the state of being of the universe, did not see it as centered on the salvation of the individual soul. Jews wished to gain their "share in the next world," but this desire lacked the metaphysical drama attached by Catholicism to the theme of salvation, as well as the awesome apparatus of hell and damnation, fall and grace, purgatory and last judgment. The Jews thought of the next world as a continued existence in a better mode, of which they become worthy by keeping the laws of the Torah; but, primarily they were anxious to keep the commandments because this practice had made them Jews, the people chosen by God, who had given them his Law. God's transcendence was mitigated by his immanence in the laws and rites of the Torah, and daily, this-worldly affairs thus gained an additional, sacred dimension. The Jew, in order to partake of the divine, did not have to contemplate a transcendent world for which his life on earth was sacrificed. Daily affairs were themselves sanctified and acquired a metaphysical significance as they were organized in a network of God-given rites and sacred procedures. While not neglecting the prospect of the next world, the Jew was more disposed to think of this world and its practical concerns, which also included religious and ritual concerns—how to practice certain rules scrupulously, how to apply them correctly to different conditions, and so on. The practical attitude attributed to Jews was thus largely metaphysical, for they were concerned with a multitude of questions relating to the observance of the *mitzvot* (commandments)—concerns that to a purely utilitarian observer would appear bizarre and very impractical.

In turning to salvation as their central religious concern, the Marranos displayed both their Catholic education and the needs of their situation. The bulk of their religious life could no longer lie in practice; on the contrary, practice in their case was usually false and deceptive. Educated in a Catholic milieu where salvation was a prime issue, they superimposed a Judaic interpretation over this Catholic concept: not Jesus Christ but the Law of Moses is the true way to salvation. There was an alternate way, different from that of the multitude, which only the Judaizing Marranos possessed.

Saint Esther and Holy Bread   The mixture of religions was also manifest in secret cults. Judaizing Marranos prayed to Saint Esther, their patron saint (a concept foreign to Judaism), but was not Queen Esther particularly fitted to this role, as she was the first Marrano, disguising her true origins and finally redeeming her people—a dream nurtured by the Marranos in their own agony. Passover matzot were called "the holy bread," a name reminiscent of the Catholic sacrament. Marrano victims of the Inquisition achieved martyrdom in the style of the first Christians. Prayers for Yom Kippur—*dia pura*, as Marranos called it—were not asking only for pardon, as in Judaism, but also, for salvation and grace. Prayers and cantillations are also replete with Catholic symbolism. "O great, omnipotent God," prayed a girl, Brites Henriques, caught by the Inquisition in 1674, "you who, as a Good Shepherd [a Christian symbol] leadst the sheep back to their pastures, gather up and return the sheep that had been lost and cut off the flock [the Marranos], let them not be harmed by another, foreign shepherd [Jesus]."[2] Some Marranos interpreted their lot in terms of the Christian concept of the fall. Their fathers had sinned by betraying Judaism and converting to Christianity, and now the offspring lived in a postlapsarian state. Their own existence must be marred by sin, idolatry, duplicity, and failure to be true Jews even when Judaizing. The sense of fallenness and acute guilt adhering to one's existence—the rudiments of the idea of original sin—are basically Catholic, but it fitted the situation of the Marranos and penetrated their consciousness.

A striking example of such a mixture is the case of the Beata of Herrera. *Beatas* were popular mystical figures who made their appearance at the beginning of the sixteenth century. Most of them were Catholic (although in a radical and mystical way that irritated the Catholic establishment), but this particular beata was a Judaizing Marrano who stirred her whole region and provoked a movement of conversion and reconversion to Judaism. According to her own story, she was summoned to heaven in a dream and there, guided by an angel, she saw "those in pain and those in glory," as well as "purgatory with the souls suffering there." This Christian, even Dantesque, picture took a surprising Marrano turn when the girl saw the just sitting in glory and the angel told her that they are "those burned on earth"—a direct reference to Marrano martyrs. On later trips to heaven, the beata brought down the message that God was ready to lead the conversos to the Promised Land. "And she told us at great length," a witness told the Inquisition, "how Elijah and the Messiah were to come," and that it was good to keep the Law of Moses for in it lay salvation.[3] As a result, many conversos started observing the Sabbath and otherwise Judaizing until the beata was arrested.

Religious duality penetrated the consciousness (and the subconsciousness) of the most ardent Judaizers. Even the Marrano martyrs and heroes were rarely Jews in the conventional sense. The clandestine character of worship, the Catholic education, the lack of Jewish instruction, the mental mixture of faiths, and the isolation from Jewish communities outside Iberia created a special phenomenon in the history and sociology of religion: a form of faith that is neither Christian nor Jewish.

Exile within Exile

The faithful Judaizers suffered a triple alienation. First, by identifying themselves even abstractly with the Jews as God's chosen people, they thereby shared the exile of the Jews and their alienated state. Second, as Jews by intent but not in real life, they were also alienated from their own essence, from what was supposed to be the deepest and most genuine element of their existence. Another duality emerged in their lives between existence and essence, between the reality of life and what was supposed to be its most authentic meaning. The Judaizing Marrano thus lived in alienation not only from his Catholic environment, but also from his own inner being, which he was unable to express in his life; and so, in effect, his life and his essence remained in mutual opposition. This existential alienation acquired a practical and social aspect, cutting the Judaizers off from the Jewish life that flourished outside Iberia. They were exiles within an exile—exiled, as Jews, among the nations, and exiled also from the Jews themselves. In this sense, Iberia was their Babylon, and their messianic yearnings were directed not so much toward the historical Zion as toward the symbolic Zion—toward the lost essence of Judaism, which was still projecting meaning into their lives and nourishing them with a sense of power and secret self-esteem, but from which their actual life was drawing farther and farther away. Their true essence became an abstract ideal, constantly fading, while their daily life and actual existence became a play of masks, an externality that stood in direct opposition to that inner essence and was unable to unite with it and to express it.

This was a classic case of alienation, almost in accord with the original philosophical sense of this category. Moreover, it was *self*-alienation, involving a measure of conscious responsibility. Some Marranos had an opportunity to leave the peninsula; this was true of Portuguese Marranos in the 1540s, and of resolute individuals throughout the century. For these people, living as exiles within an exile was a matter of choice—not an active choice but rather the confirmation of inertia. However, it cannot be said that no alternative to emigration existed in the sixteenth century. By that passive choice the real severance took place between Judaizing Marranos and professing Jews, and the Marranos grew into a special hybrid phenomenon—perhaps even sui generis—creating its own phenomenological category.

This fact was recognized by the Jews; many rabbis kept their distance from the Judaizing Marranos, refusing to recognize them as Jews. It is ironic that while these Marranos were risking their lives in order to be faithful to what they thought was the religion of their forefathers, the official Jewish world refused to welcome them as brethren, at least not without misgivings and thorough examination. The rabbinical responsa are full of cases (some of tragic family splits) in which rabbis refused to recognize Marranos as Jews. There were also many theoretical discussions of the principle. Rabbis were divided, but the majority tended toward severity. The rejection of Marranos in principle was partly due not to ideological fundamentalism but to concrete legal questions concerning such matters as *agunot*,* and inheritance. Often it was only by denying the Jewishness of the Marranos that rabbis could arrive at a liberal and humane solution to such difficult personal issues. And yet it is a fact that even from this aspect Marranos faced alienation.

Judaizers, however, comprised only part of the Marranos, and certainly the minority. Two other groups should also be mentioned: those—undoubtedly the largest group—who were finally absorbed into the Christian culture and were faithful to the new religion in varying degrees (ranging from passive submission to devotion and fanatic zeal); and those, especially important to our story, who were led by the confusion of both religions into skepticism and secularism, preferring the life of this world, or even (as happened to some) arriving at a positive rationalist philosophy, either in a deist form or even in a neopagan spirit.

Christian Zeal among Conversos

There were conversos who embraced their new religion with zeal and devotion. Some became bishops and inquisitors; others, in the lower ranks, affirmed their new identity by overemphasizing it—partly as a means of shedding their old Jewish identity—and that led many of them into sometimes venomous anti-Jewish polemics. Injecting the Jewish messianic zeal into the Catholic Church, along with the sense of election and universal mission among the nations, contributed to the reinforcement of the trend that had already started in Spain at the end of the Middle Ages: the feeling of an elect people, devout and unwavering in its Christian faith and fulfilling a divine mission on earth. In the Portugal of the later sixteenth century, this idea assumed a different tone when the death of King Sebastian in a disastrous military adventure in Morocco spurred a short-lived but intensive messianic movement in which the popular mind refused to admit his death and saw in him a secret savior who would one day reappear and liberate Portugal. Sebastianism supplied a distinctly Portuguese outlet, a channel into which was diverted part of the messianic undercurrent that had penetrated the soil of Christian society together with the Marranos.

The feeling of divine mission, the sense of election, the messianic

* *Aguna*: a wife whose husband disappears without divorcing her, leaving her unable to remarry.

enthusiasm—these are Judaic forms of consciousness that the mass conversions added to the Iberian experience, serving as catalyst to processes already under way. Marranism also interjected its distinctive color into the anti-Jewish propaganda in Iberia, as former Jews embraced their new identity with a zeal fomented by a villifying negation of the Jewish identity they sought to abandon. In both cases, the war waged against Judaism was in part a war against the former ego and a residue that haunted the convert's mind.

There was another spiritual contribution that the Marrano experience made to Spain. I mean the experience *as such*, regardless of the beliefs and views it entails. At the beginning of the sixteenth century, two related trends of religious reform and purification made their appearance in Spain. First, the teachings of Erasmus gained a strong hold in Spanish monastic circles (especially among the Franciscans) and among certain major intellectuals, including Juan Luis Vives and Juan de Valdes. Both of these men—and a surprising proportion of other followers of Erasmus—were of Jewish origin. The movement demanded the return to the pure origins of Christianity—to the gospel of Jesus and his disciples—overcoming the corruption, institutional bureaucracy, and overemphasis on external, mechanical cult at the expense of the true heart and inner religious awareness, with which the established Catholic Church was supposed to be affected. The large number of New Christians among Erasmus's followers has not been satisfactorily explained; there was mention only of demographic concentrations and of the "spirit of the Hebrew prophets"—a rather remote cause. This phenomenon may be better understood if one considers two facts. First, someone who has converted to a new religion, or has been born to a religion new in his family, tends to seek in it a deeper spiritual significance than one who has been accustomed to his old religion as a matter of routine. Searching for the deeper meaning of Christianity as a living awareness, beyond the external apparatus of cult and institution, could well be construed as Erasmus's message. More important, the very experience of Marranism created a tendency to prefer the inner heart to external works, which are seen as false, empty shells. This may have developed in Marrano families with a Judaizing history. It produced the sense that what counts is the inner experience, the heart, and the direct awareness of one's spiritual truth, downplaying the value of externals. From a more phenomenological viewpoint—regardless of the content of the religion at hand—this may be seen as preparing the ground for a critique of merely external acts even when the individual converts to Christianity.

This explanation applies even better to the second spiritual trend that came to the fore in sixteenth-century Spain—Spanish mysticism, or the *alumbrados* (the illuminated). A large number of Spanish mystics were also conversos, including Saint Teresa of Ávila, the greatest figure of the movement and the teacher of Saint John of the Cross. She was born to a family of former Jews who had suffered inquisitorial prosecution. This point is important because here is a pattern of experience that was first internalized in the state of secret Judaizing, and later transported into and preserved within Christianity, where it took the form of a secret spiritual yearning. The esoteric nature of Judaizing Marranos, the rejection of external acts as meaningless, interiorization and concentration on the inner self as a way to reach God and attain salvation—these are patterns of life and experience that, by force of necessity, took shape among the Judaizing Marranos and were transformed and translated into basic features of the Spanish schools of the alumbrados.

Skeptics, Rationalists, and Secularists

The confusion of Judaism and Christianity led in many cases to the loss of both. Religious skepticism and secularism were frequent results. Conversos who lost their Jewish faith without acquiring a Christian one found their attention directed to the secular, earthly affairs of this world, either in the form of work, commerce, and everyday life, or else in subtler forms of secularism—developing tastes for art and learning, cherishing one's own life, exploits, and career. These objectives were pursued not only for their utilitarian sake but also as aesthetic and existential values (and as metaphysical substitutes), expressing and developing the self in a world without transcendence.

This type of converso was known, in various forms, from early times to Spinoza's day. Before and during the Great Expulsion, the descendants of the noble former Jewish family, de la Caballeria, were even prosecuted by the Inquisition. Pedro de la Caballeria, author of a violently anti-Jewish book, was accused of having secretly dined in the company of Jews, and of bragging about his religious insincerity, which—free of ideological constraints—let him pursue a career of freedom and luxury. His portrait, drawn convincingly by Baer,[4] is that of a worldly man who did not take seriously the views of any religion, especially those concerning salvation and the next world, but who saw his life in this world as the sole area worthy of effort and concern. His nephew, Fernando de la Caballeria, a brilliant jurist and close associate of King Ferdinand the Catholic in imposing the Inquisition on the unwilling capital of Barcelona, was himself prosecuted by the Inquisition as a secret Judaizer and an agent of the Jews. In his case even more than in his uncle's, politics, law, personal talent, exploits, career, aesthetic enjoyment, and achievements in this world replaced the transcendent burden of either Judaism or Christianity.

Other examples of the same period are Fernando de Rojas, whom I shall discuss in chapter 4, and his father-in-law, Alvaro de Montalban.[5] Rojas's *La Celestina* is an outburst of the spirit of freedom, this-worldliness, and the forfeiture of all transcendent perspectives from life and the universe. Neither Jewish nor Christian, it is neopagan in mood, with a philosophy of pure immanence, regarding the existing universe as all there is, a constant play of forces, opposing one another in eternal strife, and (unlike Heraclitus's view) not controlled by an overall logos. The power of excess is supreme ruler, exemplified by earthly love, which achieves cosmic dimensions as a symbol of the basic structure of the universe. Rojas was, in many ways, a forerunner of Spinoza, but also his opposite. To Rojas, the loss of all transcendence left the universe a metaphysical desert, an abyss. Rojas was not really pagan, but remained bound by the Christian view that a world without an external God is an abyss. Spinoza, on the other hand, turned immanence into a divinity, identifying the universe with God and attributing to it the supreme qualities that religious tradition had placed upon the transcendent Creator. Spinoza's immanent universe was orderly, meaningful, the object of absolute knowledge and overpowering love that leads to salvation; to Rojas and the early secularists, the loss of transcendence led to a somber view of life and the universe, as (in a different mood) it did to modern nonreligious existentialists and to Nietzsche.

Rojas's father-in-law was twice sentenced by the Inquisition, once for Judaizing (although he broke the laws of both Judaism and Christianity by eating meat and dairy products during the fast of Lent), and the second time, decades later, he was imprisoned as a *relapso* for having twice denied the existence of the next world (see chapter 4). His secularism was a dimming of both religions rather than a strong positive position. As such, however, it was far from exceptional.

The undercurrent of secularism and skeptic rationalism attended the life of the conversos for generations. But until the early seventeenth century it was confined to the Iberian peninsula and affected the life only of individuals without becoming a movement. That started a century after the expulsion, when emigration from the Iberian peninsula started on a significant scale—and when the cultural atmosphere in Europe was more prone to skeptical quests.

MARRANO PATTERNS IN SPINOZA

The main patterns of Marrano experience I discern in Spinoza are: (1) heterodoxy and the transcendence of revealed religion; (2) a skill for equivocation and dual language; (3) a dual life—inner and external; (4) a dual career with a break between; (5) toleration versus the Inquisition; (6) a zeal for salvation, to be gained by alternate ways to that of tradition; and—coupled with it—this-wordliness, secularism, and the denial of transcendence. All of these Marrano features can be traced in Spinoza, even if in a somewhat different guise. They are reflected not only in his thought but even more in his life or existential case.

(1) Heterodoxy and the Rejection of Revealed Religion

In the Marrano experience in Iberia, a mixture of Judaism and Christianity led to various cases of skepticism, secularism, neopaganism, rationalist deism, or (in most of these cases) to a rather inarticulate confusion of symbols and traditions. This mixture affected the minds of even the most ardent secret Judaizers. In the early seventeenth century, when former Marranos started emigrating to Holland and elsewhere to rejoin official Judaism and reconstruct their identity along traditional Jewish lines, they carried with them a residue of their former experience and education. As New Jews, they suffered from a new duality. Living in the relatively tolerant Netherlands, with no fear of the Inquisition, their lives were no longer divided between a true self and a false appearance. This old duality was now internalized and became a split within the authentic self—between its desired Judaism and its residual Christianity. No longer a tension between truth and appearance, the new duality affected the true, authentic person who was determined to become Jewish again, yet in the process carried over with him a universe of Catholic symbols, attitudes, and world images in which his recovered Judaism was inevitably couched and interpreted. Thus, what in Iberia was a tension between the false official culture and an abstract inner truth, was now transformed into a tension within the official culture itself.

The outcome, however, was much the same: religious ambivalence and a ground ready for dissent (see chapter 3). Heterodox phenomena drew also upon skeptic, rationalist trends that had developed in Iberia and were transported into the New Jewish life in Holland—one case, that of Juan de Prado, catapulting directly into Spinoza's close circle.

Prado and Spinoza himself were the extreme cases of dissent, stepping beyond all revealed religions. Others remained within the fold of revelation but gave it new interpretations, or challenged its particulars, or combined elements from the competing revelations of Christ and Moses, or (as in the case of Uriel Da Costa) sought to reform the rabbinical establishment in light of spiritual ideals they had drawn from their former Christian phase. If Spinoza's case brought these forms of dissent to an extreme, it certainly sprang from the same psychocultural milieu and should be understood against its background.

Spinoza's heresy has been explained by more direct and localized impacts, whether the impact of certain heterodox ideas found here and there among medieval Jewish philosophers, whom Spinoza read as a youngster (Wolfson), or the personal impact of such figures as Prado (Revah) or Isaac la Peyrère (Popkin), with whom Spinoza had socialized shortly prior to the *herem*. But, as I shall argue in chapter 3, none of these direct contacts supplies a sufficient explanation, so long as the larger psychocultural milieu of Marranism is not seen as the background. Why should the young Baruch plunge into old philosophical works, drawing doubts from passages that, taken in themselves, smack of dangerous heresies, although in their systematic context they can be accommodated to tradition and still count as legitimate? And why, later, should he seek the company of such marginal and unsettling characters as Prado or La Peyrère (assuming with Popkin that indeed the two did meet)? If Spinoza turned to the books and the company he did, it must be explained by a propensity for rationalist quest and religious disquiet, drawn from his psychocultural milieu and throwing the nonconformist potential of Marranism into strong relief.

(2) Equivocation and Dual Language

Spinoza was a grand master of dual language and equivocation. He spoke to different audiences in different ways, using the same sentence or phrase in varying senses, masking his true intention to some while disclosing it to others. He would pass a covert message to anyone capable of grasping it, while using a phrase whose literal sense was the opposite, thus misleading the innocent reader. This technique is manifest in those of Spinoza's writings published during his lifetime, especially the *Theologico-Political Treatise* and the *Letters*, and much less in the *Ethics*, a work destined for a more restricted and homogeneous audience. While Spinoza advocated a literal hermeneutic method for the Bible, applying this method to Spinoza's own published works would be a mistake. As chapter 5 will argue—following Leo Strauss's suggestion—for Spinoza's language, a rather complex and subtle hermeneutics is required, far removed from the literal reading of the text.

In looking for a precedent for Spinoza's use of language, Strauss
went back to Maimonides, but this is too great a leap. Just as Wolfson
bypassed Marranism in seeking Spinoza's Jewish roots, so did Strauss
bypass a crucial step concerning the use of language. The direct and
relevant tradition that Spinoza continued almost uninterruptedly is
that of the Marrano culture and linguistic habits. Spinoza's mastery of
equivocation and dual language brings to a climax devices and sensibilities in which the Marranos had excelled for generations.

New Christian intellectuals, whether Judaizing or not, had for many
years before Spinoza developed the art of playing the overt meaning
against the covert one, deciphering hidden messages, using several
voices at a time or (as readers) learning to reverse the declared intention
of authors, or to draw illicit information from texts not intended to
convey it. This ability also assumed artistic dimensions. As we shall
see, it produced famous and typically Spanish art forms, first in Rojas's
La Celestina, the remarkably original classic, and later in the picaresque
novel, a genre given to the world by Spain in which New Christian
allusions and undercurrents abound. The picaresque literature and its
antecedents offer ample evidence of a use of language characteristic of
in-group communication and of esoteric minorities. It has provided
readers and writers alike with opportunities to indulge in the search
for meanings and allusions that only the initiated could grasp and appreciate.

Starting with *La Celestina*, the pragmatic needs of concealment by
language were transformed into aesthetic values in themselves. What
started as a practical necessity gave rise, as I argue in chapter 4, to new
forms of artistic pleasure. Equivocation, mask play, and dual language
became highly valued and enjoyable artistic devices, even when no
longer serving a specific practical need. This helped shape, if not the
language of the Marranos, as I am tempted to call it, then at least the
special *linguistic sensibilities* and gifts of the Marranos, which Spinoza
inherited and brought to a new peak.

(3) Dual Life

The use of dual language, for both Spinoza and the Marranos, betrayed
a deeper existential fact: life on two levels, one inner and one outer,
concealed and overt. Just as the Marranos lived in this dual way because
of the danger of the Inquisition, Spinoza repeated this life pattern twice
in the relatively free Netherlands: first as a young dissenter within the
Jewish community and then, after the *herem*, as a freethinker and reputed atheist in Calvinist-dominated Holland. In both phases, though

in somewhat different ways, Spinoza led the life of a Marrano of reason. Like the old Judaizing Marranos, he, too, possessed a secret metaphysical truth, the genuine key to salvation and the worthwhile life, which the multitude would never grasp and always despise. Like the Marranos, he, too, had to conceal his deeper thoughts from the eyes of the general public—and even, to some extent, from his own friends and disciples. The reason was not only prudence, but a sense of the depth and intimacy of the rational truth, which can hardly be shared by the vulgar and which even devoted rationalists may lack the depth and the subtlety to grasp. This made Spinoza an extremely lonely thinker—not socially, but intellectually. Even without an Inquisition, there were, in the ferment of the Netherlands and in the aftermath of the wars of religion, enough social pressures and political dangers that the prudent philosopher, in quest of peace for study and contemplation, would do best to avoid. The emblem on Spinoza's ring said, *caute* (carefully). But beyond these pragmatic considerations, there was also a purely philosophical one, relating to Spinoza's view of the multitude. Even if, in principle, reason is open to all, Spinoza remained an elitist in his view of the actual capacities of humanity. That *ratio*, let alone *scientia intuitiva*, will become the lot of the multitude is an illusion. Although Spinoza's theory of reason was potentially modern and democratic, his view of the sage and the multitude was still medieval, very much marked by Maimonides' views and by Spinoza's own experience and appreciation of the vulcanic nature and fluctuations of that beast, the *vulgus*.

Given human nature and the overwhelming power of the *imaginatio*, true metaphysical knowledge can be possessed only by the happy few. This raises the question of the multitude and how the philosopher deals with it. Part of the answer was, for Spinoza, that the wise man will not impose his truth on others, or flaunt it, or even disclose its existence to those unable to grasp it. Rational wisdom thus becomes esoteric, having an internal, intimate side that cannot be shared with the uninitiated without being violated and falsified. This can happen even on the level of mere *ratio*, which, lacking the intuitive and synoptic qualities of the "third kind of knowledge" (see chapter 6), is still unable to transform the inner person and the quality of his emotions. Duality of life and of discourse is thus not only a pragmatic need but also a matter of principle and (as Nietzsche might say) of good philosophical taste. What cannot be vulgarized in principle should not be made accessible to the masses.

The true philosopher will thus be a Marrano of reason even where no pragmatic needs arise. But this is an imaginary situation, for most people are ruled by the imagination and the ensuing fluctuations of the soul, with their violent outbursts, and so the need to conceal and be prudent is almost an inherent part of the wise man's lot.

Spinoza's adoption of this view cannot be unrelated to the long Marrano experience which he inherited and shared. In the same way, his persistent defense of tolerance and rejection of all forms of fanatic imposition of beliefs cannot be totally divorced from his background as an offspring of the community that suffered most from the Inquisition. *Caute* is the slogan of the son of the Marranos who, while proclaiming the antithesis of the Inquisition as his principle, knew that human nature cannot make possible a true sharing of truth, and that, therefore, tolerance (inter alia, the freedom to err or be subject to *imaginatio*) must be offered the multitude.

In chapter 5 I discuss what Spinoza proposed for the multitude. Basically, he devised the apparatus of the state and of rationalized (universal) religion as two complementary institutions with the aim of turning the activity of the imagination into an external imitation of reason, using the power of authority and obedience. This means that, without passing from *imaginatio* to *ratio*, the multitude will, out of its own transformed imagination, be held together by obedience to rational authority, producing the same behavior that reason would produce out of its own sources, so that externally they would coincide. This is the main goal of political organization and religious reform. Eventually, in the best of cases, it will neutralize the destructive and violent potential of the *imaginatio*, making the life of all, including the philosophers, safer and more secure. Philosophers, like other people, would then be freer to express themselves without fear. But if Spinoza the thinker might have believed this to be possible at some future time, Spinoza the son of the Marranos still clung realistically to the inscription on his ring.

(4) Dual Career

Spinoza's career as a Marrano of reason is divided. Among the Jews, he lived concealing his inner truth, while conforming to the outer customs and rites of the community, until this was no longer possible. Then, breaking away from the community and suffering the *herem*, he repeated, as it were, the act of his former Marrano fathers, who left Iberia to live in freedom elsewhere. Even in the atmosphere of Gentile Holland, Spinoza went on concealing his new truth from most of his fellow men. Neither Jew nor Christian, futilely fighting his notoriety

as an atheist and called by all a Jew, he neither found the external freedom necessary for a life without concealment nor the intellectual part-
nership of others who could fathom the depth or share the intensity of
his unconditional mystical faith in reason—this new alternate way to
salvation, which lies neither in Christ nor in the Law of Moses, but in
the third kind of knowledge.[6]

It was typical of many Marranos, especially those returning to Judaism, that their lives were divided into two opposing periods, often
radically severed from each other. As Yerushalmi has pointed out, Spinoza's career before and after the *herem* repeats a pattern known from
other Marranos and former Marranos.[7] Fernando Cardoso (the subject
of Yerushalmi's monograph) started as a highly placed Catholic courtier and doctor in Spain, then made a full turn and became a Jewish
scholar and apologist in the ghetto of Venice. His brother, Miguel Cardoso, also started as a Catholic and ended as a militant Jew, though a
mystic and a Sabbatian messianic, to his brother's great dismay. From
Uriel Da Costa to Isaac Orobio de Castro, not only intellectuals but
many less renowned people shed their former existence, career, name,
and identity to become something very different, in Amsterdam and
Altona, Venice and Leghorn, later in London, and even in Bayonne,
Toulouse, and Bordeaux. In this respect, Spinoza's dual career repeats
a well-known Marrano pattern; although he did not leave a Jewish career for a Christian one, he stepped out of both toward a religion of
reason.

What happened in most of these cases, including Spinoza's, is that
the duality that marked one's existence at any given moment or place
was translated into a two-chapter life history. This required that the
person do something to overcome the original duality and choose the
full realization of one of its sides at the expense of the other. Thus, the
secret Judaizer in Iberia opted for open Jewish life in Amsterdam or
Venice. His career and social identity were radically changed, and the
duality marking his life now took the form of a breach between two
periods. Yet it will be too simple to suppose that all the determinative
elements of the former life disappeared. In subtler ways, duality persisted even after the break; this may be true of Spinoza no less than of
former Judaizing Marranos in his former community.

Translating a Marrano duality into a two-chapter career is not necessarily a pattern of former Marranos alone. It can be found also in the
lives of conversos who never reverted to Judaism or who never really
Judaized in the first place; thus it seems to be a larger converso pattern.
As we shall see, Rojas was neither Christian nor Jewish, but a skeptic,

a neopagan, a Heraclitean without the logos. The effects of the converso duality on his mind were clear and typical, as was his incessant use of equivocation, dual language, and play of masks, all similarly rooted in the Marrano experience and frequently alluding to it. As a young man, Rojas composed *La Celestina* as a celebration of freedom, this-worldliness, and aesthetic pleasure mixed with his pessimistic and Heraclitean metaphysics. Then he married, moved to a small town, and led the life of a respectable provincial jurist, bourgeois, a master of prudence, sidestepping the Inquisition, which nonetheless reached the doorstep of his family at least twice in his lifetime. Rojas lived to his last moments the concealed life of a Marrano of reason (or rather of an artistic reason—religious skepticism turned into art) and died as one.

Rojas never left Iberia; Spinoza's forbears and former Marrano colleagues did, and Spinoza himself repeated the act by leaving his own Iberia—the Jewish community. But as we shall see, even afterward he did not, and could not, live his inner truth in outer freedom. Part of the reason was the esoteric nature of this truth, which in its purity could serve only the few. But there was another, no less significant reason. Spinoza, unlike other former Marranos, left one religious community without joining another—there was still no social framework capable of manifesting Spinoza's new thought. Spinoza represented a principle that was not yet instituted in communal life. There was no laicized community to identify with; one still had to be identified as a Catholic, Calvinist, Jew, Lutheran, and so on. The social frame of reference of any individual was still religious. The idea of a genuine individual, marked only by his rational powers—a universalist capacity, with no root or affiliation in a particular religious community—was too novel. It was actualized but not yet institutionalized in Spinoza: he was a living manifestation of this principle, a special case, anticipating something to come, but not yet a social reality. Thus he was, necessarily, alienated from the social reality of his time even after leaving the Jewish community. In this sense, the alienation of the Marrano, transformed into a new form, still persisted in the case of this Marrano of reason, in both periods of his career.

(5) Toleration versus the Inquisition

Spinoza's political philosophy echoed his Marrano background in other ways as well. Most evident is his philosophy of toleration, which stands out as the antithesis of the Inquisition. As an early and outspoken philosopher of toleration, Spinoza crystallized the liberal spirit of the new urban classes of his native Netherlands as it evolved in conflict with absolutist Spain. He also, perhaps primarily, drew on the lessons, the needs, and the memories of his own Marrano "nation," which had been the prime target of Spanish and Portuguese intolerance. Spinoza's principle of toleration opposed the Inquisition for what it was and for its role in the political modernization of Europe. The Iberian Inquisition had used Europe's medieval past as a principal lever in building the modern absolutist state, whereas Spinoza broke with this past (as he did with the medieval Jewish past) and, in his theory of toleration, provided the new era with a political principle commensurate with its novelty. That his political theories were, existentially, nourished by his Marrano background did not exclude, of course, their having these broader aims and implications.

Not that all former Marranos drew the same lesson from their experience. The Amsterdam New Jews had adopted political forms from their former Spanish foes as they did from their Dutch hosts. Their communal system of government was inspired by the oligarchic model of the Amsterdam burgomasters; in addition they sometimes practiced their own kind of inquisition—an incomparably more humane version, to be sure, but one that also investigated religious dissent and forced the culprits to either repent and be publicly "reconciled" to orthodox Judaism (Da Costa, Prado) or to be cast out (Spinoza). In responding to this so-called "Jewish inquisition" (a name it deserves only metaphorically), Spinoza's concept of toleration is linked to his Marrano background in yet another, more complex, and ironic way.

Toleration, however, also has a deeper significance: it means that people must be free to err. In principle, truth is unique: whoever lacks it or departs from it is, strictly speaking, in error. To that extent Spinoza resembled a religious absolutist. But Spinoza could tolerate error. He objected to making truth the source of fanatic oppression or state ideology. Spinoza rather demanded that all opinions (i.e., a great many errors) be accepted as politically legitimate, provided they do not claim to supersede the state's sovereignty and that their holder's behavior conforms to the laws of the land. Thus the price of toleration is a break between many people's inner convictions and the laws they observe in practice. In other words, a certain Marrano-like feature is essential to Spinoza's theory of toleration.

Marrano-like conformity had an even broader dimension in Spinoza. Good politics is based upon the principle of semirationality, whereby the multitude is led to abide by the same rules that reason recommends, using such nonrational motives as fear, obedience, and respect for authority. Rechanneling the common people's nonrational drives in this way is the essence of universal religion and the proper use of state authority. The multitude, although by definition unable to live the life of reason, will under proper political conditions behave externally as if it did. As for the rational person—if living in a state that is not rational (but also is not an outright tyranny), the most *rational* thing for him or her to do is to abide by the less-than-rational laws of the state even though they conflict with his inner consciousness. Thus on both sides of the multitude/rational person distinction, a certain Marrano-like gap between inner belief and social conformity is an essential condition of politics and of human society in general.

(6) An Alternate Way to Salvation

Finally, Spinoza reiterated a strong Marrano pattern in his attachment to an alternate way to salvation (see chapter 6). Here we are dealing with Spinoza's thought no less than with his life. The fifth book of the *Ethics*, where its whole essence and goal lies, offers the individual a way to the salvation and even the eternity of his soul, that challenges all of the established religious and mystical ways, and yet is motivated by a similar absolute drive. Not only knowledge, but *beatitudo*, an ethical objective, relating to the supreme state of the soul, is what Spinoza's philosophy sought and offered. This may seem, at first, a revival of the classic ideal of the sage. Yet Spinoza was writing in the midst of a scientific revolution that began an era where that supreme ideal was no longer the issue. Indeed, Spinoza was almost unique among modern philosophers, in setting forth this almost archaic ambition; others were more modest in their goals, a modesty that almost became the distinctive mark of modern philosophy in general.[8] If one looks closer, the ideal of salvation in Spinoza is not borrowed directly from Greek philosophy (which he scarcely knew) or even from the Roman Stoics (whom he did know and absorbed). It stems first of all from Spinoza's religious and mystical concerns in their translation into the language of reason, and historically it echoes his Marrano background. Salvation was a revived concern in Spain (and France) at the end of the Middle Ages. It helped fire the mind of Catholic Spain and nourish the Inquisition. It played a part—alongside Marranism—in the rise of the Spanish alumbrados in the sixteenth century. And it was a central concept in all accounts of Judaizing Marranos, who declared that salvation was to be found in the Law of Moses, not in Christ. This recurrent Marrano formula indicated that Marranos saw their secret religion as an alternative way to salvation. They knew better than the multitude, for they had a secret key to true eternity. Spinoza—infinitely more sophisticated, subtle, and solitary—shared this self-consciousness. A second-order Marrano (a Marrano of *reason*, rather than of some revealed religion) it was he, not they, who knew the true way to salvation: it did not pass through any historical religion, either that of Moses or of Christ, but through the third kind of knowledge and the intellectual love of God it produced.

Reason thus inherits the supreme goals and ambitions that were traditionally assigned to mysticism and to historical religion. The pursuit of rationality does not end in knowledge but in beatitude, eternity, and rational love. For this purpose however, reason cannot be mere *ratio* (as in the second kind of knowledge), but must, as in the third, take the shape of *scientia intuitiva*; it cannot be merely analytic and discursive, but must be also construed as synoptic and intuitive. The distinction between these two types of rationality—between the second and third kinds of knowledge—is thus tightly related to the absolute task of reason, to serve not only as a way to knowing the world, but to the supreme ethical and spiritual goals that religion calls salvation.

In stressing this Marrano-like aspect of Spinoza I attribute to him an affinity with the ideals of mysticism and revealed religion, although the way he suggested is radically opposed to theirs. Unlike other modern philosophers, Spinoza never gave up the absolute spiritual goals of the religious mystics, but he thought that reason itself, shaped as *scientia intuitiva* and as the most potent mental power, can lead to these goals, and is the only way to reach them. Mysticism is irrational, confused, a form of the *imaginatio*; its goals are to be attained only by its opposite, and insofar as they require love and unity with God, this love must be intellectual, based upon the third kind of knowledge, and God and the soul's unity with God must be duly understood and interpreted—that is, outside all historical religion. Neither the love of Christ, the Law of Moses, or the confused and ineffable mystical experience can lead the soul to where it necessarily aspires by its nature; this can only be done in ways that, while retaining the basic ambitions of the mystic and the religious devotee, are utterly opposed to their practices.

In this respect, Spinoza resembles Plato and, in a different way, Hegel. Despite the great differences in the nature of their systems, all three were rationalists seeking to attain semimystical results by the power of reason—and distinguishing, as they had to, between two kinds of rationality, a lower, analytic, scientific kind and a higher, synoptic, semi-intuitive kind. Spinoza can be seen also as secularizing religion without giving up its absolute pathos, or as sacralizing reason by giving it the supreme spiritual tasks that were wrongly attributed to religious mysticism. Spinoza saw his kind of rationalism as offering an alternate way to salvation, opposing the way that religion leads (or misleads) the multitude—and in this respect, too, his thought betrays a powerful Marrano pattern.

Conclusion: Note on the Sixteenth Century

A full historical and phenomenological account of Marranism would require a different kind of book. Focusing on Spinoza, this chapter maps the Marrano patterns that, transformed, were preserved in his life and thought. The following chapters will flesh this map out and draw its contours in greater detail. Meanwhile, let me outline what further evidence the sixteenth century can offer our analysis.

Alongside religious skepticism and this-worldliness, the sixteenth century gave rise to the picaresque novel, a distinctly Spanish literary genre in which converso authors were predominant. This new genre contains covert allusions to the Marrano situation; invariably it practices the art of equivocation (like Rojas in *La Celestina* and Spinoza in his *Theologico-Political Treatise*); in addition, it often masks a revolt against established Spanish values. Picaros were anti-hidalgos; they paraded their lowly origins as opposed to the Spanish cult of noble stock and "pure blood"; in their inverted, ironic way they challenged the Spanish obsession with nobility or *hidalguia*. Conversos were predominant in the rising bourgeoisie and therefore apt to find human worth in achievement, work, and acquired wealth. They resented oppressive religious rigor and, of course, the Inquisition. In speaking through the mouth of a rogue and vagabond, the author and many of his readers could use the picaro's adventures as an ironic means to dissociate themselves from established values and find a defying aesthetic liberation where a social one was slow to come.

Conversos were also prominent in a different cultural movement which left its mark on sixteenth-century Spain: the mystical alumbrados and their Erasmian predecessors and colleagues. Unlike the picaros, these were intensely devout, if unorthodox, Christians; although their work inevitably merged with the struggles of the Reformation and Counter-Reformation, it also bore a distinct Spanish and converso specificity. Some, denigrating outer works, were persuaded by the Lutheran claim of justification by subjective faith, but their number was small. Lutheranism in Spain was the utmost heresy, and conversos willing to go that far had a more readily available option in Judaizing. Distinctly more important were the Spanish Erasmians and, especially, the alumbrados. These groups tried to revitalize Catholicism from within by devaluing its concern with externalities and injecting a new spirit into it that was at least in part animated by Marrano-like features: a concern with pure spiritual origin and an emphasis on the inner life and "dark night of the soul" as the authentic vehicles of salvation.

Thus the two movements that made a distinct contribution to Spanish culture in the sixteenth century—one impudently terrestrial, the other intensely spiritual—could partly claim a common converso ancestry. The picaresque novel and mystical theology are remote from one another in substance, but not necessarily in origin. If the picaro dwells on his base origin, which his whole career embodies,[9] and the Erasmian (frequently a precursor of alumbrados) aspires to a *spiritually* pure origin—are they not united, despite their distance, by a common converso situation to which they react in different ways? And if the alumbrado debates the proper techniques for spiritual ascent, bypassing outer works and church cults on the road to salvation—is he merely reiterating some perennial mystical credo, or rather, in sixteenth-century Spain, is he not also echoing the interiorized effects of Marranism, and thereby responding to his country's *specific* mental situation? Moreover, placing a person's worth in his or her inner mental progress is the spiritual analogue to the converso ideology that severs the link between birth and worth and places the latter in the individual's own achievement; it is also a prelude to the kind of subjective individualism that the Protestants have initiated elsewhere and to which, in Spain, conversos were prone to respond most keenly.

Finally, one may wonder which of these two movements is closer to Spinoza. Structurally, he shares Marrano patterns with both. With the alumbrados, he has in common a striving for an alternative way to salvation; with the picaresque authors he shares a this-worldly sense and a gift for dual language. The Marrano phenomenon allows, then, for structural analogies that traverse opposing systems and can be transformed from one context to another without losing essential phenomenological traits.

Now let us turn to a more detailed scrutiny of these Marrano patterns, as they were embodied in historical fact and textual detail.

The Split Mind:
New Jews in Amsterdam

The Jewish community of Amsterdam was a brand plucked from the fire; it soon became a diadem of gold. Many in the community were former Marranos of the first generation, who returned to Judaism after having fled from the Iberian peninsula, where the Inquisition continued to burn their brethren at the stake. Spinoza himself was born a Jew, but was surrounded by New Jews who had returned to their ancient religion after their ancestors had lived for generations as New Christians in Iberia. The Netherlands was then, relatively speaking, the most tolerant country in Europe and a budding commercial empire. The rulers of the young republic—who appreciated the prominence of the Portuguese Marranos in foreign trade—after some hesitation and misgivings granted the Jews refuge and a foothold in their country. In Amsterdam the Jews managed to create a flourishing life for themselves, not only economically but also in a social and a cultural sense. With the union of the three founding congregations, Amsterdam spawned a network of Jewish education, publishing, and printing that was one reason for the community winning the sobriquet *the New Jerusalem.*[1] Innovation was not, perhaps, the outstanding feature of the Amsterdam rabbis' intellectual endeavor; their principal efforts went toward revitalizing the extant Jewish culture, framing it in the languages of the Iberian peninsula (Spanish and Portuguese), and reshaping the life of the New Jews in its light. But one cannot fail to see the extent of the originality, the resolution, and the imagination that was required of the community's spiritual leaders in order to meet this test of forging a new Jewish life on the basis of the complex and disjunctive Marrano experience, the effects of which could no longer be wholly obliterated.

"Catholics without faith and Jews without knowledge, albeit Jews by their will"—this is how Gebhardt characterized the Marranos in a poignant dictum that, however, calls for some reservation (see below on Da Costa, and note 12).[2] The problem confronting the rabbis of Amsterdam, along with its teachers, printers, and popularizers, was to invest this raw and vague desire with renewed Jewish knowledge and, in particular, to weave around it the fabric of Jewish customs and practices that had distinguished the life of the Jews for ages. At the same time, they could not altogether eschew a theoretical approach that stressed the theological and not just the practical side of their readopted Judaism. The New Jews came to Amsterdam after having led Christian lives in which theology had a prominent role, and their very return to Judasim implied an act of existential polemic against Christianity, which now had to be complemented by theoretical polemics, explicating the concepts and principles that rendered Judaism superior to Christianity on a theoretical level.

Moreover, the Christian background of the former Marranos continued to inhabit their consciousness and inform the historical experience that determined their individual and collective character. People do not discard their past simply because they make new decisions or embark upon a new course; a being endowed with consciousness and memory cannot simply return to the point of departure, even when reverting to a position once held in the past and then abandoned. The Marranos had lived among Christians for generations, partaken of their mores and education, practiced their customs—at least outwardly—and internalized the same symbolic universe and mode of thinking. Many Marranos even belonged to the Iberian elite that acquired an excellent education and attended universities, thereby sharing in the learning of their time and in its latest innovations. Though Spain and Portugal were the lands of the Inquisition, it is a mistake to view them as provinces of ignorance and darkness or as transfixed in the Middle Ages. The learning of the age was expressed in Iberia by a cultural revival that took place in the sixteenth and seventeenth centuries, shaping the so-called Golden Age; the religious zeal frequently reinforced this cultural revival in its own way. The Spain of Charles V, Philip II, and their successors was not waging a purely defensive war against ascendant Protestantism. In effect, the Iberian Counter-Reformation engendered a new Catholic renaissance that revitalized the old faith not only by use of the sword and the political establishment but also by a resurgent cultural and spiritual drive. The Marranos, who lived and were educated in this climate, must have seen this militant Catholicism as an oppressive force that confined and threatened to destroy them, but they certainly did not regard it as a power in decline, fighting for its life against fresh spirits. Rather, a fresh spirit had invaded Catholic Christianity itself.

The progeny of the Marrano experience gradually began to gather in Amsterdam. By the time Spinoza was born, the community was more than twenty-five years old and boasted a network of social, cultural, mutual-aid, and educational institutions. Those who arrived in Amsterdam as New Christians—many of them at a mature age and coming from a mixed cultural and personal background—returned to Judaism openly by undergoing circumcision, rejoining the community of their brethren and beginning to reacquire a Jewish mode of life. Together with those who returned solely out of religious motives were some who may have been seeking social and economic integration within a more liberal framework—albeit while pursuing a Jewish life but not one especially charged with religious intensity. Balancing them, however, were those who had returned to Judaism with soaring expectations and intense spiritual ardor. It is precisely among this latter group—and not fortuitously—that we find some of the more provocative and scandalous figures, the first instances of deviation and heresy. The most prominent example is Uriel Da Costa.

URIEL DA COSTA: BEYOND THE SPHERES OF IDENTITY

Uriel Da Costa's tragedy is fairly well known and has furnished material for several melodramas. Until recently the story of his life was based mainly upon his presumed autobiography, the *Exemplar humanae vitae* (a model of human life), published by a Calvinist theologian many years after Da Costa's death; it has been suspected and partly proven, however, that this text departs from the truth on several points, either because of Da Costa's polemical bias or because of the anti-Jewish tendency of the author of the many apocryphal parts that the book seems to contain, or both. The revised and more complex portrait of Da Costa that later research imposes upon the reader supports with even greater force the thesis about the split identity and confused religious affinities that Marranism offers in significant cases.[3]

Before suggesting a critical interpretation, let us briefly rephrase Da Costa's own version.[4] A New Christian from Pôrto, Portugal, and a former student of canon law at the university of Coimbra, Gabriel (the future Uriel) Da Costa rose to the post of church treasurer in his native town. Disenchanted with Catholicism, however, and doubting the existence of the afterlife, he turned his back on the religion in which he had been brought up in favor of the ancient covenant of the Jews, which he supposed to contain the word of God in its original purity.

The Bible, Da Costa claims, was his source and model for knowing and preferring Judaism. For a while Da Costa exhorted other New Christians to return to Judaism. In order to live his beliefs openly, he finally decided, and persuaded other members of his family, to leave Portugal and seek their fortune among a community of their erstwhile people.

Yet when Da Costa reached Amsterdam and returned openly to Judaism, he suffered, so he claims, a great disappointment. Instead of the original religion of the Bible, he found a religion fraught with irrelevant precepts and rules and already possessed of a rabbinical and exegetical tradition that, by its very existence, betrayed the original message of Judaism. The discrepancy between his ideal of a pristine religion and the reality of rabbinical Judaism allegedly came as a brutal shock. Rather than shedding the historical burden of religion and returning to its pure source through Judaism, the religion of the Old Testament, Da Costa was dismayed to discover that rabbinical Judaism had gone far astray from the biblical original and was crushed by historical irrelevancies; thus the historical nature of all religions was impressed upon Da Costa's mind. He concluded that neither Judaism nor Christianity holds eternal truth; they are but beliefs, opinions, and precepts that had evolved out of human needs and changing conditions and are essentially man-made. Thus Da Costa, who had started his life as a non-Christian Christian and went on to become a non-Jewish Jew, explains how he ended up a sworn deist who believed only in reason and the law of nature. "There are people," he says, "who always proclaim: 'I am a Jew,' 'I am a Christian.' . . . Yet he who pretends to be neither is preferable to them by far."[5]

Whatever the truth about Da Costa's spiritual itinerary, his attempt to live as a "universal" man was premature, and, in his time and circumstances, doomed to failure. After taking up arms against the authority of the rabbis and the oral Law (and writing a treatise, soon to be destroyed, denying the immortality of the soul),[6] Da Costa was banned by the Jews of Amsterdam. For years he lived in isolation and misery. Then, unable to continue, he broke down and recanted outwardly. He thus became a kind of Marrano within a community of former Marranos. In the *Exemplar*, he says that he resolved to live "like an ape (an imitator) among apes." But the conflict between his convictions and his outer life again led him to a confrontation with the synagogue, resulting in a second *herem*. Once again Da Costa lived in torment, an outcast for seven years; and once again he broke down and recanted. This time his punishment was far more humiliating. He was required to confess his sins in public, to submit to thirty-nine lashes, and to prostrate himself on the doorstep of the synagogue while the members of the congregation trod over his body. Finally, deeply shattered, bitter, and discouraged, he put a bullet in his head, but not before writing down his life and reflections on religion—including the statement that all religions are purely of man's making.

This is the version given by the *Exemplar humanae vitae*. Serious doubts have been raised about the authenticity of this work. Even if it is not a forgery, it certainly contains apocryphal material and interpolations—some (as those against the Pharisees) by a heavy anti-Jewish hand—as well as many points of misinformation. But it could have been Da Costa himself who misled his readers, to maintain the self-image he had created and sought to project. On the whole, I accept the critical line of Revah, who made the reader of the *Exemplar* aware of its serious flaws (and ready to find even more) without, however, dismissing the work in principle.[7] At the present stage of knowledge, such a wholesale dismissal would be rather rash and, as P.-F. Moreau aptly says, would deal Da Costa an undeserved "fortieth lash."[8]

It is indeed probable that the picaresque genre—in which allusions to the converso situation abound—served the *Exemplar* as a literary model in producing a kind of mental picaresque novel: a first-person account of the origins, itinerary, vicissitudes, and humiliations of someone outside established society, an intellectual wanderer who remained a dissident and social outcast wherever he turned. Incidentally, the best-known picaresque novel, *Guzman of Alfarache*, had the subtitle, *A Rogue's Way of Human Life*, and Cervantes's semipicaresque stories are included in a collection he entitled *Novelas Ejemplares*. Yet Da Costa's humorless tale is full of self-pity rather than self-irony—which makes it basically unpicaresque.

Revah on Da Costa's Trial

Following up on a pioneering work of A. de Magalhães Basto, Revah searched the records of the Pôrto Inquisition for firsthand information about Da Costa and his milieu. The documents he found have shed light on Da Costa's life in Portugal, especially the question of how much Da Costa knew about postbiblical Judaism. While some of the claims of the *Exemplar* were thereby corroborated, others were shown to be false or misleading. For example, Revah confirmed that Da Costa's father had been a devout Catholic with no Judaizing inclinations; that Da Costa had indeed held the post of church treasurer; that he had returned to Judaism by his own choice; that he had successfully ex-

horted others to do the same; and—most important in this context—
that it was by comparing the Old with the New Testament that Da
Costa had definitely detached himself from Catholicism. On the other
hand, the author of the *Exemplar* fails to report (or intentionally conceals) that there was a Judaizing tradition in Da Costa's mother's family; that his mother, Branca Da Costa, was an active Judaizer by her
upbringing and choice; that Pôrto was full of other Judaizers (with 143
convicted and subjected to *autos-da-fé* between 1618 and 1625); and that
Da Costa and the other members of his family did not leave Portugal
for purely spiritual reasons but were escaping the Inquisition, which
by then was in full assault in Pôrto and was gathering devastating personal evidence against Da Costa.

In studying the customs that Branca Da Costa and others in Gabriel
Da Costa's secret circle used to practice, Revah found not only rites
and precepts mentioned in the Bible, but several others, which no
reading of the Old Testament could possibly have yielded. Some of
these had rabbinical sources,[9] while others were peculiar to the Marranos and unknown among the Jews.[10] Da Costa may not have been
able to distinguish between these two kinds, but at least he had known
and undoubtedly had practiced several *post*biblical customs for about
four years while still living in Iberia.

All of this permits Revah to conclude, "What Uriel Da Costa did
not tell in the *Exemplar humanae vitae* is that in abandoning Catholicism
he had adhered neither to a personal Biblical Judaism, nor to traditional rabbinical Judaism, but to the normal kind of Marranism that
prevailed at the beginning of the seventeenth century," enriched with
a few further rituals specific to his milieu.[11] This "normal Marranism,"
Revah goes on to say, "constitutes an impoverished form of rabbinical
Judaism"—a conclusion that does not quite follow from his data. What
Revah had actually shown is that an "impoverished rabbinical Judasim" was only one ingredient of the Marrano religion, which included
other rites as well that are neither Biblical *nor* rabbinical, but are *specifically Marrano* ("true innovations," Revah calls them). This point is of
crucial importance when studying the phenomenology of Marranism
in general; here, however, it does not change the main conclusion concerning Da Costa.

Thus one can no longer accept at face value the contention of the
Exemplar that only when he met with Jewish life outside Iberia did Da
Costa discover the rabbinical heritage of Judaism, thereby suffering a
shocking surprise. Even if his early knowledge of rabbinical Judaism
was meager and impoverished, it nevertheless existed.

A Revised View of Da Costa

Clearly, a revised picture of Da Costa is necessary. In offering one, I am not committing myself to dismiss all elements of surprise and disappointment from Da Costa's story. They can be retained in a modified version.

Yerushalmi has demonstrated that learned Marranos could have collected rich (if fragmentary and indirect) information about Judaism from overt Christian sources.[12] The thesis is sound, but all it proves is the scattered *availability* of such material. How much of this was actually sought and acquired? To decide this question, one needs to know more about each individual, his conditions, and especially his motivation. Paradoxically, someone with no knowledge of Jewish rites may have been more disposed to such investigation than a person who, like Da Costa, did possess a scant knowledge handed down by Marrano tradition. Yerushalmi, even without using Revah's findings, raises an interesting a priori question. Da Costa, he says, was well aware that the Christianity of his time was a far cry from that of Jesus; why should he have expected the Judaism of his time to be that of Moses?[13] The logic of this remark is impeccable, but the intricacies of human psychology do not always follow logic and common sense. From the fact that a certain course of conduct is the most reasonable, it does not follow that it has actually been pursued—especially when dealing with a person whose mind is known to have been affected by dualities and ambiguities. Wishful thinking, self-deception, and ideological and emotional investments are some of the best-known causes of a biased perception of reality or of unfounded expectations. One can offer many reasons that the restless Da Costa with his torn identity—a non-integral Catholic obsessed with the idea of "pure (religious) origins" and yearning to find them in an ideal picture of his own Jewish origins—should have drawn a picture of Judaism that was more influenced by his own aspirations than by what seem to be the dictates of common sense.

Of course Da Costa could not actually have believed Judaism to be purely biblical; this claim of the *Exemplar* can no longer be maintained. However ambiguously, in a mode of self-deception, Da Costa *was* aware of the existence of postbiblical Judaism. But his knowledge of it was meager and suppressed; above all, he did not realize the prodigal extent to which rabbinical laws and precepts had taken over in Jewish life, or the rigid and powerful resistance they would therefore show to any attempt at reform. Da Costa, I suggest, expected Judaism to be more amenable to a purifying reform than the Catholicism of inquisitorial Iberia, especially within the New Jewish communities. Here was Da Costa's mistake and the source of his surprise and disenchantment.

We may now reconsider his case in this light. Da Costa had started as a religious reformer, perhaps with Erasmian leanings, *within* the Christian fold.[14] It was not unusual for conversos, even when they were sincere Christians, to become religious reformers and innovators with a characteristic preference for the authentic experience of the inner heart above external ritual. A century prior to Da Costa, this had produced some of the more vivifying and contested religious trends in Iberia, such as the Spanish Erasmians and the new mystical movement of the *alumbrados* (the illuminated). Many leaders of these movements were of converso origin with a history of Judaizing in their families.[15] Whether Da Costa was a direct heir to these trends remains to be shown, but the structural similarities are apparent, especially with the Erasmian tendency toward the pure origins of religion (ad fontes).

Marranos with Judaizing family backgrounds had been schooled in the distinction between a spurious external cult and the authentic, inner message of religion. When this disposition was translated into the inner-Catholic context, it encouraged new forms of Christian devotion and called for religious purification. Moreover, the more devout forms of Christianity enabled conversos to preserve a certain sense of superiority—even a challenging otherness—within the Christian fold itself. Being overtly (and differently) devout can express a subtle form of revolt; in any case, it is another sign of the conversos' not being fully integrated into their host society.[16]

Most of these factors apply in Da Costa's case. His quest for religious authenticity had first made him a reformer within the Christian context; when he later crossed to Judaism, he did so from within Christianity. On the other hand, as my analysis has suggested, even his reformist tendencies as a Christian had been nourished, at least in part, by his specific Marrano background, which made him sensitive to the problem of religious authenticity and aware of his nonintegral position in Catholic society. It may even be that Da Costa's passion for the idea of pure religious origins was partly a response to the stain of "impure *racial* origins" (the "impurity of blood") that stung him as a converso. In any case, Da Costa eventually combined these two issues—the theological and the racial (or existential),—within a single answer. The true word of God lay in the Bible—and the authentic Bible was the Old Testament, the holy book of Da Costa's ancestors, the ancient Jews. It was thus by plunging deep into his own existential origins that Da Costa could best satisfy his desire for the original truth of religion and also acquire (in accordance with Iberian norms) a superior and "purer" identity. The authenticity of the Christian religion and the authenticity of his own descent were focused in a single object. But that meant returning to the original religion of the Bible, not to a Judaism already burdened with its own "ecclesiastical" history and semi-"Catholic" distortions (including the belief in an afterlife).

Thus, I suggest, Da Costa returned to Judaism as a conscious reformer from the outset. Of course he did not expect to find biblical Judaism existing ready-made outside Iberia. He never believed, as the *Exemplar* might make us think, that the religion of Moses had been petrified for over two millenia, waiting for Uriel Da Costa to perform an unhistorical leap into it. However vaguely and unwillingly, Da Costa was aware that post-biblical Judaism was different from the original model. But he hoped and believed that the fluid New Jewish situation offered a historical opportunity to remedy this. In this respect he displayed historically minded reasoning. Having witnessed the triumph of the Counter-Reformation in Iberia, Da Costa expected that (unlike the Catholicism of which he had despaired) Judaism *could* lend itself to a purifying reform in the original direction of the Bible, especially within the New Jewish communities where, out of a minimal and shattered basis, former Marranos were trying to reconstruct a Jewish life for themselves. Since these New Jews were already engaged in an effort to recapture their lost essence, they may as well have regressed further back to their origins and restored the purer biblical Judaism that elsewhere had been obliterated.

This, however, was Da Costa's great mistake and the source of his genuine surprise. He failed to realize (as perhaps it was impossible a priori) that quite the opposite was then true: The only way for New Jews to coalesce into a unified community was by adhering to the orthodox rabbinical model as it already existed elsewhere. No other normative power was available by which to forge a unified group out of such diversity of newcomers, each with his own ambiguities and all lacking a shared standard tradition as Jews. The same fluid situation upon which Da Costa had presumably built his hopes thus turned out to be the cause of his greatest disappointment.

This revised picture of Da Costa only underscores the typical Marrano ambiguities under discussion here, especially the Jewish-Catholic duality, which already presupposes a subtler duality in each of its ingredients, and whose different configurations marked Da Costa's life in its four main stages: as disenchanted Catholic; as secret Judaizer in Portugal; as neo-Karaite in Amsterdam; and finally, as deist.

Da Costa has been called "the first modern man to abandon the Judeo-Christian tradition."[17] But in fact he did not succeed in doing so, and his futile attempt led him to despair and brought upon him humiliation and ruin. When he tried to step completely outside the views and beliefs of both Judaism and Christianity, he found that in order to do so he must also abandon Judaism and Christianity as concrete historical entities. But the time was not yet ripe for this and, in a succession of inquisitorial persecutions and two acts of *herem*, the historical nature of religion that Da Costa strove to transcend reaffirmed itself as a social and existential barrier. Given these conditions, it was precisely because Da Costa strove to identify directly with mankind in general that he ended his days estranged from himself and from all other men.[18]

It is sometimes the exceptional, almost pathological, case that sheds light on the underlying state of affairs and on an entire mental structure. The Marrano living in an alien culture projects an idealized object of yearning, with which he has no real contact—either by his life or by his knowledge—and yet he attempts to gain by this object a new identity and sense of belonging. In effect, therefore, he lives divorced from both his natural environment and his idealized object of yearning. And when he perceives the discrepancy between that idealized object and the historical reality that is supposed to achieve it, he is liable to lose his footing altogether and, like Da Costa, fall outside all spheres of identity and belonging. From this standpoint, Da Costa's case should not be regarded as a simplistic expression of the struggle between orthodoxy and freedom of thought, but as a manifestation (albeit extreme) of a specific internal schism inherent in the Marrano experience per se. Wherever he turns, the Marrano is an outsider and someone "new" (he is a New Christian or a New Jew). He does not belong to any cultural context simply or naturally, and feels both inside and outside any one of them. If he seems to have solved his problem and found an identity for himself (through assimilation into Christian society or by returning to the Jewish fold), this identity does not adhere to him simply or directly, for he must constantly struggle to engender and preserve it, overcoming the internal contradictions it entails. Hence he is doomed to a life of mental ferment and upheaval, to manifestations of doubt, and to a rupture with himself, his past, and his future—far more so than any member of a traditional society, or even of a revolutionary group such as the Reformers. The unassimilated Marrano is the true wandering Jew, roaming between Christianity and Judaism and drifting between the two and universalism. As such he is among the precursors of modernity, with its skepticism and its breakdown of traditional structures. In this respect, the life of Uriel Da

Costa, for all its pathos and melodrama, is, in the words of his own book, an *exemplar humanae vitae* lived in conditions of deracinating ferment.

Da Costa and Spinoza

Spinoza was eight years old when Uriel Da Costa shattered his skull with a bullet. Echoes of the scandal and tragedy were undoubtedly the talk of the day among the cliques of children in the classrooms. Was it so common for someone to shoot himself in the Jewish community? It is possible that Da Costa, even before his suicide, was something of a mysterious figure to the children—a banned and ostracized man, sinister and maligned, of whom the adults constantly warned—and the pathetic player in a humiliating scene of repentance. As such, he may have been the subject of talk and insinuations, a target of derision and of the cruelty of children, and the protagonist of many tales and legends produced by youthful fancy.[19] The young Spinoza did not know that Da Costa's naturalism presaged portions of his own doctrine, as Gebhardt saw in retrospect,[20] but the affair must have been deeply etched in the memory of the eight-year-old and provided him with something to reflect upon as a grown man. Once Spinoza was able to understand Da Costa's act, he could have found ample food for thought not only in the man's personal fate but in his theories as well.[21]

Revah and Gebhardt are divided on the question of Da Costa's direct influence on Spinoza. Gebhardt details the points of resemblance between their outlooks but adds cautiously that this does not necessarily imply the existence of influence.[22] Revah, however, is convinced that Spinoza gave much thought to Da Costa's case, adding that from a perusal of documents that he has uncovered, it is even likely that there was a remote family tie between the two.[23] Revah may well be right about the facts, yet the association between Spinoza and Da Costa does not stand or fall on the existence of a direct link between them. If such a link exists, all the better; even without it, one could contend that both of these men—like other dissidents and heretics of the period—unwittingly personified a broader spiritual problem that was implicit in the condition of the New Jews. Revah seems inclined to explain mental phenomena in a linear approach, as if one person has been influenced or pushed toward heresy by some other dissenting individual.[24] But, without minimizing the role of personal contacts, we must seek the source of the phenomenon of dissent in a larger, full-fledged cultural structure, which these cases enable us to identify but which extends beyond them, providing the individual cases with a fundamental background on which they can be better and more concretely understood.[25]

TESTIMONY BY OROBIO AND CARDOSO

Not all who returned to Judaism out of spiritual tension were disappointed like Da Costa. On the contrary, a number of them became militant champions of the traditional Jewish outlook and carried on a vigorous polemic with the heretics. Prominent among them was Baltasar Orobio de Castro, a Marrano physician and holder of a chair in metaphysics at a Spanish university, who was later arrested by the Inquisition for Judaizing. Interrogated, tortured, and divested of his property, Orobio finally confessed and was reconciled to the church in an *auto-da-fé* that, quite coincidentally, took place at about the time of Spinoza's *herem* (June 1656). Later Orobio taught medicine as a fake Christian in Toulouse, and finally, when he could no longer bear a life of secrecy and subterfuge, went to Amsterdam and overtly returned to Judaism, taking the name Isaac.[26] From then on Orobio became an enthusiastic defender of Judaism against all opposition and dissent and a missionary urging other Marranos to return to the religion of their forefathers. He remonstrated with Prado, attacked Spinoza, and argued with the Arminian theologian Philip van Limborch and with other Christian polemicists.

On at least two occasions Orobio depicted the heresy of the former Marranos. In a polemic against his former friend Prado, he divided the New Jews into two groups: those who return to the faith of their forefathers in sincerity and humility, sick only of ignorance but guilty of pride, and therefore ready to learn and to observe the Law; and those who

> return to Judaism after having studied some secular sciences such as logic, physics, mathematics, and medicine in the land of idolatry [the Iberian peninsula]. They, too, arrive no less ignorant in God's law than the former, but they are full of vanity, pride, and arrogance, confident that they are thoroughly learned in all subjects; despite their ignorance about the most essential thing, they pretend to know it all. And when they enter under the said yoke of Judaism and begin to hear what they don't know from those who do know, their vanity and pride prevent them from receiving instructions so that they may emerge from their ignorance. They think they will lose credit as erudite men if they consent to learn from those who are indeed educated in the sacred Law, and so

they feign great science by contradicting what they do not understand . . . In venturing their groundless sophist arguments, they
believe they are making a name for themselves as ingenious and
learned men. And what is worse, they do acquire this reputation
among some people who, due to their youth or natural evil, presume to be clever.[27]

Here Orobio designates the Marrano experience as a source of heresy among the New Jews. In his polemics against the heretics, Orobio
himself betrays the same background, for he calls to his aid such Catholic Scholastic authors as Thomas Aquinas, Duns Scotus, and Guil-
laume Durand,[28] and he brands all manifestations of independent
thought as "pride," a rather Christian denunciation. Although Orobio
is aiming his barbs at one man above all (Prado, who will be introduced below), he portrays at the same time the broader scene of doubts
and ambivalence that marked the community of New Jews in Amsterdam, as Gebhardt was first to realize.[29] Indeed, if one disregards Orobio's polemics against his erstwhile friend and benefactor Prado, the
picture he draws will appear symptomatic of a broader dilemma, affecting a whole class of people, educated in a high cultural milieu, but
lacking organic identification with any given tradition (Jewish or
Christian), who suddenly must embrace a diverse doctrine in which
they do not quite find themselves and that was never an integral part
of their lives or upbringing. This tradition now confronts them as an
alien, extrinsic order to which they must adapt themselves (or, more
precisely, which they must assimilate) because it is the tradition of the
nation with which they identify by an emotional and abstract choice.
Ultimately, most of the New Jews stood up to this test—albeit not
without inner turmoil; cases of heresy, however, including that of
Prado, illustrate on a magnified scale the kind of problem that others
faced as well. As Yerushalmi points out, the wonder is not that so
many had failed to become integrated Jews, but that so many had succeeded.[30]

That this was a widespread problem is clearly seen from the fact that
Orobio's *Epistola Invectiva* against Prado is arguing at length with different heretics, whom Orobio divides into three classes:

First, "unspeakable atheists" who dare to reject Holy Scripture and
believe only in a First Cause. The direct reference is to such deists as
Uriel Da Costa and Juan de Prado, but in a certain sense it could apply
to Spinoza as well.

Second, those who believe in God and Holy Scripture but look with
contempt on the oral Law, denying its divine source.

And third, those who believe both in the written Law and the oral Law but reject the body of rules established by the rabbis, in which they see a fatuous system that runs counter to the original Law of God.[31]

Orobio considers the latter two categories of heretics to be Jews but not the first category. The third type poses a considerable threat, in his view, because they are liable to shift from one group to another until they reach total atheism.

Further testimony to the same effect is supplied by another former Marrano, the mystic and messianic agitator Abraham (Miguel) Cardoso, who contended with both Orobio and his own brother Isaac about what he saw as their excessive rationalism. Abraham Cardoso, who is thought to have written independently of Orobio (though they may have had a common source), describes several groups of New Jews: the simple folk who "attach themselves to every saying of the sages," and two kinds of heretics.[32] The first class comprises mainly "philosophers and scientists," who demand a rational demonstration for everything and dismiss the sayings of the sages of Israel, including the sacred Law, when they lack such grounding. To Cardoso "they remain bad Jews, though not Christians." Some such inquisitive minds "place their necks under the legal maxims" and, studying them, end up as "wise and obedient"; but there are others who "remain neither Jews nor Christians, but naturalists." To Cardoso, "this sect is the most vile"; he would have written a work against them were he not busy preparing for the imminent coming of the Messiah. Even so, he had convinced someone in this group to change his mind. On Cardoso's report, then, the phenomenon evidently was generalized.

The second class comprises "haughty" people, who demand for everything not a rational but a scriptural ground. They will admit nothing without a biblical text, and for this reason they also refuse to accept the true Messiah, as do "Doctor [Isaac] Cardoso (his brother) and Doctor Orobio." Abraham Cardoso's characterization thus applies not only to neo-Karaites who reject the oral and the rabbinical Law, but also to normative Jews who accept all layers of Jewish Law but reject the Messianic frenzy of Sabbetai Zevi.

Somewhat like Da Costa, Abraham Cardoso also found the ordinary Judaism of the Rabbis lacking in spirituality and falling short of its true essence, which to him was the *messianic* calling of Judaism. Its task to pursue historic and metaphysical redemption. Cardoso thus manifested a Marrano mentality both in structure and in content, for he wished to impose his Marrano esperanza—the yearning for redemption—upon the Judaism he found when coming out of Iberia. In branding even his brother Isaac and "Doctor Orobio" as heretics, Abraham Cardoso ironically uses the best-known Christian charge against the Jews, who are blamed for having rejected the true Messiah. This charge, it is true, was current among the followers of Sabbetai Zevi in general, but coming from a former Marrano who had been brought up as a Catholic, it has a special ring.[33]

Except for an outburst of Messianism around 1666, soon to be extinguished in anguished disillusionment, it was the active, Sabbatian kind of Messianism that rabbinical Judaism usually viewed as suspicious and on the fringes of heresy. That former Marranos like Abraham Cardoso were active in this movement; that it fired the imagination of the Amsterdam community, composed largely of former Marranos who had experienced "mini-redemption" from the "Egyptian bondage" in Iberia; that after Sabbetai Zevi's fall and shocking conversion to Islam, former Marranos were among the unswerving believers who saw this as the deepest mystical secret (a "Marrano Messiah"!)—are other forms of New Jewish heresy and nonconformity motivated by the former Marrano experience.[34]

It should be stressed that Marranism had various offshoots and varieties. It is a specific historical structure, a kind of condition that overtook a large and diverse community, and the response of each individual to this condition and to the meeting of cultures and fates it entailed was radically different in each case. Features of the Marrano condition can be found among New Christians who adopted Catholicism wholeheartedly—some becoming priests, mystics, and religious reformers—and also among Judaizers who secretly preserved the memory of Jewish identity and practices, as well as among those who openly returned to Jewish orthodoxy, including rationalists and philosophers, cabalists and Sabbatians, quasi heretics and skeptics, and even complete atheists. The Amsterdam rabbis Saul Levi Morteira and Isaac Aboab reflect the Marrano background no less than Da Costa, Orobio, Abraham Farrar (the Sabbatian), Menasseh Ben Israel, the enemy-brothers Cardoso, or Daniel Levi de Barrios, the poet and adventurer; yet the manner in which this condition expressed itself took contrasting forms in different persons, and sometimes even within the same person.[35]

A Mirror of Tombs

The split mind of the "New Jews" has an extraordinary plastic and visual expression engraved in stone. At the very outset, the Portuguese community established an elegant cemetery for itself in Ouderkerk, near Amsterdam. The elaborate tombstones arranged in neat rows serve even now as eloquent (and somewhat puzzling) testimony to the life of this unique community.[36] Here are found the graves of the pillars of the community—rabbis, dignitaries, merchants—men of rank and outstanding achievement. Some of the tombstones, such as those of the rabbis Saul Levi Morteira and Menasseh ben Israel, and even of Spinoza's parents, Michael and Hannah-Deborah, are simple and smooth, without any ornamentation or drawings of figures—as was the custom of pious Jews from ancient times. But many other stones are fashioned as exquisite art, with graceful typographical design, engravings, ornaments, and family crests, and above all—in violation of the second commandment—with representations of human and animal figures. Some of these appear individually, others merge into friezes portraying scenes from the Bible. It is as though the visitor has entered a baroque cemetery of the aristocracy or upper bourgeoisie in one of the Catholic states of southern Europe, except that many of the epitaphs are in Hebrew, the names are Jewish, and the old ritualistic formula TNZBH (in Hebrew) is engraved in the stones.

Here is the grave of Mordechai Franco Mendes and his wife, Sara: the friezes on their tombstone portraying the sacrifice of Isaac, Jacob's dream, David playing the lyre, and Abraham's covenant with Abimelech. And here is the grave of Ribka (Rebecca) Ximenez and her daughter Esther: a bull and crossbones, half-naked boys shedding a tear, and in the center a tableau of the matriarch Rebecca and her maidens coming to draw water from the well. The two grieving youths on the grave of Abraham Levi Vitoria and his wife are almost completely naked; they look as though they belong in a Christian palace; and the two figures (a king and a patriarch) who, on the grave of Mozes van Mordechai Senior, stand on both sides of Moses holding the Tablets of the Law, are shaped in a grotesque style as figures on the façade of a cathedral. This same tombstone also shows the Biblical Mordechai riding a horse, the Queen of Sheba visiting Solomon, and eight other scenes from the Bible. But the visitor will reach the heights of astonishment standing before the tomb of Samuel Senior Teixeira: here, engraved in stone, is no less than the figure of God himself, beams of light gleaming about his head as he is revealed to the boy Samuel.

The tombstones in the Ouderkerk cemetery have yet to receive the full scholarly attention they deserve. From an artistic point of view, they are unrivaled—both in other Jewish cemeteries (not even in Curaçao, an extension of the Amsterdam community)[37] and in the Dutch visual art of the period. Little is known about the artists who, for a century and a half, produced these surprising headstones. But two things are beyond doubt: the vanity of this Jewish art form and the fact that the tombstones reflect not only a social class but also the Christian and south European background of Amsterdam's Portuguese New Jews and their descendants. One cannot contend that these tombstones are not Jewish art: since the members of the community were Jews, their creative efforts for one hundred and fifty years are undeniably a part of Jewish art, even if they are inconsistent with more widespread features of this art or with the second commandment (forbidding graven images). At the same time, the rows of gravestones in Ouderkerk underscore the degree to which the lives of these Jews were internally discordant and how far their consciousness was permeated by Christian symbols and images that carried over into their new lives as Jews. Adding some further, more intuitive reflections on what Ouderkerk seems to reveal, one can discern here a measure of freedom that attached to the lives of the Portuguese emigrant elite—the aristocracy, and the merchant class—even when they accepted the yoke of Judaism without demur or dissent. Their attitude toward religion seems to have included an element of enjoyment, not only of obedience and sacrifice, enjoying the recapture of their lost essence and of the relative freedom in which they could finally exist as Jews of distinction, living among themselves and their own people. A similar mixture of aesthetic impulse and religious devotion had, to a considerable extent, characterized the life of the Iberian aristocracy; and the Jewish-Portuguese elite in Amsterdam seems to have discovered that they could live in the same manner and style—but within their own element and professing the religion of their forefathers. From this point of view, they had an interest—both mental and social—in preserving the integrity of their religious institutions against any undermining influence, without, however, imposing excessive religious stringency on their personal lives. On the contrary, a good many Jews lived their reembraced religion with a much freer feeling, like people rediscovering a lost and dear treasure rather than like people bearing the heavy weight of a transcendent world on their shoulders, as did Dutch Calvinists, with their intense piety and somber, almost morbid, seriousness about religion. Of course, there were also other New Jews (people of perhaps stronger religious conviction) who gravely repented of their former lives as Christians and lived with a sense of guilt; this phenomenon is well known also in other communities of former Marranos.[38] In addition, the scholars and rabbis of the community (whose tombstones are usually simple and invariably free of figures)[39] lived with a much heavier burden, even with a sense of historic responsibility. It was their task to forge the life of the New Jews as actual Jews in every way, initiating them into the lost and practically forgotten tradition, and picking up the threads of the historical continuity where they had been dropped. Needless to say, this mission was not easily accomplished. It is impossible to impose organic continuity where rupture and crisis have occurred, and it was impossible to accord the New Jews a simple and contradiction-free Jewish identity while ignoring their Marrano past. The great achievement of the Amsterdam community was, therefore, not that it turned back the clock of history but that on the basis of the Marrano universe and experience, it managed to shape a new Jew, whose Catholicism was still active in his veins and in his consciousness, even as he struggled to suppress and assimilate it. This dialectic seems to be visually reflected in the rows of magnificent graves in Ouderkerk.

DR. PRADO IN SPAIN

Of all of the complex figures preceding Spinoza, special consideration must be given the physician Juan (Daniel) de Prado. Spinoza and Prado took center stage in a scandal that rocked the Amsterdam community in the mid-1650s and culminated in their excommunication. Gebhardt and Revah are even calling the incident the Prado-Spinoza affair, for the issue concerning them is proximate in nature and chronology and they belong to a single continuum of events.

Who was Juan de Prado? Gebhardt was the first to call attention to the heterodox physician whom he regarded, rather exaggeratedly, as Spinoza's mentor (a view I must question). Revah went even further by describing Prado as the villain of the piece—the man who, in less than a year, induced Spinoza toward heretical thoughts and led to his expulsion from the community. One may well doubt that Spinoza's mind was so weak that in so short a time he could be transformed from a "zealous member of the community"[40] into a villified and excommunicated heretic merely through the influence of a man of inferior intellectual caliber.[41] But let us leave this question for the end of the chapter, and look first at the basic facts and testimonies—most of which have been uncovered by the diligent and impressive research of Revah.

During the 1635–1636 academic year, two young men, whose paths and feelings would henceforth cross and clash for many years, met at the University of Alcalá de Henares in Spain. One was Juan de Prados (Prado), about twenty-three years old, a third-year theology student who had already devoted a number of years to medicine, philosophy, and related subjects. His younger friend, Baltasar Alvarez de Orobio (the same Orobio de Castro, we met above), had just entered the university. He, too, studied medicine, but devoted considerable time to theology. The two students became close friends. Apparently they were brought together by their common origin as the sons of Marranos and by that immediate and somewhat clandestine attachment that may well arise between young people with an exceptional background and a shared religious and intellectual unrest. Juan de Prado, five years older than his friend, extended significant aid to Orobio (the nature of which is not entirely clear), and many years later, even when the two found themselves involved in a bitter dispute, Orobio continued to consider Prado his benefactor and treated him with an ambivalent intimacy.[42]

About a year later, Prado went off to Toledo to complete his medical studies and the two friends parted ways. Mentally, both embarked on their paths as sworn secret Judaizers. Only fragmentary knowledge of Prado's activities is extant for the next two decades, but it is clear that he not only returned to the Jewish faith but became an active, militant Marrano, winning souls for Judaism among his family and friends, preaching a clandestine return to the Law of Moses, and shoring up the spirits of Marranos who were snared by the Inquisition. Some of his friends (including Orobio) were caught and made to confess, so that the files of the Inquisition, uncovered by Revah, echo in their dry way the mental and actual adventures of Prado during this period of his life.[43]

A Marrano Missionary

In 1654 the Inquisition arrested one of Prado's relatives, Francisco Gómez, better known as "Romano." Interrogated and tortured, Romano made a confession. He said that in 1639 (a year after Prado had finished his studies) the two men had met in the city of Lopera, and for a long while Prado had tried to persuade his kinsman to abandon the Christian faith and secretly return to Judaism. Romano reported that Prado was vigorous and determined in his attempt.

> He began by telling me that God had given Moses the written Law on Mount Sinai and miraculously parted the waters of the Red Sea so that the Hebrews could pass through it on dry ground. Then the doctor picked up the Bible in Latin and translated selections into Spanish for me. Finally, he said that the true Law, the one in which one can be saved, is the ancient Law. Consequently I should observe and practice this Law, for in it I shall find my salvation.[44]

Prado's efforts at persuasion were finally successful. When interrogated about the motives that led him to convert, Romano explained:

Dr. Prado's words moved me especially because he said that he was one of the most learned people in Alcalá, and since he himself practiced the Law of Moses, so could I. Prado said that no one had led him to convert to the Law of Moses and no one had taught him this Law. He had learnt by himself, through his books and his university education.[45]

This portion of the report shows that Prado, the son of Marranos, returned to Judaism of his own free will and took pride in this fact.[46] It is therefore unlikely that later he was the victim of "inducement" by someone else. Prado set himself as an example to persuade his listeners, yet the salient point here is not his boasting about his education so much as the emphasis he places on the change that occurred in him because of it. On the other hand, this same quotation certainly supports what Orobio de Castro would write later in his *Epistola Invectiva*—that the skepticism and heresy of some of the Marranos could be traced back to their university education and the pride that it instilled in them, as if their personal views were the highest authority. Orobio's general description rings true, at least in Prado's case—and in fact, he had Prado in mind.

Romano added in his testimony that Prado also succeeded in converting his wife to Judaism along with Prado's own wife and mother. In each case, the conversion was marked by a special profession of faith in which a secret covenant was made among all the new Judaizers.[47]

Underground Leader and Conspirator

Ten years later, we still find Prado involved in secret ceremonies and the dissemination of Marrano ideas. By then he was living and practicing medicine in the city of Andújar in Andalusia. In 1650, the Inquisition trapped a Marrano by the name of Duarte Rodrígues Díaz, who was cast into prison and given the attention of the Holy Office for two years until he confessed and betrayed his partners in crime. Among the names he mentioned was Dr. Juan de Prados who, according to Rodrígues Díaz, in 1649 conducted an occult Marrano ceremony to conjur up the soul of the deceased wife of Pedro Marcos de Espinosa. The deceased was a relative of the doctor's wife. Fortunately for Prado and his wife, the Inquisition did not view this testimony as sufficient grounds for instituting proceedings against them, and they were exempted from punishment.[48]

Nevertheless, this was a difficult period for the Marranos of Andalusia. In 1650 forty of them fell victim to a New Christian informer by the name of Vasco and were cast into the Inquisition's prison in Granada. Ironically, among them was Prado's wife, even though her name did not appear on the informer's list; her imprisonment was a bureaucratic error. Two others arrested on that occasion were Pedro Marcos de Espinosa and his brother Juan. Prado and his closest associates took steps to aid the internees. He smuggled into the prison a letter addressed to the Espinosa brothers in which he urged the prisoners to take heart and informed them of the actions being taken on their behalf. The letter spoke of a group of witnesses who were organizing to defame the informer Vasco and said that "Romano" (the one who was to be tried later on) was on his way to the capital to present a list of charges against the informer before the Inquisition's supreme council. The strategy of Prado and his associates may well have been to fabricate a web of false testimony in order to clear the accused and to indict the accusing traitor in his place (a common defense among underground groups). The end of the story is unclear, but it is known that Prado's letter came to the attention of the Inquisition (and thus also came down to us) through the confession of one of its addressees, Pedro Marcos de Espinosa.

This picture is complemented by the testimony of another physician, a devout Judaizing Marrano by the name of Dr. Antonio de Fonseca. Caught by the Inquisition in 1661 and falsely repented, he was trapped again and, as a *relapso*, sentenced to burn at the stake. Mercifully, he died before his sentence was carried out. At his trial, Dr. Fonseca confessed that throughout his life he had been faithful to the Law of Moses. In 1651, as a secret convert to Judaism, he maintained contact with a "Portuguese" doctor by the name of Juan de Prados. If, as is almost certain, this is the same Prado we have been following here, then there is further evidence that even in the early 1650s Prado was still an active and militant Judaizer, taking constant risks for his Jewish-Marrano faith.

This is surprising. The early 1650s were only a few years before the Spinoza affair and the ban pronounced in Amsterdam on Juan de Prado himself. Did he undergo such a swift change of heart? Or can it be that the first doubts had already begun to ferment in Prado's mind while he was still in the proselytizing underground in Spain, before he came to Amsterdam?

The Third Man: Ribera

In one of his articles, Revah tried to prove that Prado, supposedly Spinoza's beguiler, was himself "beguiled" upon his arrival in Amsterdam by another Jewish heretic, Daniel de Ribera. Revah arrived at this theory by an interesting route that did not lack the ingredients of detective work. First he pondered a section in Orobio de Castro's *Epistola Invectiva* that ascribes Prado's downfall to an unnamed third figure. When looking for the identity of this third man, Revah concluded that it must be Ribera, whom the rabbis of Amsterdam interrogated in 1658 and whose file Revah found and published along with that of Prado.[49] Thereafter, however, Revah, who painstakingly compared various versions of Orobio's writings, discovered three versions in which Orobio identified the third man by name—not Ribera but one Pinhero[50] whom both Orobio and Prado had known in Spain. Moreover, other documents show that Ribera had no Jewish ancestry; he was a Spanish former monk who found his way to Jewish Amsterdam via Italy and Brazil. In that community he served as a teacher, but was reputed to be a heretic and, after investigation, he was expelled along with Prado. His ban, quite curiously, is not inscribed in the records of the Portuguese congregation. Ribera then moved to England, where he reconverted and became an Anglican. At the same time, it is possible that he spied on the newly formed Portuguese-Jewish community of London and reported to the Inquisition. At the end of his life, Revah discovered, Ribera left England and rejoined Catholicism with his two daughters. While Ribera's curious and fascinating case still needs clarification,[51] it is certain that he was not the third man; so Revah adopts Orobio's view that it was Juan Piñero, their "detestable" former colleague, who had led Prado astray while they all were still living in Spain.

Prado's Ambivalence Compounded: The Budding Deist

And indeed, some time later, again studying the files of the Inquisition, Revah found a document that supported his view.[52] The person under inquisitorial interrogation this time was Baltasar Orobio himself, Prado's erstwhile comrade at the University of Alcalá and his adversary in years to come. Orobio was arrested in Seville in 1654 and at the beginning of 1656 was committed to torture. Unable to bear the pain, he called for the torture to stop, and confessed to being a secret Judaizer. Among his accomplices, Orobio mentioned Dr. Prado, who had in the meantime escaped from Spain and was already in Amsterdam criticizing Judaism. Orobio told of the days when he had entered into a covenant of Judaizers with Prado, but the most interesting and puzzling part of his testimony concerned an incident a year later. In 1643, Orobio told the inquisitors, he met again with Prado in Lopera and was amazed to discover that his old friend had undergone a strange metamorphosis. Prado now spoke with him in evasive terms and, with some hesitation, finally told Orobio that in his view all religions were equal and all men—Jews, Christians, and Moslems—could achieve salvation, each through the laws of his own religion, since the purpose of all these laws was merely political and derived from the law of Nature, which is the First Cause posited by Aristotle. Also present during that conversation, Orobio added, was Prado's brother-in-law, Dr. Diego Duarte Serrano, who supported Prado's position.

In summing up that position two days later, Orobio ascribed to Prado a somewhat different stance. This time he said that Prado claimed that all religions were identical because their laws are aimed at the same objective, "namely to know God, and this suffices for salvation." Orobio's two versions are obviously inconsistent. Are the laws of religion political or exclusively pragmatic (as Spinoza more or less claimed), or are religions aimed at knowing God (which Spinoza denied)? One must not take Orobio to task, for he was speaking from memory here. Neither should we be too hard on Prado, who was certainly not a systematic philosopher. The important point is that according to Orobio's recollection and testimony—which must also be viewed in light of the terrifying circumstances—by 1643 Prado had already arrived at heterodox thoughts and was displaying the first signs of deism.

How is one to construe Orobio's testimony? Does it not contradict the fact that during that time, and for a long while thereafter, Prado continued to work—and to imperil himself—for the sake of his secret Judaism and the Marrano rites he practiced?

Revah suggests that Prado was playing a double game, acting as a believer while being a heretic at heart. But this approach views Prado as more coherent and rational than he seems to have been. If he were so rational and in such control of his thoughts and feelings, why did he continue taking such risks for the sake of Judaism? Masquerading is worthwhile when it adds to a person's security, not when it detracts from that security and places him in grave peril. It therefore appears that we must trace the contradiction to Prado's own mind and impute to him an ambivalent and dualistic position on the inside as well. Ranged against the first buds of deism in Prado's mind may have been his dedication to the Marrano brotherhood—a devotion not tempered by any theory or system of ideas, but thriving on the simple camaraderie of persecuted people who share a common fate—and this feeling may have inhibited the development of his more theoretical ideas by keeping them in an embryonic or suppressed state.

Prado may not have been a profound thinker, but he had a complex and ambivalent mind. Contradictory motives may have dwelt in his mind at the same time, and it is doubtful whether he always acted—or spoke—in full awareness of his position. It was not uncommon for him to take both sides of a question, rejecting a stand and repudiating his own rejection, seeking and failing to find. When banned by the Jews, he claimed that they had misjudged him; he never broke completely and irreparably with Christianity, as attested by his ambivalent attempts later in life to approach it again. It is doubtful whether one can fully decipher his mind. Not a rational man in the ordinary sense, he must be understood through his split and searching mind and a multiplicity of personas and motives. In spite of his many paradoxes, one can, however, trace a pattern of development: from Christianity to original (or fundamentalist) Judaism, from there to the view that all religions can lead equally to salvation, and finally to the view that no religion can lead to salvation, for reason alone is the source of truth. But for all that, no station along his path was entirely explicit, definitive, or free of contradiction. Even when he wore a mask on the exterior, this did not reflect an inner, integral self, which only posed as something else to the outer world, but rather revealed a duality that prevailed in his *inner* self as well. The outer mask partly covered, partly reflected, an inward one.

Even Orobio, a connoisseur of ambivalence, was struck by Prado's paradoxes. In a terse, personal passage he compares his own case with Prado's. "I had lived in Spain pretending I was a Christian because life there was pleasant," he confesses, "but I had not been a good pretender, and so it was discovered that indeed I was nothing but a Jew." Orobio continues:

> Now if over there, where at the risk of my freedom, honor, and home—and even of my life—I was a Jew in truth and a Christian in lying, it stands to reason [*bien se deja creer*] that where I enjoy freedom, with God's mercy, I shall be a Jew. [53]

The logic is impeccable; Orobio is the rational former Marrano. Not so Prado, who exasperates him:

> It is only to you that it so happened, to be a fake Christian and a true Jew where you could not be a Jew, and to be a fake Jew where [finally] you could be truly Jewish. [54]

A perceptive résumé of Prado's vicissitudes! Does this suggest that what Prado really sought was the experience of Marranism as such—duality for duality's sake? Not even this, for Prado spoke his objections aloud in Amsterdam—which to Orobio was his worst offense. In another personal address,[55] Orobio reproaches Prado less for having had heterodox thoughts than for having voiced them—in other words, for not having been a good Marrano!

Some paradoxes, after all, have also tinged the "rationalist" and faithful Orobio—and how could it be otherwise?

PRADO IN AMSTERDAM: THE CRISIS OF THE 1650S

It is not known precisely how Prado escaped from Spain. He seems to have seized the opportunity to accompany a Spanish cardinal traveling to Rome, from where Prado went to northern Europe—first to Hamburg and then to Amsterdam. He also managed to get his wife and mother out of Spain, the latter establishing a temporary residence in Hamburg. In the registry of the Amsterdam community, Prado's name appears at a relatively late date (October 1655) as having pledged three florins and eighteen stuivers to the synagogue. Prado returned to Judaism overtly and took the name Daniel; in a certain sense, however, he found himself in a situation not unlike that of Da Costa—though with a different pattern. Until then he knew Judaism only as an underground reality, fighting for its continued life while cut off from the roots of its traditions. Now, suddenly, Prado stood before the bulk of official, normative Judaism, with its traditions, rabbis, and network of detailed beliefs and practices that he was required to accept as cogent and finished doctrine. Faced with this new situation, Prado found that the heretical ideas that had been partly dormant and partly fermenting in his mind during his days in the Marrano underground, now burst forth into the open.

It might be said that in leaving the Iberian peninsula behind him, Prado moved from Judaism as an existential and fraternal condition to Judaism as a normative and doctrinal system.[56] In Spain it was a reality of Marranos fighting for their special kind of existence and of links between men and women sharing a common fate; now, in Amsterdam, Judaism posited itself as a system of norms, regulations, and articles of faith, a system that had not been an organic part of Prado's education—or even of his life as a secret Judaizer—but which, nevertheless, he was now required to embrace as an absolute condition of his reentry into historical Judaism and for his participation in it. Many others have faced this problem, but in Prado's case it produced a new conflict. Once again the demands of his daring opinions, of his pride and his vague, somewhat diffuse quest for intellectual freedom, which were so vital to his struggle against Christian theology, now returned to the fore—above all the demand that he, as an individual, should subject all tradition to the judgment of his own reason and knowledge. Moreover, in face of the doctrinal demands made by official Judaism and its rabbis, and seeing the Jews living in relative freedom in northern Europe, Prado was liberated from many inhibitions that had constrained him in Spain. The deist ingredient in his multicontradictory mind began taking over and dominating his thoughts. Why did God elect Israel over all the nations? Who is this God that elects one nation over another? Is God a person, or perhaps only an eternal First Cause whose laws are none other than the laws of nature itself? Yet, by ostensibly approaching the resolution of an earlier contradiction in his mind, Prado reached a new (and for us more interesting) contradiction, namely, the clash between his theoretical attitude toward Judaism and his continued, real and concrete link with the Jews. Once he refused to accept the authority of Judaism as a theoretical system, the basis for his continued participation in the common life of the Jews crumbled under him. Yet Prado vehemently refused to be cut off from the community of his fellow Jews, as attested by his relentless struggle to have the ban against him lifted. In this he differs completely from Spinoza.

Orobio Contra Prado

A polemical picture of what happened to Prado in Amsterdam is contained in Orobio's generalized description of Marrano dissenters, which includes a tacit vignette of Prado. Orobio oversimplifies when he indentifies Prado's pride as vain pomposity. It is plausible that Prado tended to boast about his learning; this is corroborated by his conversation with his relative Romano. Yet the essence of pride (as we have already suggested) is not conceit but the philosophical demand for personal conviction and consent. Faced with an external tradition, the individual demands to be able to find the exercise and consent of his own intelligence and personal knowledge at the bottom of all his judgments, confused and devoid of depth as they may be. Thus in setting out to learn and appropriate the Torah of his forefathers, it is he, Prado, not the Torah as given, that must be the ultimate judge. Prado's pride consisted in confronting the Law and tradition with his personal judgment and appointing himself as judge over them. In that sense, his sin of pride is that of modern man in general; Prado is one of the minor figures who heralded modernism while being crushed by the burden of their message.

The man of pride, Orobio says, is especially dangerous to callow, weak-minded youths, whom his sophisms enchant and attract. After depicting the skeptical unrest of the 1650s in polemic colors, Orobio goes on to identify the culprit:

> This whole miserable precipice had its origin in the ignorance of one student or physician whose pride did not allow him to understand the divine antidote [to be found] in the doctrine of our ancient and contemporary Sages and Doctors. And because someone, to the great scandal of our nation, arrived by this path at his extreme ruin and contaminated others who, outside Judaism, gave credit to him and to his foolish sophisms, I deemed it necessary . . . to oppose the opinions which his malice has tried to introduce into the minds of simple people.[57]

Who precisely are the villains of this piece? As Gebhardt recognized, the "student or physician"[58] who is said to have instigated the scandal refers obviously to Prado. But who is the "someone" (*uno*) who followed these steps into his "extreme ruin" and, to the disgrace of his people, gained recognition outside Judaism? As the description could perfectly fit Spinoza, Gebhardt raises strong arguments to prove that indeed "this *uno* could have been no other than Spinoza." Revah accepted this conclusion wholeheartedly, praising Gebhardt for seeing "immediately" that there was indeed no other candidate,[59] but later he found a version of Orobio's text in which the world *someone* (*uno*) was missing and in its place was the demonstrative adjective *this one* (*este*).[60] This could suggest that Orobio (or his transcriber) did not have Spinoza in mind, but continued to refer to Prado. Unlikely as this possibility may seem,[61] it no longer permits us to assert with certainty that Orobio held Prado responsible for Spinoza's heresies. At the same time, Orobio does employ the notion of linear "corruption," for he attributes to his protagonist (be it Prado or Spinoza) the role of having "contaminated" others; and, moreover, he claims to know who had corrupted Prado himself: it was another deist of their old company in Spain, the aforementioned Piñero (Pinhero), whom Orobio seems to detest,[62] yet of whom he sketches a rather peceptive and eloquent vignette:

> Hebrew of nation, at first a Christian, then a Jew, then neither Jew nor Christian, a man of very limited judgment, a small philosopher and even less of a physician, mad in his reasoning, dauntless in his talk, the friend of novelties, solicitor of paradoxes, and what is worst, abominable in his morals [*costumbres*].[63]

Gebhardt thought this description applied to Prado, but later the name of Pinheyro was found in the margin of several versions of the text. Gebhardt, however, was not far wrong. Orobio's words could apply to Prado as well—and fit a whole class of educated Marranos whose religious ambiguity was joined to intellectual unrest and the "love of novelty."

Thus, Orobio believed Piñero had corrupted Prado, just as Revah (and possibly Orobio himself) said that Prado in turn corrupted Spinoza. If we take this linear explanation, the reader may halt and ask: And who corrupted Piñero? And who corrupted his corruptor? Whoever looks for the corruptor of the corruptor is liable to end only with the "self-corrupting corruptor"—none other than the devil. Instead of this approach, we would do better to trace the heterodox phenomenon to a much broader psycho-cultural structure, allowing for independent developments in various individuals whose intercourse affected each other's itinerary but did not causally determine it.

Prado's shifts and paradoxes mark indeed, the stations in his own itinerary. Having been converted by choice into clandestine Judaism, Prado was unlikely to be so easily pushed into deism by Piñero. The latter, incidentally, was not a pure deist but was himself torn by ambiguities; even after his death he was denounced as a Judaizer to the Inquisition in Lima.[64] It seems that, by the very nature of the phenomenon, we must be ready to admit paradoxes and ambiguities if we are to approach the Marrano mind. The dauntless and even proud attitude they showed was not merely a form of vanity; as they had lost the solid support of religious tradition and authority, all they had to lean upon was their own reasoning; this was a source of self-assurance, sometimes exaggeratedly expressed, but also of anxiety and doubt which were often dispelled by even more insistent reasoning. On the whole, the power of reason gave every individual an equal right to form an opinion, yet it was lofty and abstract, often evasive, and always open to counterarguments.

The problem of this new clan of intellectuals—a problem heightened, but also answered, in Spinoza's work—was this: how can the lofty and seemingly weaker principle of reasoning help them regain the absolute assurance and the same mental support they lost along with the solidity of religious tradition. Many—perhaps most—could not attain this stage, thereby serving as a catalyst to intellectual novelties and paradoxes that helped usher in the new rationalist attitudes of the seventeenth century, including that of Spinoza himself.

It should be noted that Orobio goes on referring to Piñero as "Hebrew by nation" even while the latter has adopted Catholicism, or rejected both Judaism and Christianity. This implies a distinction between ethnic and religious identity, which traditional Jews refuse to admit but former Marrano intellectuals were frequently led to acknowledge, because the distinction actually existed, if not as a clearcut concept (except in the blood purity regulations), then as a powerful attitude usually taken by non-Jews. Conversos continued to be called "Jews" even when they were sincere Catholics; and hostile propaganda often described them as neither Christian nor Jewish, which meant in context "worse than Jews" (not *even* Jews).

Orobio now adopts this anticonverso motif while speaking as an inner-Jewish apologist, and in the process stresses the distinction between the "Hebrew nation" and all religion. A person of "Hebrew" extraction, he implies, can be defined by ethnic roots regardless of whether his religion is Judaism, Christianity, or deism. In thus reiterating an outsider's viewpoint, which he now expresses from within Judaism—a stand no rabbis claim—Orobio tacitly admits, and partly conceptualizes, an existential distinction that Prado, Piñero, Spinoza—and Iberian Marranos generally—embodied in their actual lives. It is a distinction that he himself had personally experienced. When Prado grappled with the Jewish community, or Spinoza analyzed the Iberian Marranos as a paradigm-case in *Jewish* history (*Theologico-Political Treatise*, chap. 3), each in his own way has reiterated the same distinction implied by Orobio—which, however, in the seventeenth century, was still anachronistic and lacking a social basis upon which to build.

False Repentance and Ban

We know little about the encounter between Prado and Spinoza. But it is likely, as Revah suggests, that they met in the Keter Torah yeshiva, established and run by Rabbi Saul Levi Morteira. Faithful to its name (which refers to the crown of the Torah scroll vestments), this yeshiva was indeed the crowning achievement of the Jewish educational system in Amsterdam. It is likely that Prado had come to study in this yeshiva, intensifying his qualms and doubts in intellectual commerce with the city's greatest scholar. Spinoza and Prado were undoubtedly already in contact at the end of 1655; and although Spinoza did not find a mentor or a "corruptor" in Prado, the contact between the two men certainly helped them to boost and articulate their dissenting ideas.

In any event, less than a year after Prado's arrival in Amsterdam, the congregation opened proceedings against both him and Spinoza. It seems that by the spring of 1656 their heresy was already public knowledge. The two men, however, responded to the community's demands in diametrically opposite ways. Spinoza refused to recant, rejected all suggestions of compromise (and some say, of bribes as well), and not only decided to stand by his position even at the cost of expulsion from the community, but may even have wished to break with it himself. Prado, on the other hand, preferred to lead a double life (to which he had grown accustomed in Spain) and waged a stubborn and convoluted battle for his right to membership in the Jewish community. Thus one can read in the community's books two texts proximate in time but quite disparate in content: the ban against Spinoza and, right alongside it, Prado's statement of repentance.

On July 27, 1656, the *herem* (ban) of Baruch Spinoza was entered in the community's registry. A few days later, Prado stood before the *Tebah* (public prayer stand) of the synagogue and declared:

> Because I have held bad opinions and shown but little zeal in worship of God and His holy Law, I hereby mount this *Tebah* as ordered by the gentlemen of the *Ma 'amad* and, of my free will, confess before Blessed God and His holy Law and before this whole sacred congregation that I have sinned and erred in both word and deed, . . . scandalizing this sacred cogregation, for which I strongly repent and humbly request forgiveness . . . and accept to do the penance which the rabbis have ordered me . . . and I promise not to revert to the same or to similar delinquencies. . . . Peace upon Israel. Dr. Daniel de Prado.[65]

Nothing in these words recalls the pathos of the Da Costa affair. Woodenly, reluctantly, Prado reads a text dictated to him. His words are mere lip service, and his rebellious spirit prevents him from keeping his vow. Before long the entire community learned that he had relapsed into his evil ways. Although Prado again tried to take refuge in secrecy—as, ironically enough, he used to do as a Marrano in Spain—the rabbis heard about his deeds. The leaders of the community once again condemned Prado. On February 14, 1657, about six months after Spinoza's herem, the ban was likewise pronounced on his older friend, Daniel de Prado.

Prado and Nonreligious Judaism

Once again Prado refused to accept the sentence pronounced upon him. He wanted to remain within the community and appealed his ban. The reason for the appeal is not entirely clear. Was it a simple economic motive (Prado lived in penury, receiving financial support from the congregation), coupled with linguistic and cultural convenience? Or was there perhaps a more profound reason: a refusal to relinquish his belonging to the Jewish people, with whom he had thrown in his lot during the period of the Marrano underground, merely because of a change that occurred in his theological views? In any event, Prado's appeal placed the members of the community in a completely new kind of quandary, a problem no one before them had faced. Here was a Jew who refused to sever his ties with them and yet was a heretic in his beliefs. Would it be possible to retain within the historical framework of Judaism a man who rejects the tenets of the Jewish religion and flouts its commandments? Prado had unwittingly confronted his people with an issue they were unprepared to grapple with—namely, the possibility of nonorthodox Judaism. From this standpoint it is possible that he, rather than Spinoza (or perhaps more than Spinoza), foreshadowed the later problem of secular Judaism. Spinoza did not insist on remaining within the Jewish fold while Prado fought tenaciously both for his heterodox views and for his continued affiliation with the Jews. Here was yet another paradox marking this man of many contradictions, and perhaps it was the most interesting and telling of them all.

Nevertheless, nonreligious Judaism did not exist at that time, either as a theoretical possibility or as a social and existential reality. Rather, Prado presented to his contemporaries what they saw as a contradiction in terms, and the leaders of the community, after weighing the embarrassing matter at length, tried to reach a compromise. Two *parnasim* (elders of the community) met with Prado and offered him generous financial assistance if he would agree to take his family and emigrate someplace overseas where Jews could be found. The parnasim stressed their desire to spare him distress, but Prado nonetheless rejected their offer.

> He did not want to submit, excusing himself with reasons of little foundation; on the contrary, he was quite insistent about having the ban lifted and being granted the forgiveness he deserved.[66]

This report seems to indicate that it was not for economic reasons that Prado insisted on retaining his membership in the community. Quite the opposite, it appears that he preferred to go on suffering poverty rather than yield.[67] The embarrassment of the community leaders grew apace. They convened a special council comprised of the parnasim of that year and the previous year, together with the rabbis of Amsterdam, and after extensive consultation they reached a decision, practically amounting to an exile sentence on Prado:

> [The participants] unanimously decided that the ban on Prado will not be lifted unless he goes overseas, either with or without his family; and on condition that if he ever returns to any part of these states [the Netherlands] the same ban as before will apply.[68]

It is doubtful whether the community archives contain any other document with such a list of prominent names—parnasim of two successive terms and the great rabbis Saul Levi Morteira and Isaac Aboab. The Prado affair seems to have troubled the community even more than the Spinoza case, largely because of the unusual problem that arose with Prado's vexing refusal to yield. It would be erroneous to view the leaders of the congregation as a band of unenlightened fanatics (as Graetz portrayed them) who closed their ears to the voice of reason. From their point of view, no other solution was tenable, except at the cost of revising their own values and introducing a subversive element that would eventually undermine the social structure which they had so diligently labored to rebuild from scratch. As for Prado, it is doubtful if he would have been able to articulate the broader message embedded within his struggle, for the category of nonreligious Judaism did not yet exist—not even as a subjective concept, that the individual could employ in his inner self-identification. Rather than fight for a coherent and conscious principle, Prado seems to have been struggling for his right as an individual to live with his inner contradictions, maintaining his attachment to the Jews even while repudiating the doctrine of Judaism.

In this affair Prado displayed neither nobility of spirit nor a pure and unshakeable conscience. He was not a spiritual giant but a rather ordinary man whose fate and vicissitudes did not elevate him above his contemporaries. He was marked by vanity, quibbling, and petty pride; his suffering had endowed him with rancor and hatred, and from time to time he was prepared to recant outwardly or, alternatively, play the righteous innocent who had never sinned. Written testimonies report that he railed with vengeance and hatred against Morteira and the rest of sages, "who deserve to be killed"; he also said one should enter the synagogue with a drawn sword to create a scandal, or secretly plant offensive letters in Morteira's house. Such ideas and modes of speech were quite inconceivable in the case of Spinoza. It is not our role to pass judgment on Prado; it certainly cannot be expected that everyone who embodies the principle of free thought will be graced, like Spinoza, with the powers of spirit and nobility that mark the outstanding few. In a number of ways, it is rather the ordinary traits of Prado's personality that dramatize the unique nature of his case and the implacability of his condition.

The Jewish "Inquisition": Morteira Sets a Trap

The murky atmosphere of suspicion then prevailing in Amsterdam comes out very clearly in the sources. Rabbi Morteira was not one to forgive or forget. In conducting a thorough investigation against Prado (1658) he did not shrink from employing a spy (Monsanto) and setting a trap. As Jacob Monsanto reports in the investigation file, Morteira at first wanted to bar him from studying Latin under Prado. Finally, however, he granted permission on condition that Monsanto would draw Prado to speak out freely, and then report what he heard. The amateur detective tried his hand at it and finally achieved results:

> Three or four days ago, while giving (me) a lesson with his son present, he asked his son to leave, and the first thing he said to me was: Why are you studying Latin?[69] I replied: In order to study medicine, to which he responded that if such was the case, why was I studying Hebrew, since that language has no use whatever and is a lot of confusion, because nothing written in it makes any sense. I pretended not to hear in order to get more out of him.[70]

The informer's patience indeed paid off:

> On Monday evening before the lesson, as he sat talking to me, he said that there is no reason why we should believe in Moses any more than we believe in Mohammed. Then he asked me whether reward and punishment exist, and I replied: Is that in doubt? Don't you know that that's one of the Thirteen Articles of Faith? To which he replied sarcastically that up to now no one has returned from the Next World to ask for our help. . . .
>
> He especially mocked the wisdom of the sages regarding the resurrection of the dead, saying that such a thing is impossible and defies common sense, so that everything that has been said about the resurrection of the dead is sheer nonsense. He also says that the world was not created but has always existed in the same form and will continue to exist forever.

Here, then, are some of the tenets of Prado's deistic heresy: the world has always existed and is eternal; there is no world to come; there is no reward and punishment; all historical religions are equal. Prado, we shall remember, held a similar view in Spain, but there is a difference: in Spain he said that all religious are equal in their degree of immanent truth, whereas now he seems to say that they are all equally nonsensical. Prado also attacks the concept of revelation, contending that the Torah puts forth contingent truths; above all, he places the authority of reason over and above tradition, as the only principle binding upon man in matters concerning his conscience. Prado's arguments are specifically, and relentlessly, aimed against Morteira. He refutes the allegedly rational proofs the rabbi gave to the belief in divine revelation; and he disputes the old prejudice, repeated by Morteira and by "another barbarian" (another rabbi), that "a man who is a philosopher is wicked." Prado responds by advancing an equally long-standing (and basically valid) argument, namely, that every man philosophizes in some way; and that "they themselves [the rabbis] in saying 'yes is yes and no is no,' " are already philosophizing.

The evidence collected on Prado in 1658 shows him mixing philosophical arguments with petty taunts and derision, and proves that the mood was irascible on both sides. Even if we cannot accept all the informers' testimony without qualification, it is beyond doubt that Prado by this stage was an unabashed heretic and deist, who disseminated his ideas on the sly.

Yet Prado persisted in his campaign for rehabilitation. In 1659 he wrote a new apologia (in Latin), and his son David set out to assist his father by circulating a writ in his defense. The two challenged the propriety of the inquest conducted by Morteira and the validity of its findings. They charged the rabbi with bias and blind hatred of Prado that led his judgment astray; and they hinted at an earlier case in which Morteira acted in a similar vein (referring, of course, to Spinoza). They also mentioned the trap set by Morteira for Prado and complained that the sentence was based upon testimony from a callow student, who distorted what he had heard in order to please the rabbi and win his favor. In substance, Prado claimed that he was faithful to the religion of his forefathers; he emphasized his antagonism to Catholicism and his devotion to Judaism—for which he had forfeited important academic appointments that surely would have been offered to him had he agreed to convert to Christianity, and proclaimed that, at least practically, he had not sinned against the Mosaic Law. But all his protests were in vain. In the end Prado was forced to move to Antwerp, where he lived in the 1660s and from where he conducted his great polemic with his former friend Orobio. His end is unclear. In a moment of weakness, he seems to have made a stab at reconciling himself with the Spanish Inquisition, but the attempt did not mature and Prado died as he had lived: a faithless Jew clinging to his people and severed from them at the same time.

Inquisition Reports on Prado and Spinoza

What was Spinoza doing while Prado was fighting for acquittal? Up until recently very little was known. The four years separating Spinoza's ban from his appearance among the Collegiants in Rijnsburg (1660) were a dark period in his life. Many, perhaps most, scholars accepted Lucas's story that Morteira continued to persecute his renegade pupil and did not relent until he had secured from the burgomasters of Amsterdam an expulsion order against Spinoza. Recently some more evidence of Spinoza's activity in Amsterdam, including his relations with the Quakers, is being compiled.[71] But a strong, almost sensational light was thrown upon this dark period by Revah's discoveries. They indicate that Spinoza continued to live in Amsterdam, or visited it regularly, at least until the beginning of 1659, and that he regularly met Prado there.

Once again we are indebted to the spies of the Inquisition for the information we possess. In August 1659 two people recently returned from abroad reported to the inquisitor in Madrid: a Latin-American monk, Fr. Tomás Solano y Robles, and a Spanish soldier, Captain Miguel Pérez de Maltranilla. Both had found their way to Amsterdam and spent some time there—one seven months, the other two; and both later reported to the Inquisition in Spain on what they had seen. (The captain was summoned to report, and the monk volunteered the information in order to clear himself of suspicion because of his sojourn in hostile territory, and perhaps also to do his Catholic duty). Brother Solano wished specifically to inform on Lorenzo Escudero, a Spanish actor, but the Inquisition took a broader interest and asked to be told about the Spanish expatriates in Holland in general. So the monk tells them that

> He also made the acquaintance of Dr. Prado, a physician, who has been called Juan and whose Jewish name he did not know . . . and also one Espinosa, whom he believes was born in one of the cities of Holland, for he studied in Leiden and was a good philosopher. . . . Both of these two had formerly professed the Mosaic Law, but the synagogue expelled and chased them because they became atheists. They themselves told the witness that they were circumcised and [in the past] had observed the law of the Jews, but they changed their minds because it seemed to them that the law was not true, and that the souls die along with the bodies, and that there is no God except philosophically. For this reason they were driven out of the synagogue: and felt [with regret] the lack of the alms which the synagogue had given them and of the communication with the other Jews, they were content with maintaining the error of atheism.[72]

Brother Solano y Robles also provided a physical portrait of the two friends:

Dr. Juan de Prado is tall, thin, big-nosed, of dark complexion, black hair and black eyes. He is about thirty years old. . . . Spinosa is a short man with a handsome face, light complexion, black hair and eyes; he is twenty-four years old. He has no profession, and he was a Jew by birth [or: by nation: *de nacion*].

Unlike the monk, the captain was not so conversant with theological matters; he did describe the framework of the meetings and their content. There seems to have been a circle meeting at the house of a physician by the name of Dr. José Guerra. In addition to Prado and Spinoza, it comprised "a certain Pacheco" (probably the one who testified against Prado) and another Jewish physician named Dr. Reynoso. Guerra came to Amsterdam from the Canary Islands to convalesce from an illness, and the others frequented his home. Reynoso and Pacheco observed the laws of Judaism and refused to eat nonkosher food, but the officer often heard from Prado and Spinoza that they had abandoned the Jewish religion

because it was not good and was false, and therefore they were excommunicated; they were seeking a better law to follow, but it seems to this witness that they didn't follow any.

Captain de Maltranilla also sketches a portrait of the two:

Dr. Prado is tall with a thin face and black hair and beard; he is fifty years old; . . . Spinosa is a young man, well built, thin, with long black hair, a small moustache of the same color, and a handsome face; his age is thirty-three.[73]

Thus we have a police report of historical and philosophic interest. The physical description of the two companions may be accurate since both accounts seem to overlap. As to the statement that "there is no God except in a philosophical sense," it is consonant with what we know about both Spinoza and Prado, although in entirely different senses. Prado professed a form of deism, according to which God is identical with the First Cause of the world. God is not a person; he has no intellect or will; he does not intervene in the affairs of the world; and his laws are none other than the eternal laws of nature. But even this deism remains within the accepted framework of traditional Christian theology that assigns God a transcendent position vis-à-vis the world: the "philosophical God" is indeed the first and eternal cause upon which the world depends, but he remains distinct from the world and exalted above it. For Spinoza, however, the "philosophical God" takes on a new meaning, far bolder and infinitely more heterodox, for

(75)

he is identified with the totality of the universe itself. From this standpoint, Spinoza is at odds not only with the Jewish and Christian traditions but also with the overwhelming majority of the philosophical interpretations of God. For while Prado—like deists in general—maintains the idea of a God beyond and above the world, Spinoza's pantheism displays the heterodoxy common to deism plus an additional heresy and daring originality that comes with reshaping the image of the philosophical God himself as identical with the totality of nature.

The concept of the mortality of the soul is also found in both Prado and Spinoza, but they have different ideas of that mortality. For while Prado seems inclined toward total naturalism, Spinoza, as we shall see in chapter 6, attempts a new interpretation of the individual's eternity and even salvation—a salvation that takes place in this life by uniting the individual's mind with his "eternal essence"; but the soul in the psychological sense is destroyed with the body and neither of them enjoys the prospect of resurrection. On the other hand, Solano's statement that both men regretted the loss of the stipend they received from the synagogue and of their ties with other Jews accords only with what we know about Prado. Spinoza was a man of some means who paid taxes to the community and did not need its charity, while Prado was a pauper receiving a welfare allowance. Moreover, only Prado, to the best of our knowledge, appealed his *herem* and fought to maintain his ties with the Jews. If Spinoza, too, regretted their loss, as the monk reports, this may be true on the level of personal relations rather than on a religious or communal level. Spinoza, indeed, in the *Theologico-Political Treatise* decries the situation in which a Jew who loses his faith automatically loses his "citizenship" in his people and is considered an enemy—a clear allusion to his own fate. But we have no evidence that Spinoza wished to retain his "citizenship" in the community or made any effort in this regard. Insofar as he regretted the severance, this was a purely subjective mood with no practical consequences.

Prado and Spinoza: The Question of "Influence"

Let us return now to the autumn of 1655 and reexamine the critical period leading up to the *herem*. Spinoza was twenty-three years old when Prado arrived in Amsterdam. He had studied Hebrew, the Bible, the Talmud, and Jewish philosophy; he had also read "external books," that is, works on non-Jewish subjects, and almost certainly books in Hebrew on mathematics, physics, and astronomy (Joseph Solomon Delmedigo's works were in his library), and he had prepared himself for a career as a merchant. Spinoza had been on his own for a year. His father, a distinguished member of the community, died in 1654, leaving his business to Baruch and his younger brother, Gabriel. Together the two sons established a company called "Bento y Gabriel d'Espinosa," handling the import and export of fruit. Business was mediocre; once their merchandise apparently sank in mid-ocean. While running his business, Spinoza continued to attend the yeshiva of Rabbi Saul Levi Morteira; he may also have kept his ties with Rabbi Menasseh ben Israel, his former teacher, whose home was a meeting place for foreign scholars visiting Amsterdam. If Spinoza's mind was already riddled with doubts and heretical thoughts, he did not let them affect his practical dealings with the community. On the surface, at least, he maintained proper relations with the synagogue, was scrupulous about paying his dues and pledges, and avoided overt conflict.

His official relationship with the synagogue is known to us from the community ledgers studied by Revah. Each official member of the community was subject to three kinds of tax: (1) the *finta*, a personal tax, determined by the member's property holdings; (2) the *imposta*, a business tax, determined by the volume of imports and exports; and (3) the *promessas*, pledges made in honor of special occasions or religious events. Every six months the synagogue's treasurer would balance the account and collect the payments due.

The community's records show that on April 18, 1654, Baruch Spinoza paid half the *finta*, a total of five florins.[74] Five months later he donated another five florins to the cause of "the poor of Brazil" (Jewish refugees from Pernambuco, a short-lived overseas community that was destroyed when Brazil reverted from the Netherlands to Portugal). On the same day, September 13, 1654, it was recorded that Spinoza paid the balance of the *finta* as well as pledges amounting to eleven florins and eight stuivers, together with another sixteen florins and nineteen stuivers as the *imposta*; this indicates that he was engaged in substantial foreign commerce. The next year shows a decline in the business of the brothers d'Espinosa; Baruch, on April 11, 1655, pays an *imposta* of only six florins. The sum of his *finta* remains five florins, but his pledges grow considerably, going as high as forty-three florins and two stuviers. All this indicates an active, almost generous habit of donation.

At that time Prado had not yet made his appearance in Amsterdam, but by October 1655 his name was appearing in the ledger. His dire financial state exempts him from paying the *finta*, but his pledges reach as high as three florins and eighteen stuivers. Around the same time (on October 4, 1655), Spinoza pays half his usual *finta* and pledges in the amount of four florins and fourteen stuivers. However, for the following six-month period, ending on March 29, 1656, both Spinoza and Prado appear in the ledger as having paid only the trifling sum of twelve stuivers apiece. (Revah sees this as an expression of mutual solidarity.) Four months later Spinoza was banned,[75] while Prado ostensibly repents his evil ways. Even after his ban, Spinoza reappears in the records with another payment of twelve stuivers (evidently made before July, for the records were updated every six months), while Prado's payment goes up again to a relatively high sum, considering his circumstances: four florins and ten stuivers.

The community's tax book served Revah as major (and essentially exclusive) evidence that toward the end of 1655 Spinoza was still a devout and believing Jew who fulfilled his duties to the synagogue and regularly participated in its rites, and that it was only with Prado's arrival that a crisis occurred in his faith. Yet the community's tax records can tell us only about Spinoza's payments, not about his thoughts. There is nothing to prevent us from presuming that he only kept up appearances for the sake of peace—as long as the resolve to break with the community did not mature in him. Among Spinoza's thoughts—which we do know from his writings—there is a rule of prudence advocating to "do whatever does not interfere with our attaining our purpose," along with other practical rules such as "speak according to the power of understanding of ordinary people," "conforming to those customs of the community that do not conflict with our aims," and "seek money, or anything else, just so far as suffices for sustaining life and health (*Treatise on the Intellect*, 17). Spinoza, speaking in the first person, establishes these rules when discussing the radical change that took place in his life and in the object of his desires, when he turned from the banal pursuit of riches, prestige, and sensual pleasures to the search, through metaphysical knowledge, of the truly "highest good." And, indeed, Spinoza's later course of life confirms that, in what concerns the "ordinary people," he followed his own advice: he tried to secure the necessities of life in right measure; he never flaunted his beliefs or tried to win over simple people (like his landlords), who were not of a philosophical bent. Similarly, he took special pains to mask his thoughts, using equivocation and a good deal of religious metaphor, open to a dual and even triple interpretation. On the whole, faithful to his motto *caute* (prudently), Spinoza obeyed the rules of caution and accommodated himself to the customs of the community as long as they did not interfere with his inner life. In this he acted as a new kind of Marrano—not a Judaizing one, but a *Marrano of reason*—a stance he held in different ways, both before and after his *herem*. Spinoza's payments to the Jewish community do not therefore prove that he remained loyal to Judaism in his thoughts. On the contrary, it is more likely that, despite his heterodoxy, Spinoza had not yet reached the conclusion that allowing his mind to pursue its authentic course would require him to withdraw from the community. Thus outwardly, and in practice (which is most important for Judaism), he still tried to maintain the "ways of the multitude," expecially as only a year had passed since the death of his father, a long-time parnas and pillar of the community.

Spinoza's first-person account at the beginning of the *Treatise on the Intellect* also undercuts the assumption that it was Prado (or some other "inducer") who led him to heresy. Spinoza describes a lengthy process, starting with his pursuit of ordinary and transient goals, until he discovered that human happiness depends upon the quality of the object of desire, whether it is fixed and permanent or fleeting and dependent upon circumstances; therefore he turned to seek a "highest good" which is stable and eternal. This quite revolutionary shift did not occur at a single stroke; Spinoza eloquently describes the fear and uncertainty that attended the transition between the two positions, when he did not yet know whether the new object of his desire existed and was attainable, and had to take the risk of preferring this uncertainty to his former life and what seemed certain in it. True, this text from the *Treatise on the Intellect* is not simply an empirical document but a highly stylized autobiography, shaped to suit a literary genre. However, the text conveys that Spinoza conceived his intellectual development as a process, not a one-time event; and he describes this development in ethical terms, as basically a search after the supreme good and the highest quality of life, rather than the pursuit of a new metaphysical truth for its own sake. It therefore appears that Spinoza's thoughts and motivation have quite a different source than those of Prado.

Let us also keep in mind that Spinoza wrote a detailed apologia at the time of his ban. This text is no longer extant, but most scholars believe that it contained an early version of a number of the arguments in the *Theologico-Political Treatise*. (It is also plausible that sharp, polemical references to Judaism contained in that book are extensions of the bitter period of conflict over the *herem*.) Spinoza's arguments in *Theologico-Political Treatise* draw widely upon his Jewish education—the Bible, the nuances of the Hebrew language, Jewish exegetes, and philosophers—areas in which Prado had little or no knowledge, being a part-Spaniard who had only recently begun to study Jewish tradition and had no knowledge of Hebrew. It is therefore reasonable to assume that Spinoza's ideas and his heterodox arguments had matured long before he met Prado.

In addition, the mature Spinoza was, intellectually speaking, one of the most independent persons to emerge in many generations. Is it plausible that at the age of twenty-three he was so impressionable and insecure in his views that a man by far his intellectual inferior could induce him to such a radical change—and in so short a time? Prado arrived in Amsterdam toward the end of 1655 and Spinoza was banned in July 1656 after an extended period of inquiry and negotiations. Hence, Prado had only a few months to convert Spinoza from an "ardent" practicing Jew to a resolute and militant apostate, who not only professed entirely new beliefs but, for their sake, was prepared to sever all his ties with the Jewish community. Moreover, if Prado actually drove Spinoza to such extremes, how are we to explain their continuing friendship after Spinoza had been banned while Prado recanted? On the face of it, here is an anxious young man who had recently discovered a new and exciting world through a mentor who opened his eyes, and then the teacher betrays his pupil, acts in self-deception, and annuls the value of his own teaching by refusing to live by it. Would not this be experienced by the young man as a shock and betrayal, even as a kind of Sabbatian disillusionment?

These questions dissolve if we assume that Prado and Spinoza arrived at their heretical ideas independently and that their encounter merely galvanized those ideas. It is hard to say which of the two had more influence. The older man is not necessarily dominant. We cannot dismiss the possibility that his meeting with Spinoza liberated in Prado the deist misgivings that had been latent in his mind since his days in Spain and prompted him to give them a new shape. As for Spinoza, his contacts with Prado probably helped bring him out of his isolation—the isolation of a young man who has no outlet for his doubts and no one to converse with except old books and implicit precedents—and prompted him to take a more explicit and resolute stand. Specifically, Spinoza's encounter with Prado may have been more important from a pragmatic and psychological perspective than it was ideologically. These contacts reinforced Spinoza's resolve to assert his independence and helped him reach the final and radical decision (which Prado did not press upon him and to which he was not party) to forge his own way while severing his ties with the community. Thus we must conclude that each man arrived at his heterodox views independently, and their subsequent encounter only served as catalyst to currents that were already in train.

THE MESSIANIC HERETIC—ISAAC LA PEYRÈRE

Prado was not the only apostate with whom Spinoza was in contact. At approximately the same time, another important and colorful figure appeared in Amsterdam: Isaac La Peyrère, "the greatest heretic before Spinoza."[76] La Peyrère was born a Calvinist, but there is some reason to believe that he was of Marrano extraction. A jurist, he had served for many years as secretary to the Prince de Condé (father of the Grand Condé) and in the course of his service came to know many of the great minds and statesmen of the time. La Peyrère's main interest was, however, in theology, particularly in questions of divine history and the election of nations. Popkin even credits him with a special "Marrano theology" in which neither the Jews nor ordinary Christians stand at the center of the divine plan for history, but rather the Jews who converted to Christianity: it is they who would usher in the universal redemption, for which the way must be prepared.

La Peyrère's greatest renown derived from the scandal caused by his book on the pre-Adamites (*Prae-Adamitae*). In it he argues that even before Adam and Eve, the world was inhabited by men living in a state of nature without divine law or knowledge. The Bible begins with God transforming the Jews into the bearers of his word on earth. It is therefore a history not of mankind at large but solely of the Jews. Adam is not the first man but the first Jew (and Eve, accordingly, as Popkin puts it, "is the first Jewish mother"). To support this heretical claim, La Peyrère entered into painstaking biblical criticism, along with wide-ranging studies in anthropology that made him a leading expert on the culture of the Eskimos and of Greenland. He also started employing techniques of biblical criticism, of the kind Spinoza later grounded and expanded. Among other things, La Peyrère contended that we possess an incorrect version of the Bible and that it was not Moses who wrote the Pentateuch (a claim made also by Da Costa).

It was not uncommon in that complex age, a time of change and transition between cultural eras, to encounter men who incorporated both imagination and action, delusion and this-worldliness, messianic theology and rational science—and La Peyrère was one of them. His studies in anthropology and his work on the pre-Adamites were not carried out for scientific purposes, but for theological ones. They were congruent with an earlier work of bizarre content and extraordinary title—*Du rappel des Juifs* (The Recall of the Jews)—in which La Peyrère conceived a great vision of the approaching redemption. He divided history (after Adam) into three eras: God first choose the Jews; then, in Jesus' time, he rejected them and passed their election to the Christians, who became the bearers of his word in history; but now the final period is approaching—the messianic era—when God will recall the Jews and bring them to the Promised Land, led by Jesus, the true Messiah, and by the king of France (to whom the work was presented).

From Jerusalem the two will rule over the entire world, now utterly redeemed. Here is a mixture of heterodox Christian and heterodox Jewish visions, sprinkled with traces of a belated Crusader spirit, an early ecumenism, and a premature Zionism—and all held together by a Marrano adhesive. The Jews who will be recalled and effect the redemption will first become Christians and acknowledge the incarnation and divinity of Jesus (which, according to La Peyrère—and to the great consternation of Jews and Christians alike—is the sole essential difference between Judaism and Christianity).

But La Peyrère also recognized the existence of a secret and esoteric Jewish sect, whose members, known only to God, are blessed with the true spirit of Christianity, even though they do not wittingly admit the principle of incarnation. True to his system, La Peyrère preached against the Marrano's return to Judaism and simultaneously called upon Christians to renounce anti-Semitism and treat the Jews with tolerance and respect until the day when all would be united under the banner of the New Christianity. It is noteworthy that, in La Peyrère's thinking, these were outlines for an immediate political action, not visions of a distant future.

La Peyrère and Spinoza

La Peyrère, as we have seen, appeared in Amsterdam about the same time as Prado, six months prior to Spinoza's ban. In Amsterdam he frequented the home of his new friend Menasseh ben Israel. Menasseh was Spinoza's former teacher, and Popkin plausibly suggests that La Peyrère could have met the young Spinoza in Menasseh's home. The fact that Spinoza's biblical criticism contains echoes of La Peyrère's system may further support this surmise (although Spinoza could have known La Peyrère's ideas from his pre-Adamite work, which Spinoza kept in his library).

Despite their affinities, there is a fundamental difference between Spinoza and La Peyrère. With all his heresy, La Peyrère was concerned with theology, not philosophy; he remained a believer in divine providence and expected the mystical end of days. Spinoza, on the contrary, repudiated the historical religions with their notions of providence and redemption and, in diametric opposition to La Peyrère's biblical criticism, portrayed the history of the Jews not as *historia sacra* but as *historia profana* and as a normal phenomenon of nature. Even Spinoza's famous remark about the possibility that the Jews "will reestablish their kingdom, and God will again elect them" (a statement strikingly reminiscent of the title of La Peyrère's first book) was intended in a totally secular sense; it referred to an empirical process that might, perhaps, make the Jews return to their country in a completely natural manner, as the sheer result of sociohistorical factors and without the intervention of any divine will or providence.[77] But it is still quite probable that the young Spinoza met both Prado and La Peyrère at about the same time—and perhaps even in one another's company.[78]

Does it follow that it was La Peyrère, rather than Prado, who led Spinoza astray? Popkin has until recently been disposed toward this view, which, however, calls for the same reservations we made about Revah.[79] This premise merely exchanges Prado's mechanical role for La Peyrère's without changing the nature of the role itself. It also views Spinoza's heresy in terms of one person "inducing" another in a chain of uni-directional cause and effect. Here, too, it is preferable to surmise that doubt and heresy, being incipient in a common psychocultural structure, had their independent generation in several minds which naturally also tended to meet and exchange views. It is therefore plausible that Spinoza, upon hearing of La Peyrère, sought out his company in order to have a fellow biblical skeptic with whom he could talk and that all three men, having been aroused to their doubts independently, later happened to encounter each other, thereby serving to foster in one another thoughts and processes that were in any case already there.

This approach is congruent with all the known facts and explains them by anchoring the phenomenon of heresy within a whole mental and cultural structure underlying the life of the New Jews and in the complex and dissonant features of their consciousness. This, of course, does not yet provide us with a proximate cause of Spinoza's heresy; we do not know why Spinoza, in particular, became a heretic, or why he reached this specific position while others responded differently. In order to explain Spinoza's heresy, we need to know much more about the life of the young Spinoza, his childhood, family, reading habits, and the like; and even then we will not be able to give a full explanation of his development, for (Spinoza's own views notwithstanding), the spontaneous and idiosyncratic factors in every historical figure cannot be fully reduced to external elements alone. But if we knew more about these subjects, we would at least come closer to explaining Spinoza's particularity within a broader cultural structure. As we have tried to demonstrate, this structure is grounded in the unique Marrano condition and in the split and complex mind, a mind devoid of innocence, that necessarily attended it.[80]

Marranism and Wolfson's Thesis

Given Spinoza's Marrano background, one must review a widespread thesis that Harry A. Wolfson made famous. According to Wolfson, the young Spinoza's reading the works of the Jewish medieval philosophers may well have provided him with ample food for heterodox thought—not so much because of their strict literal meaning (though that too was a factor), but because his reading singled out the unorthodox ingredients and wrested them out of context. In other words, the tradition of Jewish philosophy itself—from Maimonides and Gersonides, Ibn Ezra and Crescas to Yehuda Abrabanel (Leone Ebreo)—provided Spinoza with ideas and clues that, in contexts, could still fall within the legitimate tradition but, standing on their own, could well inspire bold and dangerous thinking. In this sense there is some justice in Rabbi Morteira's dictum, that "he who philosophizes is evil," which echoed a whole school of polemic within Judaism. Yet in order to plunge into philosophy, a young man like Spinoza must have already possessed an inquisitive disposition and a restless mind; and this he could have drawn through a thousand arteries from the mental and educational background of his youth. Here, the Marrano culture enters the picture again; it is even more fundamental than the influence of the Jewish philosophers and helps explain it too. The combination of his specific cultural and personal background with the body of ideas and arguments in Jewish philosophy could well have sparked in Spinoza a critical and inquisitive flame—nourished mainly, if not exclusively, from Jewish life itself—long before he came into contact with outside influences and before he met other heterodox figures within the community and entered into a mutual relationship with them.

CHAPTER 4

Marranos in Mask and a World without Transcendence: Rojas and *La Celestina*

The duality in Marrano existence was not born with the New Jews returning to their old religion in the seventeenth century. It is interesting, indeed fascinating, that structural analogies to that situation exist in earlier periods as well, even in the very first generations of Iberian Marranism. Thus from the distance of a century and a half, the parallels (or antecedents) of Spinoza's mental situation can be traced in the adventures of a classic literary figure—Celestina—and in its author's metaphysical *Weltanschauung* and use of language.

The Converso "Who Composed Melibea"

A few years after the expulsion of the Jews from Spain, a young converso,[1] then in his early twenties, wrote a rich and somewhat enigmatic work that was to become a classic of Spanish literature. Officially titled "The Tragi-Comedy of Calisto and Melibea,"[2] but better known as *La Celestina* (after its protagonist), this work retains today much of the power and acuity that made it a literary success five centuries ago. Some critics consider it second only to *Don Quixote*,[3] while others put both on equal footing.[4] Americo Castro views *La Celestina* as the harbinger of modern drama and theater.[5] Others see it as the origin of the picaresque genre, Spain's unique contribution to world literature.[6]

La Celestina, however, is all of these combined, but none of them individually. Written as a play in twenty-one acts (expanded from an original sixteen), it is cumbersome to perform, and although its dialogue is remarkably rich as literature, it is usually not so fluent as a stage director may wish. *La Celestina* is better suited for reading or oral recitation, and was possibly read aloud in Rojas's circle of students and conversos.

Nor is *La Celestina* a novel, for it is written in dialogue form and takes place on a stage, without a narrator or third-person descriptions. And despite the semipicaresque elements—such as the talk of servants and prostitutes, a realistic portrayal of lower-class life with its deprivation, obscenities, and apparent lack of honor—this is not the genuine picaresque genre, which consists of an imaginary autobiography of a picaro relating his adventures in the first person. *La Celestina*, one might say, contains diverse possibilities that have been actualized in later generations. Calderon de la Barca's plays, the adventures of Lazarillo or Guzman of Alfarache (the picaros), or of Don Quixote and his Sancho Panza—are all indebted, sometimes even consciously, to *La Celestina*.

La Celestina's fame and success in the sixteenth century are comparable only to that of *Don Quixote* a century later.[7] Generations of readers have been fascinated by the eponymous protagonist, Celestina, that spicy and vital old whore, the priestess of worldly love, greedy, lascivious, tricky and conspiring, who is something of a witch but also very human, for she is capable of empathy and knows doubt, sorrow, and loneliness. Celestina manipulates the weaknesses of other people without despising or reproaching them; she cheats without malice, exploits without ill-feeling, and seduces and tricks as part of the natural course of worldly events. Thus she is a symbol of naturalism and this-worldliness. Rojas took pains to declare that his aim was to warn the public of such characters; but we may doubt whether *La Celestina*'s phenomenal success was due to this pretended moralizing.

Within a short time it became a kind of all-European bestseller. In Spain alone thirty editions of the book were published during the sixteenth century.[8] There were numerous Italian editions as well as French, Dutch, English, and even Latin translations (the last, perhaps, in order that scholars and clergymen could benefit from the moral lesson, or the amoral pleasure, found in *La Celestina*). Even a Hebrew translation (now lost) by the poet Sarfati appeared in Italy and made its contribution to the secular Jewish literature of the Renaissance.

The Plot and Its Texture

The richness and complexity of the text of *La Celestina* contrasts with its oversimplified plot. Calisto loves Melibea, who at first rejects him with cold cruelty. Calisto is a hidalgo (nobleman) of medium rank, Melibea the daughter of an eminently rich and distinguished family. Calisto's passion becomes obsessive, pushing him to the brink of madness. Seeing his master's despair, his servant Sempronio refers Calisto to Celestina, who can help him attain his "salvation." Celestina is an old procuress and go-between, specializing in all the secrets and contrivances of love. In this town alone she is said to be responsible for the breaking or restoration of five thousand virgins' maidenheads. Celestina does wonders with her needles—just as she does with her tongue, which is rough, smooth, or equivocal, as necessity demands. Apart from her talent for restoring virginity, Celestina supplies her clients with "philters of love" and other potions and sexual aids. She also has a hand in the art of disguise and cosmetics; she concocts perfumes, dyes hair, prepares tonics against bad breath; she sells, buys, seduces and panders. She practices thirty-two trades, all leading, as their final end, to the act of love and the gain that Celestina will draw from it. In her days of glory she managed a big house where gentlemen and senior servants, bishops, noblemen, and monks kept their regular girls; it was, in the words of Germond de Lavigne, "an academy of love," where, we may add, the church and the laity met for common worship. In her old age, Celestina is left with one young prostitute living with her and another living separately. As go-between, Celestina also mediates between girls from good families and their lovers, whom she brings together by various tricks and under cover of night, sometimes on the pretext of attending midnight mass.

Calisto's servant, Sempronio, conspires with Celestina to exploit his master's weakness. The old woman will plant in Calisto the hope of seducing Melibea, but will drag him along until the conspirators bleed him dry of his money. Celestina also persuades Calisto's other servant, a boy named Parmeno, to join them; she recognizes him as the son of her late and beloved friend Claudina who, like her, was a kind of procuress and witch, and a victim of the Inquisition.

In a subtle and complex scene, full of mask-play and equivocation, Celestina succeeds in seducing Melibea.[9] Meanwhile, the two servants establish a liaison with Celestina's girls and we observe them in intimate and open discourse. As Melibea surrenders to Calisto's passion the servants quarrel with Celestina over the spoils, and in a fit of rage they kill her; they are caught by the local judge and executed. Calisto is killed falling off a ladder while leaving Melibea's house in the dark, and the unhappy girl takes her own life in despair. The work ends with a grand monologue by Pleberio, Melibea's father, bemoaning the ways of the world and the disorder and suffering that reign in it.

A simplistic plot and an excess of corpses—but this is not what makes *La Celestina* the work it is. Its strength lies in its actual texture and execution. The dialogues are rich in poetic and linguistic variation—sometimes in excess of present-day taste[10]—and abound in subtle nuances. The work has many layers of expression and meanings that sometimes play against each other. For example, an ancient philosophical dictum is ironically distorted in the mouth of a servant, or acquires an opposite meaning in the context in which it is uttered; or the covert significance of a scene reverses or obliterates its overt meaning. This seemingly earthy, this-worldly play, full of the talk of servants and prostitutes, is at the same time a work for literati, who have read Aristotle and Petrarch, Plautus and the Stoic sages, who know the nuances of Catholic dogma and the secrets of the life of the Marranos. Yet, the fact that anyone in this play can pronounce a moral and philosophical dictum does not detract from the vitality of the characters (just as a similar combination a century later does not diminish the vitality of Sancho Panza). It only adds to the diversity of the work and contributes to the message of mask-play and equivocal irony which are major aesthetic ingredients of *La Celestina*.

Rojas's Converso Background and the Inquisition

Rojas enjoyed much less fame than his work. When, at the turn of the century, Serrano y Sanz discovered documents that established Rojas's Jewish origin,[11] he was not warmly welcomed by all Spanish scholars. Some were reluctant to see one of their illustrious number excluded, as it were, from the pure Spanish stock. But in this they seem to have shown a misunderstanding of their own tradition; for the concept of pure Spanishness does not reflect a historical reality but an abstract, partly mythological ideal. An essential characteristic of modern Spain is the assimilation of seemingly un-Spanish elements, including Jews and Muslims; and a good deal of Spain's uniqueness lies in this very mixture.[12] Hence, discovering that Rojas was of Jewish descent and of "impure blood" does not mean that he was un-Spanish, but rather deepens and enriches our understanding of what being Spanish means.

Fernando de Rojas was born in or around the year 1476, in Puebla de Montalban near Toledo, into a converso family. Rojas was born a Christian, but his environment swarmed with conversos, many of whom had relations with the professing Jews (who lived in Spain until 1492). When Rojas was a child the Catholic sovereigns, Fernando and Isabel, ascended the throne and unified Spain; when he was ten the Inquisition, recently established in Spain, entered Puebla de Montalban. The usual period of grace was announced in which the inhabitants were required to confess their crimes of secret Judaizing, or to denounce others.

One of the captives was Alvaro de Montalban, later Rojas's father-in-law. He was accused of having observed some Jewish rituals, like eating matzot on Passover, keeping the festival of Sukkot,[13] and buying kosher food. At the same time, Alvaro was also charged with violating the Catholic fast of Lent by eating cheese and meat and drinking milk. This meant that Alvaro had sinned twice, both against Christianity (eating on a fast day) and against Judaism (eating meat and dairy products together)—a religious duality that would persist throughout his life.

Alvaro de Montalban was not the only member of Rojas's family standing trial. His late parents had also committed the sin of Judaizing, and the Holy Office exhumed and burned their bodily remains—in order to save their souls from the fires of hell (and also in order to enable the Inquisition, according to law, to confiscate their property, or part of it).[14] Alvaro's fortune was better: after having been interrogated, tortured, and condemned, he was sentenced to the humiliation of a public recantation and fined—thereby being "reconciled" to the church.

There are some hints that Rojas's parents, too, were tried by the Inquisition. A document of a much later date refers to "the *Bachiller* Rojas who composed the old Celestina," and says that "the *fiscal* [prosecutor] contends that he was a son of Hernando de Rojas, *condemned as Judaizer in the year '88*" (emphasis added).[15] This is a biased and hostile testimony, for its aim was to oppose the Franco family (a relation of Rojas) in its claim to nobility (*hidalguia*). But the date fits, and it cannot be ruled out that the twelve-year-old Rojas saw his father suffer humiliation. Gilman even goes as far as to give a vivid description of the trauma of the boy seeing his father burning at the stake in an *autos de fé*.[16] Gilman thinks that Rojas's mother, too, appears in a list of persons judged by the Inquisition, together with her "minor sons" (*hijos menores*),[17] and if so, he concludes that even before his childhood ended, Rojas was fully aware of the fate of his family and of his race.

Even if the evidence is not conclusive,[18] it is undeniable that being a converso was a powerful, ever-present fact of Rojas's experience as a child and young man. This experience included two major traumas: the establishment of the Inquisition and, later, the expulsion of all the Jews from Spain. Also included was the consequent need of the Marranos to disguise their inner world, practicing subterfuge and dissimulation, addressing the initiated in one way and the rest of the world in quite another. In other words, Rojas grew up and matured in the days when the characteristic needs of the conversos took shape and became urgently pressing. For some, the need to vacillate between the secret essence and an outer make-believe; for others, the need for prudence and camouflage in order to avoid being falsely accused of Judaizing; and for all (to varying degrees), the need to devise new strategies of survival and to create allusive and equivocal forms of speech and expression in order to convey illicit messages to a group of select listeners. Such needs arose not only among Judaizers but also among those conversos who tried to be faithful to their new religion. The murky atmosphere of suspicion created by the Inquisition kept them in constant fear. Keeping up appearances in speech and deed became an imperative of life itself and took the shape of a complex and subtle art. Daily life was tenuous and fraught with danger.

Student Days in Salamanca

In 1494, when Rojas was eighteen years old, he came to the University of Salamanca to study and become a jurist. Here he made contact with groups of students and professors who were, like himself, of converso origin. The Salamanca of Rojas's time was a center of cultural ferment. The literature of the Italian Renaissance had made its way there, as had the new science, especially in its application to navigation. These were the days of the great discoveries—America, and before it, the Cape of Good Hope in Africa and the sea route to India. Among the master astronomers and cartographers assisting in these discoveries was the Jewish scholar, Rabbi Abraham Zaccuto, who had taught in Salamanca before Rojas's time and went on from there to Lisbon. This was also the first generation of printers in Spain. The world of ideas was flourishing. Works published abroad soon found their way to Salamanca.

Salamanca was also a kind of refuge for converso intellectuals. After studying the university records, Gilman concludes that a large proportion of the students, and certainly most of the faculty, must have been aware (whether they liked it or not) of their common converso origin. This fact, coupled with the folklore peculiar to universities, encouraged the growth of intimate groups of conversos, a kind of unofficial student fraternity of "blood brothers."[19] Rojas himself, in one of the prefaces to *La Celestina*, speaks of his "fellowmen" (his *socios*). Possibly this was the group in which his work grew and matured, or which served Rojas as audience for the first recitations of his text.[20] This was a time of struggles between social factions and schools of thought, or quarrels over honor, women, and even academic positions; many carried arms on the street and violent encounters between gangs—or duels between individuals—were a fact of student and urban life.[21]

The common origin of the conversos did not necessarily indicate fidelity to the Jewish religion. Some became zealous Catholics, even officers of the Inquisition. Juan de Cervantes, an ancestor of the writer,[22] and Diego de Deza, who was made bishop in Rojas's time and later succeeded Torquemada (himself a converso) as the inquisitor general of the realm, lived in Salamanca. And there were also, in the middle, conversos who out of the confusion and mixture of the two religions lost their faith in both, developing a certain measure of skepticism, distance, and ironic self-consciousness, or tending toward a kind of secularism and emphasis on temporal life as the only one that has meaning and reality—sometimes, as in the case of Rojas, returning to the sources of ancient pagan thought.

His eight years in Salamanca were among the richest and most crucial in Rojas's life. Here he wrote *La Celestina*—according to him, within a fortnight of the school vacation[23]—and was later made a *bachiller*, the basis for his future career as a jurist. Seeing that *La Celestina* had been well received and, despite his fears, had not provoked inquisitorial suppression, Rojas gained courage and composed, for the second edition, prefatory verses in acrostic which reveal his identity as follows: "The *Bachiller* Fernando de Rojas concluded the comedy of Calisto and Melibea and was born in Puebla de Montalban."[24]

In 1502 Rojas published the enlarged, twenty-one-act, tragi-comedy version of his work. In the same year he left Salamanca, returned to his hometown, and married Leonor Alvarez. Thus Rojas, like many other conversos, married within his community. Alvaro granted his daughter a generous dowry of eighty thousand marvedis, which enabled the young couple to maintain an orderly, middle-class, provincial life—the very opposite of the daring and agitated universe of *La Celestina*.

A Marrano Dual Career

Sometimes the duality marking the life of the converso takes the form of a division between two radically different periods in the life of the person. Noteworthy cases include converts and Marranos who returned to Judaism outside the Iberian peninsula. At times this Marrano duality took the form of opposite life periods—a man leading first the life of a distinguished doctor, scholar, or courtier in Iberian society, then transforming himself into a Jewish writer in the ghetto of Venice, into a Sabbatian messianic propagandist, or an Amsterdam rabbi. As Yerushalmi has pointed out, the dual life of the Marrano shapes itself here as a dual career divided by time.[25]

This phenomenon is true not only of those who changed their official religion in either direction, but also of converso descendants who lost their historical faith altogether. The most outstanding example is certainly Spinoza. Having lived at first as a "Marrano of reason" among his own people, the former Marranos of Amsterdam, he then severed his ties with this world and turned to a philosophical life, without religion, within the Christian Dutch community, where again he continued, in Marrano-like fashion, to conceal his inner thoughts and intimate philosophical truth from the multitude. From this point of view, as I pointed out in chapter 2, Spinoza's life maintained a genuine Marrano structure, even though its content had been transformed.

Rojas, like Spinoza, also led a dual life—in both senses. His inner world, if we are to judge it by *La Celestina*, was secular, philosophical, and terrestrial, without a transcendent dimension of life and with no binding historical religion. One might say that he was equally indifferent to Judaism and Christianity, but that he had to conceal this inner state from the outer world—especially when the problem concerned not his work but the banality of daily life, where he could no longer hide behind the mask and philters of an aesthetic creation. Here Rojas constructed a rigid system of defense, making a true break with his past.

Rojas's marriage initiates the second phase in his life, marked by a kind of antithesis to the vital, effervescent author who both revealed and concealed his daring mind in the dialogues of *La Celestina*. Taking his young bride, Rojas left his native town and moved to Talavera de la Reina, a city which better suited his new needs; and there, for the next thirty-five years, until his death in 1541, he led the life of a respectable provincial jurist, devoted family man, and conformist. For a short time he even served as *alcalde* (a kind of municipal judge). Over the years he succeeded in building a wall of defense around his family. This required not only a good deal of camouflage, but the routinization of conformist habits, which must eventually also affect the mind even when it does not radically transform one's basic views of life.

This seeming paradox of external interiorization is not unique to Marranos; it is relevant to many other cases of assimilation, submission to coercive authority, or even "education" in a superficial sense. In Rojas, it took the form of a dramatic duality and split. Even as he lay on his deathbed, Rojas had to keep appearances and die a good Christian according to official custom. Had he been found out at the last moment and sentenced posthumously as a secret heretic, his property would have been in danger of confiscation and his family—the nucleus of love, value, and meaning that he so assiduously cultivated in this world—would have been gravely threatened.

The Inquisition Again:
Alvaro Denies a Transcendent World

Despite all Rojas's precautions, the Inquisition repeatedly called upon him. In 1517 a friend of Rojas, Diego de Oropesa, was arrested by the Holy Office. Among other offenses he was charged with wearing a clean shirt on Saturdays and avoiding the eating of pork. Changing one's shirt on the Sabbath was a common sign of Judaizing according to the semiotic code of the Inquisition, enough to bring a person to trial and grief. The prisoner named Rojas as a decade-long acquaintance who could testify in his behalf.

Rojas was asked three questions. To the best of his knowledge, did the accused (1) live as a good Christian and keep the Catholic rites; (2) consume pork and other foods forbidden to the Jews; (3) kneel down in church, as faithful Christians do.

The documents of the Inquisition record Rojas's evasive answers as follows:

> To the [first] question he answered that he considers him [the accused] a good Christian and that he used to see him go to Mass and sermons, and that he has no more to say.
> To the [second] question, he answered that he does not know.
> To the [third] question, he answered that he believes so, but has not seen him do so.[26]

Gilman points out the drama behind Rojas's answers. Rojas does not want to abandon a friend in trouble, but has to consider the danger to his family and himself. If he lies to defend his friend when no corroborating testimony exists, he might be considered an accomplice or a fellow Judaizer—and Rojas was already held to be "suspect." Therefore, all that Rojas was prepared to say is taken, in Marrano fashion, from the world of appearances: he "saw" the accused go to church; he "considered" him to be a good Christian; but in what concerns deeper truths he knows nothing.

It is hard to avoid an ironic comparison with what Celestina does in the play: Rojas's second answer would perfectly suit her too. The inquisitorial record sounds like a quotation from Rojas's work, and Rojas sounds like one of his own characters. But if the play makes an incursion into life, it is because it has already ironically mirrored this life in the first place.

The fact that Rojas was held in suspicion emerges clearly on the second occasion. This was a real crisis. Alvaro de Montalban, already seventy years old, was again apprehended by the Inquisition. Two secret witnesses had denounced the old man, saying they had heard him deny the existence of a future world:

> After midday when they had eaten and passed time pleasurably and were returning to town, the present witness remarked: "You see how the pleasures of this world pass by. . . . Everything except gaining eternal life is foolish and illusory." At this the aforesaid Alvaro de Montalban replied saying: "Let me be well off down here, since I don't know if there is anything beyond."

The convicting words were pronounced in the presence of a priest. The witness says he winked at Alvaro and tugged at his sleeve to warn him, but Alvaro repeated his words saying, "Here let me be well off, since I know nothing about what lies beyond." Another witness, too, reported that Alvaro had said: "We can see the here and now; what lies beyond we cannot know."[27] Alvaro's talk about the exclusive existence of this world correspnds to his ways in the old days—when he mixed both religions. It also fits the mind-set of other conversos (including Rojas himself), both in the early days of Marranism and in later generations up to (and beyond) Spinoza.

Alvaro was thrown into jail as a *relapso*. During a routine investigation he said he was the father of Leonore Alvarez, "the wife of the Bachiller Rojas who composed Melibea."[28] Later, when the question of his defense counsel came up, the old man "said he would appoint as his lawyer the Bachiller Fernando de Rojas, his son-in-law, who is a converso" but—so the inquisitorial clerk remarked—his grace [the Inquisitor] rejected this request as inappropriate and demanded that the lawyer be someone "without suspicion" (*sin sospecha*).[29]

So Rojas was held in suspicion—either for the bare fact of being a converso, or as the son-in-law of the accused, or as the son of a former convict (a lesser probability), or also as the one "who composed Melibea." Given this background we must agree with Gilman's assessment of the stress under which Rojas's family must have lived during the arrest, fearing what the old man might say under torture and worrying about the fate of the dowry. (The Inquisition could confiscate whatever property convicts possessed "in the day they started to Judaize," a rule that enabled the Holy Office to confiscate assets from heirs.) But it seems that, at least economically, this family was fortunate. The Inquisition did not touch Rojas's dowry; in his will we see him return the eighty thousand maravedis to his wife, before any further distribution of his assets.[30]

It is crucial to see that Alvaro's charge was not Judaizing but heresy with respect to both religions. This pattern was encountered twice in his career. Many other conversos stressed life in this world as the only real life and rejected any transcendent views. A century and a half before Prado and Spinoza, this was a kind of early secularism and skepticism which other sources record as well. Thus Fritz Baer[31] is able to paint the portraits of notable conversos, among them Pedro and Fernando de la Caballeria (the latter, a brilliant jurist, was an assistant to King Fernando), in whom all religious, transcendent outlooks were replaced by a terrestrial concern for cultivating the mind and body, for personal career and achievement, aesthetic and intellectual pleasure, power, learning, and self-assertion—all as purely this-worldly dimensions of life. The fact that these two personalities were tried by the Inquisition for Judaizing only testifies to the short-sightedness and inanity of the Inquisitors.

The Converso-Picaro

A distant relative of Rojas, Bartolome Gallego, embodied a more tempestuous mixture of faith and conviction. He, too, was held by the Holy Office, and his arrest cast a long shadow on the fragile tranquility of Rojas and his family.[32] He left Spain at the age of six in exile and later converted to Christianity in Sardinia. Afterward he moved to North Africa, living in Fez and Oran, where he traded in various goods, from oil and chickpeas to rings and silver jewelry. When visiting the Jews he lived and behaved like a Jew. Thus Gallego was twice a pretender: he confessed neither religion but adopted the religious customs of the particular group in which he operated.

At a later date Gallego returned to Talavera where he had converso relatives (including Rojas). One day he was arrested by the Inquisition on the charge that he had praised the Moslem religion, in which the believer takes his shoes off before entering a place of worship, as against the Christian practice of wearing muddy boots in church.

Gallego was jailed, tortured, and sentenced to public humiliation and to life imprisonment. He escaped from prison—quite a feat under those conditions—and the Inquisition burned him in effigy. Serrano y Sanz sees Gallego as a kind of "picaro";[33] but his adventures express the inner disorder of a converso whose religious world had been shattered while his terrestrial world is in turmoil.

In contrast, Rojas's terrestrial world was well constructed—with prudence, moderation, and constant dissimulation. His inner world, if judged by *La Celestina*, was no less complex, free, and agitated, than that of Gallego, but in the outer world Rojas succeeded in establishing himself as a respectable, if somewhat suspect, provincial jurist. The mask, a prominent literary element in *La Celestina*, became part of the life of its author; he wore it even on his deathbed. Many people have left death masks that captured their features at the final moment of life. For Rojas, we have instead a spiritual death mask. It is not different from the mask he and many of his fellow conversos wore during life. Nor is it unrelated to the diverse forms of mask-play and equivocation that abound in *La Celestina*.

Life and the Text

Let us examine how the life of the Marranos is reflected in *La Celestina*, both in its thematic symbols, content, and allusions, and in some of its formal and aesthetic values. By the latter I mean the play of essence and appearance, truth and mask, inner and outer life, together with the rather tragic irony that sometimes emerges from their contrast and interplay. This is a fundamental element in the life and experience of the Marranos—and a major feature of *La Celestina*. *La Celestina* was written for an audience with the capacity to distinguish and identify subtle verbal masks and games of equivocation, a skill that the Marranos were forced by their special situation to develop. Rojas exploits this linguistic and semiotic skill and the sensibilities that accompany it, and uses them aesthetically.

Let me, however, begin with a word of methodological caution. *La Celestina* is a complex work that defies any attempt at a pat interpretation that would reduce it to a single dimension. Therefore, in emphasizing the life experience of the Marranos I wish only to set in relief a hermeneutic and aesthetic viewpoint that is necessary, though certainly not sufficient, for understanding *La Celestina*. While reading many passages from the perspective that interests me here, I do not exclude the possibility, indeed the need, to reread them from complementary points of view as well. On the contrary, because the interpretation I offer emphasizes the plurality of meanings in the text of *La Celestina*, I must be the first to urge reading it from more than a single perspective.[34]

Further, a work like *La Celestina* has its own substance and coherence, which transcend the meanings and intentions the author may have had when composing it. In the same way, the aesthetic unity of the work is autonomous with respect to the historical and biographical context from which it sprang; like any major literary or theoretical work, its meaning is, above all, a function of the relations among its ingredients in their own context. Yet no work is born ex nihilo. The unity of meaning in this work is at the same time a transformation of the elements that were fed into it by its cultural context and by the individual who wrote it; these elements have to be seen in their complementarity. The independent meaning of the work transcends the historical material from which it sprang—but it must be understood as this transcendence, that is, also as springing from the material, although it cannot be reduced to it. History is preserved within it as something that has been transformed into the work's inner coherence, but as such it is a vital ingredient. Moreover, sometimes, as in the case of *La Celestina*, it becomes possible to glimpse the deep structures of a whole epoch and subculture through their aesthetic reflection in a single major work of art. Rojas was the spiritual predecessor of another heretic—Spinoza—himself an offshoot of the Marrano culture. In his great and somewhat enigmatic work, Rojas evinces a similar outlook, a similar relation to language, to masks, and most important, to metaphysics, clearing a path outside both Judaism and Christianity that Spinoza was to follow over a century later.

Having set the methodological boundaries of the investigation, I shall look for traces of the Marrano experience in three levels of *La Celestina*: in direct though covert allusions to Marranism, the Inquisition, and feigned religious cults; in the play of masks and equivocal language, which this work contains much beyond the practical necessity; and in the metaphysical world view implied in *La Celestina*, which is neither Christian nor Jewish.

(1) COVERT ALLUSIONS TO THE MARRANOS

From a distance of half a millennium, we can decipher only a few of the covert allusions to the Marranos in *La Celestina*. The subtleties of a passing hint, or topical allusions whose time has long passed, will elude us. Many hints must rely on information which the author could presume his educated readers to possess, but which we no longer have.[35]

"Hope" and "Salvation"

What will be most readily apparent to the alert contemporary reader are the references to a life of constant dissimulation, and the allusions to the Inquisition and its trials and *autos-de-fé*; such references abound in *La Celestina* and are, of course, related to the basic Marrano experience. They are also couched in expressions that were typically associated with the Marranos, such as "hope" (*esperanza*) and "salvation" (*salud*). Old Christians used to say that the conversos lived by their

esperanza—the futile hope that they would be reunited with their erstwhile people and be redeemed by their God. This Marrano "hope" was
a constant object of derision by their foes. The concept of *salud* was
also attached to the life of the Marranos in two ways.* Salvation was
the object of hope, redeeming the Marrano and returning him to God.
Also the Judaizing conversos were constantly characterized as believing that salvation lay in the Law of Moses and not in Christ's Church,
to which they officially belonged. In hundreds of inquisitorial records,
the wish to be "saved by the Law of Moses" is restated almost ritually.
To Jewish ears this sounds rather un-Jewish. Jews were less concerned
with individual salvation than with national redemption in this world
and in the daily fulfillment of the commandments. But the curious
blend of this formula is precisely what expresses the split identity that
marks Marrano life. The most profound hope and desire are directed
to a fundamentally Christian ideal—salvation; yet salvation is deemed
attainable only by rejecting the Christian Messiah and accepting the
Law of Moses (again a rather un-Jewish appellation), whose modali-
ties, moreover, were constantly fading from memory and receding
into the past.

Is it a mere accident that the words *salvation* and *hope* occur frequently in *La Celestina*, too? Their use is transferred, to be sure, from
the religious to the erotic context; but the alert reader does not have to
exert herself in order to grasp the parallel. Celestina is to mediate between Calisto and his salvation; this formula is stressed more than
once.[36] Speaking to herself, the old woman plans to arouse Calisto's
esperanza even further, and he, later, complains that this *esperanza* is
the cause of his doom. Moreover, Melibea—the object of Calisto's
hope and the agent of his salvation—is described by her lover as his
only God. Besides its other meanings, this blasphemy hints to the
reader that the love affair can also be interpreted as a theological metaphor. It also reinforces, from the standpoint of the play's overall
structure, that such phrases as *salud* and *esperanza* do not recur acciden-
tally.

Celestina's role is to mediate between Calisto and his salvation. Such
mediation was the traditional role of the church, but here it is fulfilled
by a whore. Whoever is shocked by the thought that the holy church
takes on the image of a whore (perhaps even of "the great whore of

---

* Although the primary meaning of *salud* is "health," in a secondary sense it also
means "salvation" (or "state of spiritual grace," "attainment of eternal glory"; see definitions of *salud* in Diccionario de la Langua Española [Real Academia Española, 1970]).
The choice of a term in which the idea of salvation, with its theological connotations,
hides behind the more innocent concept of health is itself an equivocation and a Mar-
rano-related use of language.

Babylon" in the Book of Revelation) can take comfort in the fact that this is only one side of the equivocation. Judaism does not fare any better. Celestina is supposed to foster *esperanza* and assure its satisfaction; and this may well parodize the hope of the Judaizing Marranos, whose disguised ways are also compared to the painted, posturing harlot. On a deeper level, the comparison may touch upon a fierce anti-Jewish motif already voiced by some of the church fathers (John Chrysostom), who compare Judaism to a brothel. In her multiple guises, Celestina reflects both Judaism and the church in a warped, distorting mirror, while she herself expresses a primitive natural force that transcends both religions.

This duality of Judaism and Christianity, the impossibility of identifying completely with either, the confusion of hostile motifs borrowed from their conflict—all provide an almost archetypal expression of the Marrano experience, marked by a dual identity and tension. The tension existed not only among Judaizing Marranos but also among those who accepted Christianity sincerely, and certainly among those who—like Alvaro and Rojas, and a century and a half later, Spinoza—left both religions because of the confusion and duality that beset them. Spinoza, as I shall show in Chapter 6, reiterates a similar predisposition in abandoning the historical religions altogether and in powerfully reinstating the goal and craving for *salvation* within the new philosophy of reason that is to replace religion in leading to beatitude and the true love of God. If Spinoza had read *La Celestina* (Spanish literature was his favorite recreational reading, and *La Celestina*, although it was not in his library, was then a popular book), he must have recognized the old whore's grotesquely inverted role as the mediator of salvation, and approved of her as symbolizing the naturalistic and this-worldly nature of salvation, free of transcendent commands and a theology of revelation, although he would rather place this role in the *rational* principle in nature and in the intellectual kind of love.

Religious Hypocrisy

The two servants, on their way to a voluptuous feast in Celestina's house (opening of act 9), pass through the church to check if the old whore "has finished her devotions" (*devociones*). Meanwhile they discuss Celestina's religious hypocrisies. When in church, says Sempronio, she either prays for her sinful schemes to succeed (and thus cannot be really praying to the Christian God) or she does not pray at all. In rolling her prayer beads she actually "counts the number of maidenheads she's got on hand for repair," and "when she moves her lips she is rehearsing lies and thinking up new schemes to make money." What looks like prayer is indeed such muttering as: "he'll say this or that; I'll reply thus" and so on.

At the time, religious hypocrisy was specifically associated with the Marranos, many of whom indeed developed strategems to avoid or attenuate the sin of "idolatry" they attached to Catholic cult. Some pronounced silent annulments or whispered reservations when entering church, a custom preserved even in the twentieth century by some good Spanish Catholics, who do not suspect that the unintelligible, but presumably pious words they have been taught by their parents to mutter before entering church are really anti-Catholic blasphemy in broken Hebrew. More specifically, Sempronio's words about Celestina correspond to a well-known anticonverso stereotype of the time, which they probably were meant to invoke. After the riots in Toledo (1449), many vicious pamphlets were distributed against the conversos. One extant pamphlet represents a sarcastic "privilege" that the king grants some converso. Among other things, the converso is permitted to have "two faces" and, in church, to pretend praying while holding his tax-farming register in place of the prayer book and murmuring his accounts to himself. This is almost the same as Sempronio's words about Celestina; and even if Rojas did not read this particular pamphlet, he certainly knew the stereotype well—and could rely on his public to know it.[37]

The Danger of Exposure

Calisto, in church, prays on and on. Sempronio warns him:

> Look, sir, you've been here so long that people are beginning to notice it. . . . They call an overly devout man a hypocrite. (Opening of act 11)

This admonition fits the Marranos equally well: hypocrisy must be practiced in moderation if it is to be effective. An excess of pious gestures will arouse suspicion no less than their absence. Sempronio then adds more timely advice, which also fits the Judaizing Marranos:

> If you have a passion [a malady?], suffer it at home, don't let the world feel it. Don't let strangers guess your trouble, since the tambourine is in the hands of those who will know how to play it [i.e, informers]. (Ibid.)

This warning would not fall on deaf ears in the era of spies and denunciations.

The Inquisition and its *autos-de-fé* are referred to in the text quite evidently—though through a screen of equivocation and metaphor.

When Parmeno describes Celestina's modus operandi to his master, he tells how she would have lovers meet under the cover of prayer and midnight mass. Using a show of religious devotion to disguise secret practices is of course a feature of Marrano life; but this passage contains even more specific hints to Marranism:

> She was a great friend of students, purveyors, and priests' servants, and sold them the innocent blood of those poor girls which they had foolishly risked for the repair that she had promised them. She flew even higher and through her girls reached the most sheltered females, this on honest occasions, such as the Stations of the Cross, nocturnal processions, early Mass, and other secret devotions. I've seen many such enter her house, their faces covered, with men behind him, barefoot, penitent, muffled, their shoes unlatched, who were going there to do penance for their sins! You can't imagine the traffic she carried on. (Act 1, Simpson, pp. 17–18)

This picture perfectly fits the Judaizers. They also used worship in church and pious Christian symbols to cover a diametrically opposed reality; they too "never missed a Mass nor Vespers" while their minds and hearts were elsewhere. Moreover, the pious night procession, where false penitents follow barefoot the objects of their lust, can be seen as a parody of the most terrible procession of penitents—the *autos de fé*. As further irony it may suggest what everyone knew—that the *autos de fé* was frequently a cover for false repentence.

Even clearer (though more sophisticated) is the other hint implied in the description of the parading young men: their mask (marching barefoot and half-naked) is there to disguise their true feeling (sexual lust) because it suggests its opposite, ascetic repentance; but seen from a different perspective, *it is rather the mask itself that reveals their true essence* (half-naked, they prepare for an act of carnal love). This may resemble the masks that Rojas himself puts over his characters; his text, too, contains hints and equivocal signs which, if only seen in their proper light, suddenly become transparent.

Marranos among the Clerics

Describing Celestina's diligence, the servant remarks, "She did not overlook any convent." This phrase has a special sting to it. Irony is here twice removed; it is irony under the cover of irony. On the first level, this is a conventional swipe at the clergy: monks, too, are Celestina's clients. No monastery in the land is free of sin. But on a more covert level this statement alludes ironically to the Marranos, about whom it was equally said that no monastery in the land was free of them. It is indeed a fact, documented in the files of the Inquisition, that many Judaizers chose monasteries as their refuge, posing as monks and sustaining their devotion to Moses under the protection of the Crucified. Moreover, conversos in general (and not only Judaizers) made their way, in the first generation, into major sectors of Spanish society, including the ecclesiastical hierarchy and the major monasteries.

This is also the context for understanding Sempronio's words in act 1. The servant draws up a list of potentially surprising news, and includes the item, "so-and-so has been appointed bishop." Apparently this is an ordinary anticlerical barb: a common man, unlearned, a sinner, or otherwise undeserving, has been made bishop. But on a second level, this can be (and probably was) read as a reference to former Jews who indeed rose to high ecclesiastical ranks; in the first generations of Marranism, the best-known cases were Pablo de Santa Maria, alias Shlomo HaLevi, bishop of Burgos, and Alonso de Cartagena, his son, born a Jew and circumcised, who later was also bishop in Burgos. In Rojas's own time there was Fray Diego de Deza, a converso teaching in Salamanca who was appointed bishop and later (after the publication of La Celestina) even succeeded the converso Torquemada as inquisitor-general of the realm.[38]

When the other servant, Parmeno, describes Celestina to his master, he puts special emphasis on her power to conceal, to put a mask upon a mask. Of her first profession he says it was "a cover for others." He also endows her with expertise in makeup, which is essentially an art of concealment and make-believe. Moreover, Celestina fakes even the makeup! Parmeno concludes his speech with the exclamation, perhaps partly a lament, that "it was nothing but lies and mockery" (act 1, Simpson, p. 19). In context, this sentence, too, can be read as summing up the life and situation of the Marranos.

Celestina's power to restore maidenheads is stressed several times. Parmeno tells how the old woman succeeded in selling the same girl to the French ambassador three times as a virgin. Is this not a miracle—a kind of rude and terrestrial miracle of virginity—reflecting in its coarse mirror another, holier and better-known miracle of virginity? Celestina's talent also signifies that she fabricates innocence, which is what so many Marranos were doing in their external lives.

Celestina as Mock-Bishop and the Clergy as Mirror-Marranos

Celestina's role as an inverted religious figure reaches a powerful climax in act 9. In a semipicaresque feast with her girls and their lovers, the old whore invokes memories of her days of glory, when numerous girls served in her house and brought her power and honors:

> They brought me plenty of customers: old gentlemen and young, and clergymen of all ranks, from bishops to sextons. Why, the moment I entered a church, hats would come off in my honor as if I were a duchess! When they saw me half a league off they'd leave their prayers, and one by one and two by two they'd come running to greet me and ask whether there wasn't some little thing they could do for me, and each would ask me about his girl. Some, even while they were saying Mass, seeing me come in, would get so flustered that they'd say everything wrong. Some called me "mistress"; others, "aunt"; others, "sweetheart"; others "honorable old woman." There they arranged their visits to my house, and mine to theirs. There they'd offer me money or gifts, or they'd kiss the hem of my gown or my cheek, to keep me happy. (Act 9, Simpson, p. 110)

This is a picture of an inverted universe. Celestina usurps the place of the man of God and becomes the object of worship. The traditional values of honor are also inverted. She is no longer a *puta vieja* (old whore) but *vieja honrada* (honorable old woman); it is those who do not patronize her who are considered low and despicable.

The priests, Celestina goes on, used to send her all kinds of food, "which they had received from their flock as the tithe of God," then came to her house to consume them in the company of their girls. The best Spanish wine also flowed from ecclesiastical casks, until Celestina became an expert, able to identify regional wines from Madrigal to San Martin. On special occasions, Celestina adds, to the consternation of the public, the Holy Bread (*el bodigo*) was also offered her (*ofrecito*).

As the priestess of illicit love, Celestina herself becomes the object of worship. Those who offer her their tithe, or sacrifice, are the official clerics and men of God, who draw their offering from what they themselves are offered by the faithful. In this respect Celestina stands above the usual ecclesiastical hierarchy. But in another respect she is well within it; hats and miters are doffed when she enters church, and the devotees kiss her gown—as if she were another archbishop or cardinal. (Since Celestina gains this position by her terrestrial influence over the clergy, satire is here directed, not only at the morals of the clergy but also at the mundane and political character of the church, where positions are determined by earthly games of power, bribes, extortion, and the like, and not necessarily by the measure of one's devotion to God.)

Behind the sharp cynicism, the priests are a mirror image of the Judaizing Marranos. They too have an external official devotion and another, true devotion opposing it. Outwardly the priests serve in the churches of God and collect his tithes, but in fact they practice the cult of the priestess of lechery and pass God's tithes over to her as the harlot's fee. Thus they, too, live in the duality of two opposing cults—to God and to Eros. This is no longer ordinary anticlerical satire; it is a grotesque reflection of the Judaizing Marranos.

"Who Is without Falsity?"

The atmosphere "of all was nothing but lies and mockery" merges with a more somber one: murky suspicion and mistrust among relatives and close friends, the outcome of the Inquisition. Rojas expresses this too in the attire of a love story.

After having his hopes and expectations raised by Celestina, Calisto arrives at the home of Melibea, who receives him with a show of prudence. Feeling deceived, the agitated lover bitterly complains:

> O Celestina, deceitful and cunning woman! Wouldn't you have done better to let me die, rather than coming to animate my hope [*esperanza*] and blow up the fire that was already consuming me? Why did you falsify the words of this lady, whom I worship?

He goes on, in a passage laden with meaning:

> Where is truth? Who is without falsity? In what place shall I not find impostors? Where shall I find a frank enemy, a true friend? Which is the land where treachery is unknown? Alas, why plant in me this hope [*esperanza*] that leads to my destruction? (Act 12, Simpson, p. 131)

Calisto's lament aptly describes the converso predicament in the Spain of the Inquisition, a land full of fakers and pretenders, both among the Marranos and among their persecutors; a country stricken by treason and secret denunciations, where each person was liable to betray his friends and could not trust even his own relatives, and where the Marrano's hope—*esperanza*—threatens to bring destruction. Calisto's words are incisive in both of these parallel meanings, which seem to have been intended equally by Rojas. This is one of the play's most direct passages when the essence of Marrano life springs explicitly, almost declaratively, to the foreground.

Prudence and Trust

The same atmosphere was evoked in Celestina's earlier conversation with Parmeno. Just as Calisto will say later; "Where is truth, who is not affected by lies?" here this motif is evidenced in Parmeno. Celestina tries to seduce the boy into joining her plot, and Parmeno says in confusion, "Upon my life, mother, I no longer believe anyone." To which the old woman responds, "It is exaggerated to believe everyone; not to believe anyone is a mistake." This seems to be one of the many aphorisms scattered throughout the play, here serving Celestina's immediate purpose. But it is also a cardinal rule of survival for Marranos under the Inquisition: trusting everyone is a fatal mistake, yet to survive, one must trust *someone*. The Marrano's terrible dilemma is therefore to decide whom to trust. Celestina suggests to Parmeno that she deserves his trust—a remark that on one level sounds cynical and self-serving, but that makes good sense on another, tacit level. Celestina used to be an intimate friend of Parmeno's late mother, Claudina, whom she loved dearly and still mourns. Thus it is the wily whore—who is, to be sure, also very human—whom this play portrays as deserving what little trust a person can afford in this world, especially in the Spain of the Inquisition.

The Victims of the Inquisition as Martyrs

A clearer and even more direct allusion to the Inquisition surfaces when Celestina describes to young Parmeno the first time that she and Claudina were arrested for sorcery. Parmeno responds with theological babbling about "the first error" and "persevering in sin." Man, he declaims, is not responsible for his first movements; what counts is not the first error but the persevering. This is one of the ironic speeches that Rojas puts in the mouth of servants; its hidden meaning would not be lost on readers who knew that Marranos were burned at the stake not as first offenders, but because they "persevered," either by refusing to confess and repent or, more commonly, by "relapsing" into their sin after having repented of it. At this point Celestina loses her patience. In a rare, impulsive decision, she discards her mask and utters not official truths, but truth itself. And the truth she unveils turns out to be a hymn of praise, an ode to the victims of the Inquisition—here represented by the prostitute Claudina—whose heroism consists precisely in "persevering in her sin" and to whom, of all people, the kingdom of heaven is due!

Parmeno.	What did you say, mother?
Celestina.	I was saying, my son, that, not counting that occasion, they arrested your mother (whom God cherishes) four other times. Once they accused her of being a witch, because one night they found her working by candlelight at some crossroads in a public square, with a painted witch's cap on her head. But these are trifles; *people must suffer some [such] things in this world in order to maintain their lives and their honor!* And how little did she mind it, or let it change her sense! *She did not give up her profession on that account, not she! She even got better at it. So much for what you said about persevering in sin.*
	She did everything with grace, and, before God and my conscience, so calm was she, even on her ladder, that you'd thought she didn't give a penny for the people down below! *And so it is with those who are like her, and have the same worth, and know something like her.* (Act 7, Simpson, p. 83, trans. revised; emphasis added)

Celestina's speech about "persevering in sin" thus becomes a covert hymn to the victims of the Inquisition. The sentence, "People must suffer such things in this world in order to maintain their lives and their honor," will serve as cold comfort to the Marranos, who will recognize their own judgment of the *autos-de-fé* in the claim that Claudina's public humiliation actually upheld her honor. Celestina praises her suffering friend's stand as an example of nobility and glorifies her ability to prevail in the face of torment. This is precisely the "persevering in sin" that, by an ironic reversal, here becomes the sign of valor and greatness of soul for which the Marrano martyrs of the Inquisition were best known. Moreover, Claudina was arrested as a witch on account of certain vague signs, including *candlelight*—an allusion to the way Marranos were arrested. The Inquisition when entering a city, used to publish a list of signs by which Judaizers could be identified—an awesome semiotic code in which the lighting of Sabbath candles was prominent.

And who are those who are "like Claudina, and have the same worth, and know something like her"? They are apparently sinners like her, who have the same worth as a whore and a witch; but this verbal mask actually points to a group of courageous people, men and women well trained in suffering, who have inner worth and "know something" unknown to others—a select, esoteric group whose devotion to inner truth commands admiration and leads to deeds of greatness and valor.

Celestina clearly mourns Claudina; in speaking of those who "are like her and have the same worth" she expresses genuine admiration. On a deeper level, an inner identification takes place between Celestina and her dead friend, who serves Celestina as a kind of alter ego.

All this lays the groundwork for what is to follow. Celestina continues: "that priest . . . knew better who said, when they came to console him at his execution, that the Scriptures hold blessed those who suffer persecution by the authorities, for theirs will be the Kingdom of Heaven" (Simpson trans.: the word *justicia* means both "justice" and "those who dispense justice"). This is open blasphemy, for it promises salvation to the victims of the Inquisition (the *relapsos,* those "persevering in sin," and so forth), who are thus portrayed as martyrs (while the Inquisitors appear as the true offenders). It is true that the blasphemy is spoken by one whore talking of another, but we cannot expect Rojas to speak openly, without hiding behind a negative character. That Celestina quotes a priest who, in an ironic twist, cites a verse from the New Testament,[39] may suggest that the priest had blasphemed, too, and might even have been a Marrano.

Again, Rojas exploits a well-known Marrano motif. In the early days of the Inquisition, many Church dignitaries in Spain were troubled by the possible analogy between the Marranos' burning at the stake and the early Christian martyrs worshiped by the populace. It was even suggested on this account to keep the public away from the burnings, an idea that of course went contrary to the whole point of the act and the intentions of the Holy Office, and had no possibility of being adopted. The issue was real and pressing, though, and Rojas seems to make use of it.

In portraying the victims of the Inquisition as martyrs, Rojas does not have only the Judaizing Marranos in mind. As everyone knew, many sincere Catholics had also been falsely accused and cruelly punished. Rojas wavers between the two as he lets Celestina continue depicting Claudina as a heroine and martyr:

She was wrongfully and unreasonably accused; and with false witnesses, and with cruel tortures, was forced to confess to being what she was not.[40] But since she had courage, and since a heart inured to suffering can better support evil treatment, all this was nothing to her.

Who is "the heart inured to suffering" by way of torture and false accusations? What Marrano, reading these words could fail to think immediately of his own plight?[41]

Celestina concludes under the mask of a sermonizing priest:

> Thinking of what your good mother endured here on earth, we must believe that God rewarded her up in heaven, if what our priest said is true; and this consoles me.

To unsuspecting readers these words will sound cynical, coming as they do from a sinful whore whose world is upside down. But it is enough to reverse the perspective and these words will stand out literally—as, indeed, many readers of the *Celestina* were led by their experience to read them.

(2) THE AESTHETICS OF MASK AND EQUIVOCATION

In *La Celestina* equivocal language and the play of essence and appearance emerge as a central artistic theme in itself. As such, there is a high correlation between these elements and the life of the Marranos. It is no accident that what was so dominant in the actual experience of this group should attain such prominent artistic expression in the work of one of its representatives. The duality of consciousness, the opposition between the inner and the outer world, together with reciprocal influence and even confusion between them, were part of the actual experience of readers and author. These finely developed and highly pitched sensitivities were transmitted by the work and met with empathy and comprehension on the part of its readers.

Of course, a play of masks is a conventional dramatic device, not limited to the Marrano experience alone. But there is no denying that in the life of the Marranos it became almost universalized and acquired a dominant existential force. The very existence of the Marranos was built upon the opposition between a hidden truth and its feigned externality, and their survival depended upon the careful interplay between the two. This daily situation required all Marranos to sharpen their skills at camouflage and disguised language, comprehensible only to the initiated. These linguistic needs arose suddenly in the first generation, and *La Celestina* is strikingly attuned to the special sensitivities they demanded. The texture of the work is rich in plays of meanings and masks, much beyond what is required by its plot and intrigue, to the point where this formal and aesthetic element becomes a theme in itself.

Equivocation is evinced even in the names of the protagonists. Celestina—the "celestial"—is the name of the most earthy character conceivable. Pleberio—the man of the *plebs*, the "plebeian"—is the name of the most noble character in this play, both in station and in spirit.

The first scene (after the prologue) is immediately constructed as a play of masks. Calisto reveals his passion to Sempronio who tries at first to placate him. Sempronio speaks in two voices, loudly to his master and silently to himself. Even with respect to his master he wears many masks; he is now the voice of religion, now the voice of reason, without believing in either. Moreover, even when Sempronio speaks to himself the discerning reader will notice that he assumes a clownish posture.[42] Rojas uses a theatrical convention that signifies frankness (a character talking to himself) in order to express the opposite (dissimulation) and this creates a sharply cynical effect.[43]

Calisto is aware of Sempronio's game. After the servant has inveighed against love affairs as a pious man of God, his master rebukes him for his dissimulation.

> *Calisto.* It is a wicked thing to lie when preaching to others, you who are boastful of your Elicia [the prostitute Sempronio is keeping]!
>
> *Sempronio.* You should do the good I say, and not the evil I do.

This is a form of clowning; but in a deeper sense it legitimizes the opposition of word and deed, the inner and the outer. Sempronio is unruffled when Calisto unmasks him, for the mask itself now has its own value. The acts and thoughts behind it have no importance. Truth appears here as its own mask, and *as such* becomes a model for imitation. This is also the role Sempronio assigns to language, ritual, and nonverbal expressions. These acquire an autonomous weight, having a life of their own, independent of reality.[44] A cognitive statement, for instance, or a moral exhortation (or a ritual gesture), are given the semantics of some "truth in itself," regardless of the conditions in which they are uttered (or performed). But we know that in real life the contrary holds true: a merely verbal truth behind which there is no speaker of truth is empty hypocrisy. This is the case of preachers whose tongue does not reflect their heart (and at whom Sempronio's words snipe in passing), of fawning servants (whom Sempronio himself represents)—and this is also a major characteristic of the Marranos, who imitate convention of speech and behavior contrary to their own inner lives. Indeed, when Sempronio identifies truth solely by its external appearance, he not only makes an ironic allusion to clerical hypocrisy, but a tragic allusion to the state of the Marranos as well.

The play of masks goes on in Calisto's relationship to his servants.

Sempronio cheats him, flatters him, and helps him to deceive himself. Calisto says, "Henceforth, too, be as faithful to me as you are now" (act 2). The audience snickers, as does Sempronio in secret. But Calisto may also smile: he knows very well that he is being cheated, and in a certain sense invites this. Later, Parmeno, the young servant, arrives and Calisto asks his opinion about his love affair. He encourages the boy to speak openly. "Truth is so strong that it will even take command over the tongues of its enemies," Calisto declares without believing his own words, and thus he defines the tacit theme of the whole scene. The inexperienced Parmeno takes his master's words at face value and, with bold wisdom, warns Calisto against getting entangled in this affair. Calisto bursts out in anger: "You pretend to be loyal to me, but you're nothing but a lump of flattery." The roles have been reversed. The faithful Parmeno betrays his master by being faithful and honest. And the traitor Sempronio is faithful to his master in that he guesses his mind and helps him to deceive himself. "You know very well," Calisto shouts at Parmeno, "that my pain and waves of suffering cannot be treated by reason . . . they don't want to be advised!"

Parmeno is no hero. This is not the noble Kent speaking to King Lear. "I suffer for being loyal" he complains—and joins the conspiracy against his master. What Celestina's ardent persuasions failed to do in the first act is now achieved by Parmeno's disillusioning confrontation with truth. Now he grasps that his master's fine statement about "the truth always winning" has been refuted twice: first, by the very act of being said, for it was proclaimed in self-deception; and second, by the opposite result that Parmeno had suffered in person.

Few Marranos would fail to recognize their own grappling with truth, mask, and self-deception; and many would appreciate the game for what it is and, as Jews frequently did, find consolation in its humorous and self-ironizing aspects.

Social Revaluation under Mask

Act 2 began with another play of disguise and dual meaning. Again the speaker is Sempronio. He praises Calisto for having given money, which, the audience knows, he shares with her, to Celestina: "How glorious it is to give! How miserable to receive! . . . You did yourself great honor—for what is the use of fortune except to serve honor, which is the greatest of worldly treasures?" Here a somewhat farcical, somewhat serious critique of the role of honor (*honra*, also definable as social prestige) in the life of Spanish society slips into the play. Sempronio rails on in praise of honor, with a significant equivocation. "Honor," he says, "is the prize and reward of virtue. That's why we offer it to God, for we have nothing better to give him." The last part of the statement can be read: "nothing *in general* can be better than honor"; but equally it can be read: "*we* have nothing better to give God except honor" (we cannot give him virtue, since we lack it, so honor is all we can offer him). In the second case, giving honor to God is an empty ritual, a substitute for the virtue we do not possess. The end of the statement thus contradicts its pious beginning. But the disguise does not end here. Even the first statement, when closely examined, entails a grave social heterodoxy; for, in opposition to the norm governing Spain, it puts honor to other tests than birth and rank.

> Some say that nobility is a glory stemming from the merit and antiquity of one's ancestors; but I say that another's light will never brighten you unless you have light of your own. Don't take too much pride, therefore, in the glory of your father, however magnificent he may be, but only in your own, for thus you gain honor which is the highest good attainable by man.

With great rhetorical power, the cynic Sempronio puts on a new mask and, as usual, uses other people's ideas for his own ends. Just as previously he spoke in the name of religion, and later in the name of reason, so here he becomes the ideological spokesman of the new bourgeoisie, which was then rising in Spain, especially among the conversos. Honor, indeed, is the highest value "outside of man"; but it is not gained by noble birth or by "purity of blood," that which the conversos lack, but rather by industrious work and the accumulation of wealth, in which the conversos excelled, being the backbone of the professional, commercial, and productive class then on the rise. Sempronio himself does not believe in this view; in act 9 he says the exact opposite (and the prostitute Areusa will say there against him, with sincerity, what Sempronio voices here insincerely). Rojas takes refuge behind the backs of the cynical servant and the courageous whore to voice some of the most trenchant pieces of criticism in his play.

Equivocation as an Aesthetic Value

Apart from its reflection in the game of meanings and the play of consciousness, equivocation attains other forms of expression as well in *La Celestina*. There is, for example, a dual meaning attached to the semiotics of an object: the belt which the "sick" Calisto asks of Melibea is in one sense a simple talisman, but in another sense it signifies the lifting of the barriers of sexual chastity (the cure Calisto actually seeks for his "malady"). Another form of dual meaning resides in situation, that is, in the ironic contrast between what a character says and the situation or context of speech which immediately refutes it, such as Calisto's words about all-triumphant truth and Sempronio's sermon about piety. A further type of equivocation is the use of philosophical aphorisms by prostitutes, servants, and the procuress Celestina. This, as Rojas declares rather boastfully, is a major aesthetic building block of the play; but it is nontheless a form of *bal masqué*. The servant who did not invent the epigram and is deemed incapable of knowing it, spouts wise sayings as an actor changes roles or faces. For him, as for Celestina in the seduction scene, language becomes a mask. Even when speech is true it is false, or at least misleading, since it does not express a subjective truth but more often its opposite, or its complete absence. This serves as a linguistic imitation of the life of the Marranos, who are also locked in double-speak and dissimulation. There is a rupture between sentences and speakers, between gestures and meanings, between the ruling social code and the life of the inner person— a rupture which, for the Marranos, almost became a way of life.

In addition, the capacity to freely exchange views and values and to manipulate them verbally points to a certain confusion which Rojas introduces into these ideas, and to a degree of distance and irony he adopts with respect to established social values. Every character in this play can say anything, injecting into it his or her own grotesque or ironic meaning. Every servant can spout wisdom like a cleric or a biblical scholar. Any sentence can be uttered in every possible mode: literally, allegorically, equivocally, in cynical clowning which is to be recognized as such—and also with agreement, passion, or criticism. Anything goes.

Rojas's words of social criticism must also be read in this spirit. He does attack the concepts of external honor and purity of blood (always behind the mask of a servant or a prostitute). In this he lent his voice to the protest of his fellow conversos whose blood was not "pure" and who, like the prostitute Areusa, demanded that honor be attached to deeds and not to the distinction of birth. Many conversos belonged to the emerging bourgeois class and wished to attain social standing by their wealth and industry in a country whose traditional values, still eminently powerful though no longer congruent with reality, looked down on labor as base and despicable. Yet *La Celestina* is not a piece of *littérature engagée*. Even while identifying with these converso values, Rojas does not write as a committed social reformer but more as an artist changing ideas like masks, and putting these and other words in the mouths of characters as he pleases. In the final analysis, language looses its univocal character in this play and functions as a carnival of masks. *This is no longer a pragmatic need but also, now, an esthetic value.*

In this game which the author plays with his readers and all the characters play with one another, it is hard to know whether language serves to communicate or to disguise; but in any case it serves both to amuse and to realize an artistic conception.

Of course, this is the only way Rojas could protect himself and ensure the survival of his work. In retrospect he succeeded. But for that purpose he had to weave a fabric of allusive and equivocative language, which established its own literary genre; and in this way he linked the formal and aesthetic values embodied by his work with his historical and existential background.

It would be impossible to mention all the cases of equivocation and mask-play in *La Celestina*. The text is filled with them. For instance, in discussing Rojas's direct allusions to the Marranos or his immanent metaphysics (see the next section), I use textual examples that frequently also illustrate equivocation and mask-play, and I invite the reader to reread them from this perspective. For, indeed, whatever else we may find in this work, equivocation will often be there too, perhaps as the carrier of the other ingredients.

To anticipate, in Parmeno's "old whore" monologue (one of the keystones of the play) there is an opposition between the joyous celebration of earthly love and the mask of blame attached to it. This is a "Marranesque" structure, where a vital truth is hiding under the veil of Christian hypocrisy. The truth is the principle of nature, passion, love, which is present in all creatures, but which Christianity has distorted and turned into an "old whore." The essence hiding behind the mask is no longer Judaism but a quasi pagan world that transcends both.

Also, the account of Celestina's machinations is a true carnival of masks. Recall the night procession in church, under cover of which lecherous encounters take place; the implied hints to the *autos-de-fé* and unmistakable allusion to the victims of the Inquisition; notice Celestina's Marranesque habits of disguising herself—never missing mass or vespers; her proficiency in cosmetics and the renewing of maidenheads—all arts of disguise; and the generalization that all was nothing but lies and mockery." Recall also the crude picaresque masks, as when Sempronio arrives at his lover's residence and now it is his turn to be deceived in a game of double meaning, which the girl and Celestina perform above his head. This piece, and its follow-up in the third act, are a brilliant illustration of a game played on two levels, that of language and that of action, where everyone cheats everyone else to the audience's delight.

The play of masks attains a high point in the complex and subtle scene of Melibea's seduction (act 4, followed up by act 6). This fascinating scene revolves around a constant game of masks, built upon a major verbal equivocation with a plethora of secondary equivocations (verbal and nonverbal) accompanying it. Melibea's seduction, which passes through several stages of self-deception, combines the two major elements we are discussing: dual language and a game of masks which takes place not only between the inner and the outer person but even (as in Melibea) within the inner person herself.

Complex Dualities: The Essence Affected by Its External Appearance

In observing the dialectic of dissimulation and dual consciousness, special emphasis must be laid on the reciprocal influence between essence and appearance. The play of masks does not follow a simple dualistic model, according to which there is, on the one hand, a complete, hidden, and integral essence, and on the other, an external and distorted appearance opposing it. Essence, or truth, is itself modified by the fact of being reflected in the appearance, and this makes it frequently ambivalent and deficient in itself. The Marrano, whose experience is reflected here, is not necessarily the Judaizer who possesses an integral, steadfast secret faith which he conceals behind a purely external Christian shell. Such Marranos constituted a minority; and even then Christianity, the shell, had itself penetrated to the interior, both because of the effects of education and the internalization of symbols, and also because of the inherent dialectic of essence and mask. It is impossible to retain and preserve untouched an essence which becomes ever more abstract, an ever more lofty ideal, and gradually loses its influence on actual life. The essential and the actual then stand at two opposite poles: the essence is supposed to reside in the lost Judaism, but because the latter becomes increasingly remote and abstract, it is life on the level of the Christian mask which becomes real. Essence thus ceases to fulfill its role—being the essential thing in life—yet the appearance is not thereby redeemed and does not acquire integral significance, for it remains devoid of some deep and true element that was severed from it. At either of these poles, one is suffering, or alienated, and cannot attain unity or reconciliation. His essence opposes his actuality and yet is reflected in it as in a warped mirror. The duality in consciousness or the split in identity thus penetrates the life of the Judaizing Marranos.

And these, in addition, were in the minority. Among the other Marranos a diversity of states is conceivable: a Marrano trying to espouse his newly won Christianity, partly in a process of self-deception; a Marrano preserving an affinity with Judaism, but without deep conviction or fervor; a Marrano eagerly embracing Christianity while maintaining an inner distance from it; a faithful Judaizing Marrano, who had lost his background of Jewish knowledge and historical fact; a Marrano who converted without conviction, with others continuing to view him as Jewish; and finally, the Marrano torn between the two religions, who no longer knows where his "essence" ends and his "mask" begins. Because of his social and existential experience, he is obliged to live in a world of camouflage and double-speak, such that the borderline between the outer and the inner becomes blurred. We should remember that Marranos of all varieties lived in the shadow and terror of the Inquisition which used to throw into its cellars at will both Judaizers and good Christians, and in order to survive it was therefore imperative to develop techniques and strategies for camouflage even where there was not so much to conceal. As Parmeno said, all was "nothing but lies and mockery."

Marrano Romeo and Juliet?

There is a view that the Marrano situation is hidden in the plot of *La Celestina*: Calisto is an Old Christian, whereas Melibea's parents are rich New Christians. Therefore marriage, which would have averted the tragedy, is inconceivable between the two lovers.[45]

A Marrano version of *Romeo and Juliet*, this interpretation is tempting but, unfortunately, refuted by the text. On several occasions Melibea is described as belonging to a high rank of nobility, higher even than Calisto's. In the banquet scene in act 9 (where frank talk prevails), Semprenio states: "Calisto is a gentleman (*caballero*), Melibea a nobleman's daughter (*hijadalgo*), and it is natural for those of noble birth (*nacidos por linaje*) to seek and choose one another." Later, Melibea's parents, unaware of her affair, discuss her marriage prospects in close quarters (where no dissimulation is necessary), and mention as a matter of fact that no family in the land would shun matrimonial links with them. These statements indicate that, if anything, it is Calisto who would rise above his rank by marrying Melibea, though their difference in social rank is not prohibitive to a possible match. If they do not marry, the reason must lie elsewhere.

It is therefore not in the plot of *La Celestina* that its Marrano side resides. Nor can it be properly discovered by the simplistic method of a roman à clef. Rather, we must examine the actual texture of this

work for its use of dual language, its specific allusions, and finally its
hidden immanent metaphysics.

(3) *LA CELESTINA*'s UNDERLYING METAPHYSICS:
LOVE AS DISORDER IN A WORLD OF PURE IMMANENCE

We have seen that many conversos were driven to question the foundations of both Christianity and Judaism, to the point of losing a
definite religious identity and transcending the theistic world view altogether in their inner consciousness. Religious skepticism, philosophical deism (whether popular or sophisticated), and the view that this
world encompasses all reality are some of the consequences. Culmi-
nating in Spinoza, such phenomena are known and documented in
conversos of many previous generations, including Rojas's own family
(his father-in-law, Alvaro de Montalban). That Rojas himself belongs
to their number cannot be left in doubt by the content of *La Celestina*.

The spiritual universe of the play is neither Christian nor Jewish. Just
as Rojas the artist was inspired by Terence and Plautus, so did Rojas
the thinker retreat from the religious universe of the Middle Ages to
that of ancient Rome, transcending—or, seemingly, retreating from—
both the Old and the New Testaments. This does not mean that Rojas
returned to the Roman world in its historical reality.[46] What he turned
to was rather an image, a reflection of the ancient world as pictured
from his own viewpoint, already affected by the Christian experience.
In this Rojas was influenced, among other things, by the contemporary
Italian Renaissance, specifically by Petrarch, but with a major difference. Rojas's return to the Roman world is not purely scholarly and
aesthetic, nor does it aim, as did Petrarch, to renew and revitalize the
Christian culture. Rojas rejoins the ancients on a deeper philosophical
and existential level, for he goes outside the universe of Christianity
and theism altogether. In this respect, as I shall argue later, Rojas's
attraction to pagan culture is not so much a positive choice as it expresses his negation of the Jewish and Christian world view and of all
transcendent dimensions of existence.

"I Am a Melibean"

Heterodox voices are heard in the play from the very beginning. Calisto, in the frenzy of his love, blasphemes. Sempronio, the corrupt
manservant, reprimands his master while putting on a pious face.

Calisto.	What are you saying?
Sempronio.	I was saying, I hope God does not hear you, for what you have said is heresy.
Calisto.	Why?
Sempronio.	Because it contradicts the Christian religion.
Calisto.	Ah! Never mind!
Sempronio.	Are you not a Christian?
Calisto.	Me? I am a Melibean! I worship Melibea, I believe in Melibea, I love Melibea.

Calisto is not a Christian but a "Melibean": his terrestrial beloved takes the place of the Savior. This is not just a brilliant slip of the pen. The same idea recurs in the subtitle of the play, and also in expressions such as Calisto's statement that Celestina is to mediate between him and his "salvation." (Incidentally, this is further evidence of Celestina's role in symbolizing the Church—the "Old Whore.") The same idea is repeated in another passage:

Calisto.	What are you reproaching me for?
Sempronio.	For submitting your man's dignity to the imperfections of a woman.
Calisto.	A woman, you brute? Say rather: a God.
Sempronio.	Do you really believe that, or are you making fun of me?
Calisto.	Making fun? I believe her to be God, I recognize her as God, and I don't believe there is in heaven a higher power than she, although she resides among us here on earth.

Calisto's blasphemous words put Eros on a higher plane than Christos. Moreover, Calisto divests heaven of all supernatural power and presents his "god," Melibea, as a terrestrial creature residing here "among us." Thus, there is nothing in existence but this world—its desires, its adventures, its pleasures.

And to whom does Rojas assign the task of defending religion? To none other than the corrupt knave, Sempronio, who defends religion by a rude joke and puts on the pious face of a devotee lamenting the loss of faith. His cynicism is heightened by the fact that he is talking to himself—a dramatic situation which usually indicates frankness but is used here for its buffoon effect.

Calisto's blasphemies were deleted by the Inquisition many years later. Had the censors been subtle enough (which they rarely are), they would have cut out not only the words of the master but those of the servant as well. Sempronio's hypocritical talk is, if anything, even more sacrilegious than the direct blasphemy of his master. Moreover, the fact that the protest against Calisto's semipagan heresy is put in the mouth of this scheming and corrupt knave, Sempronio, has a sharp, cynical effect that undercuts that very protest.[47]

The Ode to the Old Whore

Another major passage expressing a pagan sense of the world is Parmeno's monologue, in which he describes Celestina to his master, calling her "an old whore." Calisto is embarrassed, but Parmeno reassures him:

> Why are you worried? Do you think she was insulted by the name I called her? Don't believe it! Why she puffs up as much when she hears it as you do when someone says: "What a fine horseman is Calisto!" Besides, that's her proper title and the one she goes by. If she's among a hundred women and someone says "Old Whore!" with no embarrassment whatever she turns her head and answers with smiling face. At parties, festivals, weddings, guild meetings, funerals, at every kind of gathering, she's the center of merriment. If she walks among dogs, that's the name they bark. If it's birds, they sing nothing else. If it's a flock of sheep, they bleat her name. If it's asses, they bray "Old Whore!" The very frogs in their puddles croak it. If she passes a smithy, the smiths' hammers pound it out. Carpenters and armorers, farriers, tinkers, and fullers—every kind of instrument fills the air with her name. Farmers in their fields, at their plowing, in the vineyards, or at harvest, lighten their labors with her. When gamblers lose at the gaming table, then you should hear her praises ring forth! All things that make a noise, wherever she is, proclaim her. [Oh what a consumer of roasted eggs her husband was!][48] What else would you know, save that when one stone strikes against another, they cry "Old Whore!" (Act 1, Simpson, pp. 16–17)

This text can be read in two ways. On the level of disguise it is supposed to put Celestina in her place—as a decent reader would expect. Her taking pride in the title of "Old Whore" only heightens the impression of her corruption: even her values are fundamentally perverse. Similarly, her belonging to a lower order of artisans and manual laborers, devoid of social honor, and even of domestic animals, is seemingly supposed to denigrate her. Her name—Old Whore—is on everyone's lips as a common abuse which the vulgar throw at each other and "into the air."

Yet all this is but a thin veneer. In fact, and essentially, this passage is a song of praise, an ode to what Celestina represents: a free, powerful force of nature, the power of Eros and love that fills the universe and permeates all its creatures. Even in the inanimate world it operates as an embodied and secret force (cf. the "two stones" at the end of the text). Freeing ourselves of the feigned Christian context and reading this text without irony, we shall find here the poetic force of a Greek paean to nature.

But this vital cosmic power, earthly love, is here presented in the pejorative shape of an "Old Whore." This fact does not only reflect the need for literary camouflage, it also includes an essential message: look what Christianity has done to the pagan power of Eros and love—it has distorted its nature and turned it into an "Old Whore."[49] Such reversal of values—like the need to hide behind its mask—is itself a perversion of nature and reality. Christian culture has taken the cosmic power of Eros and by pouring into it the negative significance of sin and shame, has transmuted it into an Old Whore.

But the opposite, too, takes place—by Rojas's art. As we go on reading this poetic-ironic passage, the term *Old Whore* sheds its negative meaning and is transformed into a synonym for pagan natural forces that transcend and supersede the Christian context.

The ode to the Old Whore is one of the key passages in this play. It deals with earthly love in its relation to the structure of the universe. This, as I read it, is a central theme of *La Celestina*, embodied in its plot and attaining from time to time explicit expression in the text. Celestina declares with pride, "I trust in my great power" (act 3, Simpson, p. 44); and elsewhere, in an intimate talk with her cohorts, she says: "Love is so strong that it not only crosses the land, but even the seas. It has the same authority with every kind of men. It breaks through all barriers" (act 9, Simpson, p. 107).

But she hastens to cite also the sinister side of love, in accordance with the central idea of the play: "It is an anxious thing, fearful and eager; and looks upon everything in a roundabout way [*en derredor*]."

Indeed, there are two sides to this coin. Although love is a cosmic power, we must beware of romantic interpretations of love in Rojas. A natural force is not in itself an object of admiration or idealization. The excees of power disturbs the order of things and is one of the sources of the suffering, and of the pessimistic world view that ultimately emerges from *La Celestina*. True, love as such involves no sin in the Christian sense, but it does involve a moral danger in terms of pagan philosophy—the danger of irrational excess.

This is the spirit in which old Pleberio, Melibea's father, pronounces the lament that concludes (and, in an important sense, summarizes) the play. The power of love is to Pleberio a further indication of the fundamental disorder of the universe. The immense force of love is but part of the play of forces—all natural, all terrestrial, without any transcendent meaning—to whose vicissitudes we are prey. "O love," the old man cries, "who gave you such a great power!" Upon hearing these words, our ears still ring with Celestina's proud exclamation, "I trust in my great power." Celestina, indeed, as a force of nature, embodies both the vital and the sinister sides of love. From this viewpoint she is suitably described as a "witch," that is, related to the sinister and demonic dimension of existence. This complex nature of love is a major message of the whole play. Love governs and sustains the universe—but the universe it sustains is not necessarily harmonious. Celestina, as the priestess of love, is by this very role related to the sinister side of existence and to the element of chaos in the universe.[50]

Pleberio's Lament

One of the rhetorical climaxes of *La Celestina* is the concluding lament of Pleberio, Melibea's noble and wealthy father. Pleberio has been in the background through most of the play; now, in the final scene, he suddenly emerges to the forefront and we see him in his awesome lament and fall, as if he had been the hidden true hero of the drama all along. From a purely theatrical perspective, the last scene looks somewhat patchy; but in content it is the most significant of *La Celestina*, for it heightens the immanent metaphysics and areligious world view that underlie Rojas's work.

Pleberio's lament is delivered in the style of the ancient moral philosophers who, observing the world and its caprices, the vicissitudes of fate, and the inexplicable suffering that is man's lot, assess the value of life and death. This long and eloquent speech betrays no shred of Christian sentiment. Nor does it contain a single mention of God, Jesus, Mary, or any other Christian hero. Some were reminded by Pleberio of a Hebrew prophet, or of Job; but the resemblance is superficial. Pleberio's speech is also devoid of Jewish content. If he is "Job," then he is a faithless Job who takes no comfort in a God calling out of the storm or in a hidden, divine justice. On the contrary, for him the universe remains empty of any purpose and significance until the very end. As for the prophets, Pleberio echoes their style, if at all, only formally—by the high pathos pulsating in his words, or the moments in which he approaches something that could be called sublimity; but in substance he is separated from them by a deep gulf. Unlike the prophets, Pleberio does not lament the lot of a sinful people, nor the forsaking of God's word and covenant, but his personal tragedy: the death of his beloved daughter and the desolation that marks his life as a consequence. The object of Pleberio's lament has nothing to do with God in heaven or his children on earth. For him there is only his personal relationship to some other thing or person in this world. The value of life depends here completely upon one's personal lot, or upon a particular link to some other individual in the world.[51]

Pleberio thereby transcends both the Christian and the Jewish universe. Only in a world devoid of divine grace and of transcendent significance can life become so utterly empty because of a tragic this-worldly personal event, like the death of a daughter. The next world neither comforts Pleberio nor frightens him; it simply does not exist. Similarly (as various critics have pointed out), Pleberio does not regard his daughter's suicide as a sin. In a Stoic-pagan context, when life is drained of all its value, suicide can be justified and sometimes even considered sublime and heroic; but for Judaism and Christianity suicide is an unpardonable sin.

Pleberio's lament is not addressed to God. "O fortune (*fortuna*)," he cries, "O life full of affliction," "O world, world," "O love, love." All these have wronged him; it is against them that he cavails. Neither Jesus nor providence, nor any divine authority is responsible for Pleberio's suffering; it is only the way of this world, a world whose indifference Pleberio has come to know from personal experience. This realization transforms his pessimism into realism. He does not complain of the lack of metaphysical salvation, for he never believed in it. His happiness, the meaning of his life, resides in this world—a world in which he has amassed honor, inherited a fortune, planted trees, built ships—and above all, cultivated and cherished his only daughter who embodied his life, his achievements, his love, all the dimensions of his existence. All this—the very meaning of his life in this world—have vanished together with Melibea, and so, in true Stoic spirit, old Pleberio invites death to replace a life that was drained of its content.

O world, world, many have said much about you, describing and comparing your qualities from hearsay . . . I will tell it from sad experirence . . . When I was young I thought there was some order governing you and your deeds; today, having seen the pros and cons of your graces, you seem to me a labyrinth of errors, a frightful desert, a den of wild beasts, a game in which men run in circles . . . a stony field, a meadow full of serpents, a flowering but barren orchard, a spring of worries, a river of tears, a sea of suffering, a vain hope (*vana esperanza*), a false joy . . . Many have abandoned you in fear that you would abandon them; they will call themselves blessed when they see the reward you gave to this sad old man in return for such a long service. (Act 21)

This is not a Christian picture, which perceives the world as base and degraded as against a divine world to come. Rather, this world is all there is, and *as such* it is a metaphysical wasteland and "a labyrinth of error." In this state of metaphysical affairs all that can give sense to life are achievements, emotions, and objects of love *within* the world. But they, too, are annulled by the vicissitudes of fate, and man is then left in his metaphysical nakedness within an empty universe.

"Why did you forsake me sad and lonely in this vale of tears?" So Pleberio ends his lament, and the play. His concluding outcry—echoing, from a nonbeliever standpoint, that of Jesus on the cross—symbolizes man's fundamental position. The universe has been a vale of tears all along, and man is forsaken within it by his very nature. But the tumult of earthly life, including love and ambition, cover up this truth or drive it, repressed, to the margins of consciousness. The "servant of the world" must encounter some horrendous shock in order for this latent truth to hit the center of his consciousness in a sharp and painful revelation. This is what has happened to Pleberio, who now speaks "out of [his] sad experience" and no longer as an abstract philosopher. In a painful realization the world now takes for him the shape it had all along—but so painfully clear and distinct that nothing can expunge it. What happens to Pleberio anticipates what will happen a century later to a better known tragic hero, Macbeth: with the disappearance of the terrestrial element that is supposed to give life its sense (there: ambition, here: love), the universe is revealed in its *fundamental* lack of meaning. (*Macbeth*, too, is not a Christian play.)

Although Pleberio's exclamation recalls Jesus' outcry on the cross ("My God, my God, why didst thou forsake me?"), the allusion is definitely and almost provocatively heterodox. The old man does not address God, but his daughter. It is *she* who has forsaken him in the vale of tears. The daughter takes the place of God as the exclusive agent who can endow Pleberio's life with meaning and hope. Fundamentally, this heresy is similar to, and just as serious as Calisto's statement ("I am a Melibean") at the beginning of the play. Despite their difference in personal depth both characters, the lover and the father, put Melibea in the role of God.

This inner link between two heterodox expressions so separated by dramatic space (and that other commentators apparently left unnoticed) proves to me that Pleberio's lament is organically tied to the rest of the play and to the tacit metaphysics that govern it throughout. If this world has no transcendent dimension, then some particular entity within the world can possibly gain metaphysical significance, and even be sanctified by some person as the foundation of his or her life. This is not merely "paganism" but outright idolatry.

Pleberio's lament abolishes formal elements that are otherwise almost ubiquitous in the play: irony and disguise. Despite a few equivocal hints, no additional ironic expressions are found. This may heighten the exceptional position of Pleberio's speech, but it is also an inner necessity for it. A tragic lamentation is incompatible with irony. Pleberio cannot use allusions and double talk, since the dramatic impression of his words, his attempt to express greatness, and even sublimity, are only possible if he is felt to be speaking from the heart. From this viewpoint, too, the last scene lets the masks fall, and we gain a precious glimpse into the depth of Rojas's own world.

Love as Unromantic Mess

"O love, love," the old man cries, "who gave you this unfitting name. . . . If you were love, you would love those who serve you, and if you loved them, you would not afflict them with suffering." Pleberio portrays love as a chaotic, irrational force, the source of suffering and madness: "the enemy of all reason . . . why do you act without order and concert (*concierto*)?" These are the same characteristics that Pleberio ascribes to the universe at large. There is a clear analogy—set, indeed, by the whole play—between the power of love and the structure of the universe. Love represents the immanent power and disorder of nature in general; and the story of Calisto and Melibea—a story of excessive love and the mad deeds it entails—is thereby linked internally with Pleberio's comments on the universe and its meaning.

This unromantic picture of love fits in well, furthermore, with love as symbolized by the wizened Celestina, and no longer by the tender Cupid. Rojas, despite himself, is here somewhat influenced by the Christian image of physical love. True, there is no sin in love as such; love is a primal, true force of nature. Yet love is not inherently invested with beauty and harmony—just as those properties are also absent from nature in general. Rojas's naturalism—unlike that of ancient paganism, and also, in a different way, unlike that of Spinoza—is totally devoid of sacred elements. There is only nature; but nature is a play of opposed, excessive forces, without inherent value, beauty, or divine attributes. Had Rojas spelled out, poetically, the metaphysics that flashes through his work, he might have said that nature itself was an old witch.

This unromantic view of love[52] is expressed not only in the plot of *La Celestina* but also in its emotive texture. Throughout the play there is not a single love scene displaying tenderness, warmth, or beauty. Love burns in cold fire; it is more passion than love, almost obsessive and driving the lovers mad. Everything is marked by passion, seduction, and conquest. Calisto suffers from his love as from a malady, bordering on madness. Melibea returns his love as one in mortal combat with temptation. Her submission to him is indeed total, but it is devoid of tenderness. Both are driven by love to excess—without enjoying the moments of grace and joy in love itself. The sexual act, too, is conceived more as a conquest that gratifies an obsession than as an experience of joyous pleasure. Here lies also the emotive-dramatic difference between *La Celestina* and other famous love stories.[53]

On the matter of love, too, Rojas stands worlds apart from Spinoza. Both accept the strict immanence of being, but for Spinoza love, as cosmic principle, is a divine principle of order, parallel to reason itself; it is another aspect of the universe-God's all-embracing order and rationality—and is, consequently, conceived as "intellectual" love. Spinoza thereby adopts a neo-Platonic idea developed specifically by Leone Ebreo. Rojas admits only irksome, obsessive love which lacks harmony and warmth and will match, as cosmic principle, the chaos and irrationality of the world as Rojas pictures it. Immanence is all there is, and it is shaped in the image of disruptive love.

Just as love persuades the play throughout, so does the broader philosophical and metaphysical message it symbolizes. While Otis Green focuses the theme of love on its passionate and courtly expressions, Gilman tends to see the love story as relatively unimportant for understanding the meaning of *La Celestina*. Rojas, he says, centered his *attention* on the lovers and his *intention* in Pleberio,[54] whose final speech embodies the essence of the play. But even if we agree to use the concept of intention in literary analysis, we cannot simply relegate the intention to some separate, almost detached text that the author affixes to his work. In order to identify an intention as actually embodied in the work we must see it manifested in its actual texture and not just appended to it as an ideological *deux ex machina*.

This condition is fulfilled when reading Rojas's work in the following way:

First, the basic theme of *La Celestina* is the nature of love and its relation to the metaphysical structure of the universe. Love represents nature, which is the only reality; but this does not entail a romantic idealization of love. Love is a two-sided power, penetrating and vitalizing everything, but also exceeding the right measure. Love thereby represents the universe as a whole, which is a theater of conflicting and excessive forces—a kind of Heraclitean system without logos and harmony, whose play of opposites and reversals chills man's desires and dashes his hopes.

Second, this pervasive, rather sombre metaphysics gives *La Celestina* a measure of internal unity. It is not an abstract idea "glued" on to the work, but one which is embodied in the real artistic stuff of the play. It is manifest (1) in the love plot and its vicissitudes; (2) in the emotive material from which the relations between the lovers are woven; (3) in Celestina's figure as a demonic goddess, replacing the tender boy Cupid; (4) in the somewhat enigmatic prologue; and, of course, (5) in Pleberio's concluding lament, which summarizes all of these and brings their implicit metaphysical meaning into relief. Only as such can this important monologue assume its crucial place, not as a separate text but as linked organically to the rest of the play and explicating what has underlied it all along.

All this leads, indeed, as Gilman and others suggest, to a "pagan" world view; but here, too, certain qualifictions are necessary. Gilman sees the world of Pleberio (and of Rojas) as "neo-Stoic." Yet the Stoics attributed reason and internal order to the universe, even seeing the World-Reason as a divine power—and this contradicts Pleberio.

Pleberio is no Stoic sage. He is not self-sufficient; on the contrary, his dependence on Melibea is total. He has no proud self-consciousness and does not overcome the world by overcoming himself. Nor does he see any inner order in the world—neither Christian nor Stoic-rational. He does manifest certain Stoic characteristics, like fortitude, this-worldliness, greatness in the face of suffering, a philosophical stance toward death; but he has also the ingredients of a skeptical world view and what we have called Heracliteanism without the logos. For him the world is a play of clashing forces, marked by irrational excess; and his naturalism (unlike that of the Stoics before him, or Spinoza after him) allows no admiration or deification of nature as such.

This calls for additional qualification. Even if Pleberio betrays an undeniable "pagan" element, this paganism should be grasped more in negative terms—as a retreat from the Christian and Jewish universe—

than in the sense of a positive world outlook. There is a difference between the absence of a Christianity that never existed and of which no one is aware, and the negation of a Christian system that already existed but whose world has become flawed. The memory of what has been and is no more—that with respect to which the negation takes place, perhaps even in the form of a lost illusion—is, dialectically, a necessary ingredient of the process and of the meaning of its outcome. And, indeed, Rojas retreats from the theist culture without replacing it with a genuinely positive and integral pagan world. His substitute lacks the plenitude and assurance of the original pagan world. It is marked by a void, a vacuum in its center. Paganism is very much an affirmation of life, a celebration of life or—as with the Stoa—an assent to the rationality of the universe with all its compulsive necessity; but in Rojas we do not find this.

Also, paganism had room for pantheist elements: existence itself was sanctified; it became a value in itself or acquired divine attributes. Pleberio's metaphysical skepticism, and seemingly that of Rojas, is altogether devoid of pantheistic and sacred elements. His naturalism is a "naked" one, lacking inherent worth. From this rather ironic viewpoint, Rojas continues to think in Christian, that is, theistic, categories. For him, as for the theists, no divine presence is possible if it does not have a transcendent origin; if the latter disappears, then the whole domain of the divine vanishes with it, and the universe takes the shape of the labyrinth and metaphysical wasteland Rojas portrays.

Rojas's metaphysical position is thus worlds apart from Spinoza's, although he anticipates him not only in the abstract, but as a possible outcome of the Marrano culture and experience. Spinoza went much further than Rojas in shedding the remnants of a Christian (and Jewish) outlook; the world without a transcendent God does not thereby become a meaningless arena, but is deified and takes the place of God himself. Rojas, on his part, anticipates modern metaphysical skepticism more than reviving ancient paganism; and the distance between him and Nietzsche is no greater than the one that separates him from Virgil or Seneca.

Neither a Jewish prophet, nor Job, nor a Christian believer, Rojas returns to a pagan world without really reaching it, and does so mainly by negation. The name of God is absent from Pleberio's speech, that of Jesus is never mentioned, and the work does not contain even a single authentic Christian character, with the result that the role of defending Christianity is left to the cynical knave, Sempronio. Rojas presents a world outlook that negates the historical religions and, with them, all transcendence.[55]

Rojas Versus Spinoza

Herein lies the major difference between Rojas and Spinoza, the philosopher who both continued and opposed him. Spinoza's new world picture had inner power and coherence lacking in Rojas. The difference, however, does not lie in the contrast between Spinoza the systematic thinker and Rojas the poet. It transcends all matters of form, method, and rigor, penetrating to the deeper layers of their respective metaphysical outlooks. The fact that Spinoza's world is much more coherent and organized is partly due to the fact that, in its metaphysical content, it is a world enjoying intrinsic meaning and unity, not a hybrid of two lost religions but a new, positive entity, a deified nature that inherits the absolute positivity, divinity, and sublimity of the old transcendent God. It is this inner feature of Spinoza's universe, its intrinsic power and coherence, that is manifest in the logical coherence of his philosophical system. But, in addition, this is the outcome of the fact that logos, or reason, has been restored to the natural world just as the perspective of a transcendent God has been banished from it. Reason itself is deified in Spinoza, as the principle governing nature/God. Unlike Rojas before him—and unlike Nietzsche later—Spinoza sees rational meaning in natural necessity, and rational meaning is divine meaning to him. It has—or will have for the true philosopher—the same invigorating power, and even the same function—a this-worldly form of salvation, occurring immanently within this life—that belief in a transcendent God and the next world had for religious believers. Moreover, Spinoza discards the vestiges of the Christian outlook which we have found in Rojas and with which Nietzsche grapples—those vestiges which, in the Nietzschean idiom would be called "the shadows of the dead God." For Spinoza, abolishing the transcendent God does not leave the world subject to the Christian outlook of an inferior, Godless sphere; rather, it is the world itself that is deified. The absolute, or God, is relegated to where it really belongs, as opposed to its distortion in historical religion. It is above all, I think, this total liberation from the vestiges of Judaism and Christianity, which neither Rojas, nor even Nietzsche, can claim, and which elevates this world to a divine plane, that has aroused the uproar against Spinoza and branded him the most challenging atheist.

CHAPTER 5

Spinoza, the Multitude, and Dual Language

The preceding chapters have shown the origin in Marrano culture of some of Spinoza's most characteristic traits: skepticism toward historical religion, an immanent metaphysics, the use of dual language, and the quest for an alternative way to salvation. The discussion has focused so far on Marrano intellectuals preceding Spinoza. We will now return to Spinoza himself and show how these elements are used and transformed in his thought. I propose to do this by means of detailed analysis of two major issues in Spinoza's philosophy, one relating to the multitude and the other to the wise man. In this chapter I shall analyze Spinoza's use of the different levels of language as they relate to his theory of the multitude. In the next chapter I shall offer an interpretation of intuitive knowledge—the road to salvation that Spinoza suggests for the happy few. While dealing with each as a philosophical problem in itself, the discussion will also illustrate how Spinoza's role as a Maranno of reason is relevant and illuminating in understanding his thought.*

THE LANGUAGE OF THE MARRANOS

The Marrano penchant for dual language, which Rojas amply illustrates, prevailed in other works of art and discourse as well. It is particularly evident in the picaresque novel, Spain's distinctive contribution to world literature. The picaro is the antihidalgo, the person of base origin who in a distorting mirror reflects the Spanish cult of *hidalguia* and pure blood, while he himself completely discards this value

---

* When discussing *La Celestina* I made a methodological remark which applies here as well: the primary meaning of a philosophical work emerges from the meaning-relations between the ideas that comprise it; but frequently the latter transform or rearrange historical and experiential elements, which the work both transcends and partly retains.

system and makes coarse or subtle jest of it. Some of the best-known picaresque novels have been written by conversos (among them *Guzman of Alfarache* and probably *Lazarillo de Tormes*, the first of the genre); and like *La Celestina*, they abound with coded language, hints, and allusions to the Marrano experience. Later on, Cervantes, whose new art incorporated picaresque elements, and who probably was also a converso, has Sancho Panza repeatedly protest that he is a good Old Christian, and makes numerous other direct and oblique references to Marranism and its place in Spanish society.

For Spinoza, another master of the art, dual (or multiple) language served a philosophical rather than an aesthetic purpose. Just as Rojas and other writers of fiction have turned the equivocal language of the Marranos from a necessity into an artistic value, so Spinoza turned it into a philosophical instrument. In all of these cases, dual language was used beyond its social function of prudence and dissimulation; it became an ingredient of a broader cultural enterprise—be it a novel, a drama, or a philosophical system. This is one of the chief characteristics (discussed in chapter 2) that make Spinoza a Marrano of Reason.

THE MULTITUDE AS A PHILOSOPHICAL PROBLEM

The multitude was a major philosophical concern for Spinoza. The philosopher lives among the multitude, surrounded on all sides by its powerful presence. He cannot attain his goal in ascetic isolation, nor can he realistically expect all men and women to rise to the life of reason. For Spinoza, therefore, the question of how to deal with the multitude becomes a major philosophical question in itself—even part of the general question of what is the good life, what is the life of philosophy.

Spinoza regards the multitude as a category in itself. Individuals can rise above the level of *imaginatio* and attain the life of *ratio* (reason), even the supreme degree of *scientia intuitiva* (intuitive knowledge), but the great majority is incapable of this—and the multitude is defined by that majority. Therefore, the multitude will always be there, guided by the powers of the imagination and by the special psychology of the masses to which it gives rise.

In the usual course of events, the psychology of the *imaginatio* breeds conflict, discord, violence, and war, as well as fanaticism and the various forms of intolerance. It is the source of life's insecurity and of social instability. Yet, Spinoza asks, even if we must admit that the multitude will remain governed by the imagination, must we accept this behavior and its catastrophic consequences? Perhaps there is instead a natural way to reshape the imagination and to redirect its effects on the multitude, in order to neutralize its destructive results and engender behavior that is socially beneficial.

This question defines the philosophical program of Spinoza's *Theologico-Political Treatise* and informs it throughout. The overall aim of this work is to establish mental and institutional mechanisms that will transform the imagination into an external imitation of reason, using state power and a purified popular religion as vehicles of a semirational civilizing process. This program is carried out in both parts of the *Theologico-Political Treatise*—the theological and the political—conferring systematic unity upon them. It contains Spinoza's main answer to the question, What is to be done about the multitude?—a question that dominates the *Theologico-Political Treatise*'s concerns.

Spinoza's answer is not to raise the multitude to the level of reason, a task he considers impossible. Rather, accepting that the majority of people will inevitably remain dominated by *imaginatio*, Spinoza seeks to transform and institutionalize the latter's effects in semirational patterns. This civilizing intervention in the crude course of nature will be carried out by a perfectly natural mechanism, based upon scientific knowledge of the passions and their effects; there will be two such mechanisms—one religious and the other political.

The man of *imaginatio* will not base his actions on true knowledge ("adequate ideas") or purely rational motivation. He will continue believing in external authorities (God's will, the Bible, the transcendental status of moral and legal precepts, and so forth, and will require the coercive power of the state to restrain his socially destructive passions by means of still more powerful passions. In direct contrast to the philosopher, the man of the multitude will be motivated by obedience to authority and fear of punishment. And yet, these two radically different human types will manifest little or no difference in their external conduct, for each in his way will act in accordance with the rules of justice and mutual social benefit. Purified religion and the rationalized state are thus designed to engender in the multitude the same conduct that the rational model requires, even though it will be motivated by nonrational powers and by inadequate ideas.

Hence the close link between the problem of the multitude and the problem of language. Spinoza's program for the multitude cannot utilize clear and distinct ideas and their verbal correspondents as its vehicle. To have the desired effect upon its target group, it must be suited to the latter's mental powers and tendencies. This requires the philosopher to use language rhetorically, so that his discourse might trigger the desired effects in his audience. The rhetorical use of language has a social and cultural role that, far from being regarded as undignified, acquires philosophical import for Spinoza as part of his general theory of discourse. Just as people are divided into those led by the imagination and those guided by reason, so there must be different types of discourse suited to each group—and also discourse that will fit an eventual transition by allowing the rational model to inspire and externally reshape the imagination.

The Psychology of the Multitude

Given that the multitude is its underlying problem, it is no wonder that the *Theologico-Political Treatise* begins with a succinct discussion of the psychology of the multitude. The main characteristic of the multitude is uncertainty, resulting from ignorance of true causes and lack of adequate ideas. Uncertainty makes the person of the multitude prey to the alternation of fear and hope, between which he or she vacillates without sufficient reason. Controlled as he is by his passions, he pursues goals that are unstable and uncertain in themselves (riches, pleasure, fame). As a result, his fundamental state is *fluctuatio animi*, the fluctuation or vacillation of the mind,[1] which explains the notorious unreliability of the multitude, its quick reversals of position, and the fierce, intolerant way in which it takes up any stand.

Uncertainty also breeds superstition, the essence of historical religion, according to Spinoza. The greater the lack of certainty, and of rational self-confidence, the stronger the temptation to invest one's faith in superstitious explanations. *Fluctuatio animi*, vacillation between fear and hope also accounts for the multitude's volatile nature, its outbursts of cruelty and violence, and its inclination toward intolerance and fanaticism (which is a false form of self-confidence). For although the multitude is liable to change its position, it always clings to its present position with fervid ardor. Paradoxically, the basic uncertainty of the person of the *imaginatio* does not result in tolerance, but in an ever-changing cycle of absolute stands.

To complement this picture drawn from the *Theologico-Political Treatise*, one must consider what the *Ethics* has to say about the psychology of association and about anthropomorphic explanations. The world image of the multitude is based upon contingent associations of ideas to which nothing constant and objective corresponds in reality. This produces cognitive instability that both informs and compounds the mind's emotional instability. Lacking necessary order and regularity, a world picture based upon association invites superstition, which is enhanced by the anthropomorphic nature of the imagination—its tendency to explain everything in terms of anthropomorphic purposes and intentions. Together, they provoke an irresistible appeal to occult humanlike powers, which are believed to operate arbitrarily behind the natural phenomena and which must be appeased, or otherwise influenced, by flattery, submission, sacrifice, and other such irrational acts.

Vana religio *as Alienation*

Spinoza thus carries his analysis of cognitive superstition into the domain of historical religions, those based upon cult, prayer, and revelation. Each historical religion is *vana religio* to Spinoza, a spurious religion of the imagination. Its dominion over the lives and minds of its adherents is a form of repression, indeed, of self-repression, because the fear that makes this dominion possible arises from the multitude's own weaknesses and expressed its psychological needs. This mental state of servitude is exploited by and readily enhances a political form of servitude; religious superstition becomes an instrument of tyranny. The supreme secret of monarchy, Spinoza says (momentarily denouncing all monarchic governments equally), is to wrap up the fear that it instills in its subjects in a specious garb of religion so that men "may fight as bravely for their servitude as if it were their salvation." Here Spinoza seems to anticipate the concept of self-alienation that became prominent in later philosophical and psychological discussions. The psychology of the multitude, by its own dynamic and so long as it is not reformed in the semirational manner the *Theologico-Political Treatise* recommends, is liable to produce self-alienating religious and political institutions, in which the individual is made to turn against himself, viewing his bondage as freedom and as worthy of sacrifice, and thus deepening that bondage.

A Program for the Multitude

The reformed religious and political institutions suggested by Spinoza are designed to alleviate this alienation even without raising the multitude to the level of true rationality. This program is to be carried out in two stages, theological and political.

Stage 1: The Universal Popular Religion

In the first stage, historical religion as *vana religio* must be undermined. This is the negative, indeed subversive, side of the critique of religion; its role is to clear the ground for the genuine rational life in those capable of it and for a semirational substitute in the rest of the populace. The substitute is the *religio catholica* (universal religion) discussed in the theological part of the *Theologico-Political Treatise*; it is a popular version of the religion of reason that remains rooted in passion and the imagination and is rational only externally or by imitation. Designed as it is for the multitude, not for true philosophers, the universal character of this religion lies in its stress upon the same patterns of conduct that reason recommends; it does not presuppose any true knowledge, however, only obedience. Hence its universality is not self-constituted but borrowed; in order to know its own content and to set the model it has to follow, the reformed religion cannot rely upon itself but must turn to what is an external authority for it—reason. This makes the use of reason not truly rational, since contrary to its nature, reason is used here without understanding, as yet another external authority to which one shows mere obedience. Herein lies the semirational nature of this kind of religion—its being a mere imitation of reason within the realm of the imagination.

Furthermore, this form of religion has a second master: the authority of revelation—or the Bible—which the person of the imagination is disposed to obey and by which, in Spinoza's plan, the multitude could be moved to comply with the semirational model. But this requires that the content of the Bible be reinterpreted to suit the message of the new universal religion. Although Spinoza insists that biblical hermeneutics must become an objective and autonomous science, he also expects it to serve as a means for reforming historical religion by reducing the true meaning of the prophets, and what is held to be the word of God, to a concise set of general and rather secular principles, such as justice, solidarity, and mutual help.

Thus, while the authority of reason supplies the paradigm of conduct to be followed, the motivation for doing so is still drawn from revelation, or more precisely from the multitude's persistent attachment to it. Spinoza treats this attachment as a real psychocultural force by which the mechanism of the reformed imagination can be set up in a purely naturalistic manner, diverting the passions of the multitude from their normally destructive course to produce benign and socially stabilizing results.

Stage 2: State Laws Interpret the Word of God

The second—political—stage in Spinoza's program for the multitude is required both for its own sake and as a complement to the theological stage. The nuclear doctrine of justice, solidarity, and mutual help, to which revealed religion and its word of God have been reduced, is far too vague to serve as a basis for action. The principles must be spelled out in specific legislation and adapted to the social context in which they are meant to apply.

Nothing of this can be determined a priori, either by mere philosophizing or by consulting Scripture. The Bible was not meant as a concrete political constitution except for one people—the ancient Hebrews—whose state has long since been destroyed. Therefore, whatever specific commands the Bible contains are now outdated and irrelevant for Gentiles and modern Jews alike. What the Bible continues to teach validly is its abstract moral core, the general principles of social ethics that are nondenominational and therefore must be interpreted (i.e., translated into actual legislation) by the secular authorities of each state.

By making the political authorities the sole interpreters of what is considered the word of God, Spinoza grants the secular government a monopoly over the normative domain as a whole—that is, over right and wrong, justice and injustice in all their valid applications. Since no normative concept can validly exist for Spinoza except by virtue of the enforceable law of some actual state, he thereby undercuts the superior authority that priests, rabbis, and other clergy claim for themselves over the state, and denies their right to construe religion as a realm within a realm. The clergy may well participate in the battle of ideas, but they should not enjoy institutional privileges of any kind. Similarly, Spinoza will have to dismiss as meaningless the moral claims of secular intellectuals who assume a supernatural or transcendent point of view in criticizing the laws passed by the government, although he will of course not deny their right to be heard; logical and political legitimacy are sharply distinguished concepts.

Insofar as the laws of the state—which specify how justice and mutual help are to be practiced within a given community—are seen as interpreting the true word of God, the political system employs religious sentiments and authority as an auxiliary. But the state, of course, also has its own independent system of compelling obedience. In monopolizing both might and right—power and justice; in possessing undivided sovereignty and the exclusive capacity to punish, to deter, and to enforce its laws, the state is the most potent mechanism by which the power of the imagination can be reshaped in the multitude in imitation of reason.

This is particularly true of a free state whose laws come close to a rational paradigm; but Spinoza holds that even arbitrary laws are preferable to the fierce dangers of lawlessness and anarchy (of which Europeans had a recent experience in the thirty-year war). The civil state is a realistic middle term between two hypothetical extremes: the state of universal strife where no government is available, and the state of universal rationality where no government is necessary. Had all people been acting out of reason alone then, justice and solidarity would have reigned automatically and state power would have become superfluous. Although no rational person is altruistic in his motives, rational people understand what is truly beneficial and are thereby driven to act toward others in ways that (in most cases) have the same effects as altruism.

The multitude, however, which lacks such rational understanding, must have another power, another natural mechanism to redirect its passions toward socially beneficial conduct. This is supplied by the authority and legislation of the state. Using obedience, fear, and other nonrational powers, the state can elicit the desired conduct from its citizens, although it cannot change their fundamental motivations or reform the inner quality of their lives. The state, moreover, can attain this goal not through fear and intimidation only, but by the routinized practice of the laws themselves and by the remolding of the associative functions of the populace in habitual patterns that echo or imitate a rational paradigm.

The state thus becomes for Spinoza not a mechanism of power only but also a civilizing agent, an instrument of education. In both ways it uses mass psychology to create an institutionalized form of semirationality, imposed by obedience and enhanced by habit, repetition, and the memory of advantageous results. This does not mean that the state should indoctrinate its citizens with any particular opinion; on the contrary, the state must be tolerant of all conflicting views and ideologies. Yet the very functioning of the state as an institution can mold the psychology and habits of the citizens and thereby also reinforce itself.

Such a program has its dangers. Spinoza leaves too vague the difference between educating and manipulating the multitude; he gives far too little thought to the need for checks and balances that would disperse the concentrated power of the state without compromising its authority or dividing its sovereignty. More generally, he pays little heed to the danger of a despotism of reason, a concept that Spinoza must have deemed incoherent, but which historical experience has since validated and to which Spinoza's theory is not sufficiently immune.

These are all serious lacunae that deserve separate discussion. But my outline of Spinoza's program in the *Theologico-Political Treatise* indicates the importance that nonphilosophical discourse must have in its execution. Using metaphor, allusion, equivocation, and other rhetorical devices is essential to Spinoza's program (no less than strict philosophical discourse). Its indispensability is even more apparent as we consider the special nature of the *Theologico-Political Treatise*, which is not merely a theoretical work but also a form of *philosophie engagée*. This treatise was not written as a pure philosophical tract on religion, the Bible, and the state, but was meant to intervene in the social and cultural processes of its time and, by its use of discourse, to trigger and enhance the execution of its own recommendations in the very act of putting them forth. In having this practical and even performative side, the *Theologico-Political Treatise* uses several levels of discourse simultaneously, addresses different audiences in the same text, exploits the connotations of familiar words to serve radically new purposes and, in general, uses language in ways other than pure description and philosophical reasoning. Significantly for Spinoza, these rhetorical forms acquire philosophical import in themselves, because they figure in a general theory of discourse that the philosopher must work out in response to the genuinely philosophical problem of how to live among the multitude—that is, in simpler terms, of how to live.

The Learned Multitude

Two questions must be considered at this point. First, How can a book like the *Theologico-Political Treatise* be addressed to the multitude when it was written in Latin? In Spinoza's time, the general public rarely read books even in the vernacular. The answer is that Spinoza envisaged two sorts of multitude: the crude and the educated. This is similar to Maimonides, the medieval Jewish master (himself, for a while, somewhat of a Marrano) from whom Spinoza drew inspiration in the art of philosophical rhetoric. Maimonides' greatest concern was not with the totally unlearned but with those he calls "the rabbinical multitude" (or "the multitude of Law holders"), meaning the mediocre religious leaders who are no less metaphysically ignorant and bound by superstition than the common people, although they enjoy the authority and numerical power of the established orthodoxy they represent. Maimonides recognizes degrees in the learned multitude, and includes in it the lofty metaphysicians who represent God in categories drawn from this world. (In this respect, Maimonides had been the most radical philosopher of transcendence, just as his rebellious disciple half a millennium later became the most paradigmatic philosopher of immanence.) In Maimonides' *Guide of the Perplexed* it is the ordinary theologian and mainstream teacher of the Law who represent the multitude's outlook in its most pervasive and important face. Similarly for Spinoza, the learned multitude consisted first of the Jewish rabbis and then, more importantly, of Calvinist and other Christian theologians who were, as Spinoza pointed out in his letters to Oldenburg, the audience he was most concerned about. Spinoza addressed this tenacious group of the learned multitude both as a target in itself and as the medium by which reformed ideas should eventually reach the uneducated multitude.

If this is so, a second question immediately arises. Does the learned multitude include Spinozistic disciples as well? And does a rhetorical element therefore exist even in the *Ethics*, Spinoza's "geometrical" explication of truth? Generally speaking, the *Ethics* is by far the purest philosophical text Spinoza wrote, and the most univocal. Yet Spinoza does not speak to himself in it. He clearly takes into consideration his audience and its point of departure. For example, the first eleven propositions address proponents of the New Philosophy in a tacit effort—polemical and didactic—to draw them away from Descartes and toward Spinoza's position. Without this intent, Spinoza could have started his deduction otherwise. Moreover, the geometrical method itself has a subtle rhetorical function in Spinoza, as does his choice of traditional theological terms. But the rhetorical function is not necessarily deceptive; as I shall argue later in this chapter (partly revising Strauss's claim) it also has a constructive hermeneutical function. Especially, such terms as "God" and its derivatives are used in earnest, as are *pietas, religio,* or *salus.* It is not only in his knack for dual language that Spinoza was a Marrano of reason but equally in his quest for an alternative way to salvation, and he used his linguistic proficiencies to further this goal as well. He did not speak of God or salvation in order to deceive his audience but to claim that he had finally found what God truly is and how salvation can be attained.

THE SCIENTIFIC ("GEOMETRICAL") DISCOURSE

The scientific method defines, above all, the universe of discourse of the *Ethics.* Language in this domain is to serve adequate ideas only; it takes its model from a formal deductive calculus, construed *ordine geometrico* and ideally requiring an absolute degree of transparency. According to this model, everything must be fully defined and conclusively established at the outset, without an opaque margin or residuum of any sort. Definitions are considered stipulative and exhaustive; they are supposed to create the full semantic scope of each term, excluding any additional input, tacit connotations, or other satellite elements of meaning that might hover around the term in its natural use. The same clarity that is attained at the outset must be transmitted to all further steps without loss or distortion. Thus, at every stage of the explication, each unit of discourse will be subject to the same principle of absolute distinctness, with no blur or halo at its semantic boundaries.

This also mean that the scientific language is fully synchronic. What the language means depends exclusively upon the inner and simultaneous relations between its components. To understand a term we are neither allowed nor required to transcend the given linguistic system to something else—natural language, the history and etymology of words, the linguistic habits of actual speakers—or to consider the role of metaphor, connotation, and other semantic imputs and accompaniments. The entire information necessary and relevant to fully understand this language is supposed to reside in the system itself, as if it were a formal-deductive calculus.

I say "as if it were," because this ideal is neither actually implemented by Spinoza, nor can it be carried out where substantive philosophical issues are at stake. Indeed, Spinoza did not follow this model in his actual philosophical discourse. The two political tracts are not written *more geometrico*, and one of them, the *Theologico-Political Treatise*, abounds in nontheortical language, including metaphors and rhetorical devices. Moreover, even the *Ethics*, where Spinoza speaks his purest and most literal philosophical language, approaches the deductive model only from afar.

The definitions in the *Ethics* do not create the full semantic scope of their objects. Spinoza's seemingly stipulative definitions are in fact theoretical ones; they offer a new, sometimes revolutionary interpretation of a traditional philosophical issue which the redefined term invokes. Thus, when defining "God," "substance," or "freedom," Spinoza is not just laying down a convention: he exploits the existence of these terms in traditional philosophical discourse in order to put forward his own theory about their objects, stating what God, substance, and freedom actually are. His first definitions thus provide seminal philosophical doctrines, which frequently contain no less than Spinoza's major revolutionary insights, and much of the system that follows serves to further explicate them. Moreover, as readers of the *Ethics* often recognize, the order in which these insights are spelled out *more geometrico* could frequently be reversed, placing a theorem in lieu of a definition or a definition in lieu of an axiom and vice versa.

Furthermore, the linear progression allows Spinoza to spell out a fundamentally closed, circular system whose contours precede and implicitly guide the deduction (although they require the deductive process in order to take explicit shape). The full scope of the system emerges only after two necessary conditions have been fulfilled: first, the actual deductive process must be performed, and secondly, its linear form must eventually be transcended toward the synoptic overview of *scientia intuitiva*.[2]

This implies a distinction between the system of truth as it is in itself (in the "infinite intellect of God") and the cognitive order in which it is reconstructed and known by the mind. As a rough analogy we can think of a geographical map whose landmarks relate to each other in a single constant pattern, but can be approached by a variety of routes. Thus in metaphysics, the *ordo cognoscendi* (cognitive order) may be open to variation, as long as its paths follow the same logical map (and as long, of course, as it respects the logical rules of inference which alone can serve as its vehicle). But at the final stage, when the progression is supposed to be replaced by a holistic and simultaneous grasp of the map, the question of cognitive order becomes obsolete.

The Geometrical Model as Metaphor

These considerations should modify the sometimes exaggerated role which commentators of the *Ethics* attribute to the geometrical order and to its specific layout in the text. Spinoza had published a geometrical exposition of Descartes' philosophy while disagreeing with much of its content, and he avoided the geometrical form in his own political tracts. The geometrical model, then, is not as sacrosanct to Spinoza as is sometimes supposed, for it neither guarantees nor is indispensable to the attainment of truth. The geometrical model is more a matter of philosophical form and mood; it stresses the need for rigor, clarity, and step-by-step consequentiality as necessary conditions of rationality, and it also calls for philosophical detachment in dealing with the most passionate issues. Thus it dramatizes certain major features of Spinoza's philosophical message. But Spinoza makes no claim that the infinite intellect of God takes the same cognitive route as traced in the *Ethics*, nor does he actually shape his book as a formal-deductive calculus. As any readers of the work will recognize, the *Ethics* draws heavily from natural language and the traditional vocabulary of philosophy; thus it contains elements of content, allusion, connotation and the like, which an actual formal model will have to reject as opaque; and if the *Ethics* admits them, it is because its language is *not* truly "geometrical" and cannot be so by the nature of its subject matter. Spinoza's actual discourse, even in pure philosophy, is fundamentally non-formal but depends on history, natural language, and the accumulative human experience, although it is organized in weak analogy to a formal system.

Thus the geometrical model, the antithesis of metaphorical discourse in Spinoza, is in this respect itself a kind of metaphor.

The Uses of Historical Vocabulary

In a succinct and crucially important remark, Spinoza explains his use of philosophical terms and its dependence on cultural connotations:

> I know that in their common usage these words mean something else, But my purpose is to explain the nature of things, not the meaning of words. I intend to indicate these things by words whose usual meaning is not entirely opposed to the meaning with which I wish to use them. (Ethics, pt. 3, 20 exp.)

Although Spinoza makes this remark with reference to moral and psychological terms, it applies to the *Ethics* throughout. It clearly states Spinoza's preference for historical terms that have a relevance, or affinity, to the subject matter he explicates.[3] Whether it be God, substance, freedom, love, envy, or error, the subject matter is invoked by the proper term, then redefined or reinterpreted by Spinoza. His aim, as he indicates, is to give explanatory (theoretical) rather than lexical definitions, conveying not what a term signifies in ordinary usage but the true nature of the thing it invokes and is used to designate.

This presupposes, of course, that philosophical issues have historical continuity and that traditional terms are capable of properly designating such issues (or subject matter) even if the terms are given false or distorted interpretation. For example, God may well be the reference of our talk even if we misconstrue his nature. Designating a subject matter and correctly interpreting its objects are two distinct acts, one logically independent of the other: the first is best served by using traditional terms, while the second requires that these terms be given new definitions that sometimes amount to true semantic revolutions. Only the new definition is supposed to capture the actual object which other definitions have missed; but in order to know where our target lies (and to render talk about its being "missed" or "captured" meaningful), we must first delineate its general domain, be it in vague contours only; and this, Spinoza holds, is best done by retaining traditional terms even after their meaning has been submitted to a radical shift.

A further purpose for using the historical vocabulary of philosophy is to exploit the emotive and connotative halo of a traditional word and, by redefinition, transfer it to a new object to which it is believed to properly belong. To this major use of philosophical terms I shall refer later, when discussing the "hermeneutic" function of language.

In summary, as long as philosophy must deal with substantive and perennial questions it cannot, from Spinoza's standpoint, be reduced to a purely formal and synchronic form of discourse. This is why the geometrical ideal could neither be implemented nor have been intended by Spinoza in any other way than as a weak analogy. Even so, there is a valid concept of "strict" philosophizing which requires rigor, clarity, and a form of discourse that is plain, literal, and unambiguous, free of metaphor and equivocation, with no attempt to suggest, persuade, or otherwise affect the reader rhetorically. The philosopher will adhere to this kind of discourse when reasoning with himself or with others who share his viewpoint; however, there are other contexts in which, for philosophical reasons, he will have to use different types of discourse as well. To these other uses we now turn.

The Rhetorical Context

Spinoza was a master not only of clarity and rigor but equally of equivocation and double language. His rhetorical use of language was elevated to the level of art. Here Spinoza brought to perfection a style and skill in which his ancestors, the Marranos, had excelled for generations,[4] adapting it to his own situation, that of an esoteric thinker enmeshed in the world and living among the multitude.

Using inadequate ideas, the rhetorical use of language adapts to the mind of its target audience. Its aim is to affect the imagination in ways that will produce desirable (i.e., semirational) effects in the audience's perception, emotions, and especially conduct. Spinoza assigns three major functions to the rhetorical use of language: one passive, or defensive; another active, even aggressive; and the third is constructive and hermeneutical.

(a) The Passive or Defensive Function: Prudence

Caute was not merely an inscription on Spinoza's ring. Prudence to him was far more than a personal strategy or temperament: it was a philosophical issue in itself, what *ratio* must recommend to any philosopher as part of the life of reason. Given the all-embracing presence of the multitude, the question of how to handle it constitutes a major ethical concern. We have seen that the philosopher cannot attain his goal in isolation, nor can he expect all people to rise to his own level. At the same time he has to engage in public affairs (or public discourse) since part of his goal is to help others, who are capable of it, to cast away their superstitions and share in the life of reason. Yet this goal has nothing of a missionary zeal in it; motivated as it is by rational motives, it is held in check by a sense of realism and also by a kind of paternalistic benevolence on the part of the philosopher. Knowing that most common people are incapable of truly rational attitudes, he will not seek to provoke them and to shatter their lives in vain. He is also well aware of the dangers involved, which makes his benevolence join forces with his prudence, both nourished by purely rational motives. Yet some people are capable of rising above their situation, and the philosopher must seek and pick them out by a differentiated discourse which speaks in different voices to different subgroups, even though officially it is addressed to all of them alike.

In other words, the philosopher must trace the delicate and narrow path between two conflicting imperatives: provoking a rational conversion in those capable of it, and concealing his true message from those whom it will not benefit and might even threaten him for having expressed it. Both aims are dictated to him by reason; as a rational person he must both help to educate the first group and refrain from provoking the second; and since his major instrument is public discourse (which officially addresses itself to everyone alike), the rhetorical and equivocal use of language becomes rationally necessary for the philosopher.

Barred from revealing his true mind to everyone, the philosopher cannot be fully trained for a life of reason unless he learns how to use language defensively, masking his true aim and intentions and passing tacit messages to some while in the same text or phrase misleading others. One of the most efficient masks is the use of pious phrases, images, and formulae, borrowed from the Scriptures or from accepted religious beliefs.

For example, Spinoza in the *Theologico-Political Treatise* repeatedly mentions the will of God, his decisions, thoughts, and commands; he cites biblical verses, alludes to Christian dogma, to providence, to God's Son, to events where God acted as a particular agent, and otherwise cloaks himself in language which his strict philosophy would reject as superstitious. Spinoza even adduces a list of "articles of faith" which, taken literally, flatly contradict his metaphysical doctrine (they refer to a personal God, moved by justice and love and not by necessity, etc.), although practically every article contains a nucleus which can be translated into a strict Spinozistic thesis and be seen as its metaphoric mask.

In his correspondence Spinoza used a similar technique. Many of his statements have a facade that sounds like the current theological idiom, and an inner meaning that is bluntly heretical. That his prudence did not spare him the charge of atheism may testify to the limits of linguistic camouflage. After all, Spinoza was not just a reformer of revealed religion but its adamant enemy; his philosophy of immanence (or so-called pantheism) did not merely oppose the established religions but all other philosophies of reason that affirmed the transcendent status of God and the duality between God and his world. Spinoza was in this respect a loner even among the daring heterodox minority; and with such a gulf separating him from his contemporaries, he could not sufficiently mask his thoughts without compromising his intellectual identity and goals beyond what he deemed tolerable. At the same time Spinoza did practice concealment in varying degrees and lived— even in the relatively tolerant Netherlands—as his own kind of Marrano, a Marrano of Reason whose hidden esoteric truth, the one that leads to true salvation, is not Judaism in opposition to Christianity, but the immanent religion of reason in opposition to all historical religions.

(b) The Offensive Function: Persuasion and Polemics

Spinoza also uses language rhetorically in order to arouse doubts in his audience and combat the malignant effects of *vana religio*. This offensive function of language is independent of the defensive and would have existed even if there were no problem of prudence. It expressed the philosopher's need to reach out to those who may be capable of rational life and subvert their entrenched beliefs in preparation for philosophy. This is designed to produce a kind of mental purification like the one Descartes sought to achieve by his method of doubt and the free will behind it. Spinoza recognizes no free will, only causal processes, and uses language rhetorically to induce doubts and queries in his audience through a natural course of cause and effect. Whereas Maimonides, Spinoza's chief mentor in the matter of rhetoric and the multitude, had written a *Guide of the Perplexed*, Spinoza wished to start by provoking perplexities in order to loosen the grip of religious superstition over the multitude and make it ready to accept new, rationally guided authorities (including the secular state), and also, for a select few, in order to clear the ground for a genuine life of reason.

Neither goal can be reached by merely arguing *more geometrico*. In order for rational arguments to be effective against entrenched religious beliefs, the audience must already recognize the superior authority of reason over revelation. But this is precisely the iron bar which Spinoza confronts, a deep chasm over which no particular usage of reason can bridge, because nothing less than an overall conversion will do. Perhaps this is a vicious circle, but Spinoza believes that it can be broken with the assistance of less-than-rational factors that will mediate the ascent of rationality. Thus the rhetorical use of language can build an imaginary, semirational bridge where a genuinely rational one could not have been erected. Since the person of the imagination cannot share the philosopher's rational standpoint, the philosopher will have to assume his interlocutor's language and standards in order to transform their meaning and, eventually, turn their authority against itself. This requires dialectical skill and the generous use of metaphor, allegory, and equivocation. Using dual language, the philosopher can adjust his mode of speech to the multitude while always retaining a level of discourse in which his statements are philosophically true. This duality allows him to be effective without being totally deceptive. It also prefigures the rational outcome that the metaphor should eventually help emerge, and thus enhances its educational role, its only justification from Spinoza's standpoint. Thus Spinoza, the enemy of allegorization, when reading the Bible, falls back upon allegoric and metaphorical language when the text concerned is neither Scripture nor strict philosophy, but discourse that is to help the latter undermine the authority of the former.

Another familiar technique is to undermine the Bible's authority by finding contradictions in it. But this again presupposes that some credence can be given to the forces of reason. Although the contradictions are materially drawn from biblical statements, it is reason which passes the verdict, judging these contradictions as flaws (rather than, say, as signs of God's imponderable wisdom). This may remind us that the dichotomy between reason and revealed authority is frequently not as neatly defined as an abstract model presumes; religious believers who respect their rationality are often deeply disturbed when having to admit the irrationality of Scripture, even if this will not necessarily shatter their belief. On the whole, the more inquisitive or doubtful one already is, the more effective this technique will prove to be. Here again we are dealing (at most) with a tool of gradual change, not with a sweeping one-time instrument of conversion.

This kind of polemics manifests that reason is incapable of proving its superiority, but must in the last analysis affirm it. A rationalist standpoint such as Spinoza's or Descartes' involves an existential stand which no proof can guarantee. Of course, these two philosophers will not admit of any such descriptions; to them, reason is its own light or provides immediately its own justification. But even on their theory, rationality does not emerge from argument and proof but from the kind of intellectual intuition they call the *lumen naturalis*: a secular kind of revelation which is declared open to everyone and entails no religious connotations. This rational illumination either occurs, taking complete possession of the mind, or it does not. What if it does not? What should be done while the mind is still possessed by false ideas and is not ready for clear and distinct ones to emerge? The inevitable answer is that one must prefigure rationality by less-than-rational means, and suggest the horizons of reason as a temptation rather than as a self-grounding truth. Inevitably, rationality itself must in this stage be an object of persuasion.

(c) The Constructive-Hermeneutical Function

Although it is customary to view Spinoza's thought as utterly ahistorical, his theory of language and the multitude may serve as a counterexample. Here Spinoza reasons in terms of a process rather than an abstract, dichotomous model. He does not envisage a radical, one-time revolution but a gradual growth of rationality from within the domain of *imaginatio*, and he thinks it is the philosopher's task to provide tools for dealing with the various forms of this transition—as he himself does in his theory of allegory, metaphor, and nonscientific discourse generally.

While part of the multitude, whose dogmatic discourse has been shattered, will eventually move on to genuine rationality, the majority will remain in the realm of the passions and the imagination, which, in Spinoza's plan, must be reorganized as an external imitation of reason. In both cases, rhetorical discourse does not have defensive and subversive uses only but serves a constructive hermeneutical function. In the case of the first group it helps preserve the semireligious dimension which Spinoza considers essential to rational truth as well; and for the second and larger group, the hermeneutical use of metaphor and equivocation should help establish the semirational imagination which is Spinoza's answer to the problem of the multitude.

I use the term *hermeneutical* in the general sense of adding (or extracting) a new structure of meaning within a body of discourse which carries a cultural or traditional import. Spinoza's constructive use of hermeneutics is seen in two major ways: (1) in his reading of the Bible Spinoza extracts a rational message from what seems otherwise to be, and serves as, a tool of the imagination;[5] and (2) in his systematic works he exploits the affective and connotative halo of select traditional terms, especially "God" and its various derivatives, in order to give the philosophy of reason its import as a substitute for religion.

Metaphoric-Systematic Equivalence   There is a whole series of terms which serve Spinoza as metaphors, but are perfectly translatable into strict philosophical language. By redefining these traditional terms Spinoza transfers this semantic core from the realm of the imagination to that of reason. Although the literal sense of the term may be very misleading (e.g., "the will of God"), there is another, philosophical sense into which it can be translated and which constitutes its tacit new meaning.

An example of such a translation is given in the following quotation:

> To those who ask "why God did not create all men so that they should be governed by the command of reason?" I answer only: "because he did not lack material for to create all things, from the highest degree of perfection to the lowest"; or, to speak more properly [*vel magis proprie loquendo*], "because the laws of his nature have been so ample that they suffice for producing all things which can be conceived." (*Ethics*, pt. 1, end of appendix)

Spinoza sees a tacit equivalence between the first statement, which uses the common theological idiom (God as omnipotent Creator) and the second statement, which translates this imprecise metaphor into proper philosophical discourse (that of *Ethics*, pt. 1, prop. 16 and other propositions that spell out God's logical necessity to become particularized in finite things). The second statement uses adequate ideas to convey the same message which the first had couched in inept words and inadequate ideas. The philosopher using (or reading) such discourse will know that the true meaning of the first statement is actually given in the second, although for rhetorical reasons the equivalence is not allowed to appear on the surface.[6]

We may represent the relation between this type of metaphor and its rational equivalence as follows:

$$\text{(met)}$$
$$P \equiv P'$$

This is of course a special kind of equivalence; P and P' are not interchangeable in their literal senses, although each in its own idiom translates essentially the same idea. Literally taken, the two expressions have different meanings and opposing truth values; but as the modifier *(met)* indicates, only one of them is autonomous and meant to be taken literally; the other draws its meaning from the first and serves as a rhetorical envelope for it.

Given this relation, we can offer a few translations of metaphoric expressions of this kind into their systematic equivalents:

God's intellect: The totality of adequate ideas (including all individual essences, and all true propositions and theories about the universe) taken in their interrelations.

God's will: The totality of things, events, and processes in the universe, taken in their necessary causal connections.

God's power: The same as God's will (with a subjective emphasis on factuality).

Creation: The inner particularization of the substance in accordance with the logical laws of its nature (*Ethics*, pt. 1, prop. 16).

Salvation: Knowledge of the third kind coupled with intellectual love of nature-God.

God's omnipresence: The fact that all modes are in the substance.

God's decrees: The eternal laws of nature.

God loves justice and benevolence: Justice and mutual help are models for imitation in conduct.

Depending on context, the expressions on the left (and others like them) can be used either in their metaphoric capacity or as direct substitutes for the expressions on the right. Spinoza uses them both ways, to suggest or prefigure rational ideas and, in particular, to embody and encapsulate some of the major principles by which the imagination is to be reshaped as a practical imitation of reason. Metaphoric discourse serves him here in a *constructive* capacity, as building-blocks of the semirational imagination.

Illustration: The "Articles of Faith"   This is illustrated, perhaps without refinement, in the "articles of faith" which Spinoza designs for the multitude as postulates for action. Although Spinoza says they need not be true in themselves as long as the agent believes them to be true, and indeed couches these beliefs in a particularly heavy theological idiom, at least six of Spinoza's seven principles can also be given some general philosophical interpretation. That God exists; that he is one and unique, omnipresent, and possessing supreme right (power) and dominion over everything; that his worship consists exclusively in leading a life of justice and loving one's neighbor; and that only those (and all those) who obey God in leading such a life will be "saved"— all these statements are compatible with both superstition and philosophical truth, depending on the mode of interpretation.[7]

Spinoza himself explains how this duality works. In another revealing aside, he observes that the dictum that God provides the model of true life can be taken to mean either that (1) God is a person animated by justice and mercy (superstition), or that (2) God is the natural ground of all things and ideas, including the philosopher's ideas about the good life (Spinozistic truth). As we interpret each dictum in more detail, the gulf that separates their true from their superstitious construal will become more apparent; but the multitude, Spinoza insists, need not engage in a detailed interpretation in order to use these beliefs as postulates for action. In these examples Spinoza again exposes his technique of metaphoric equivalence and lets us see the constructive role he assigns it in building a semirational imagination.

God and Other Nonmetaphors: The Semi-religious Hard Core However, not all metaphoric expressions can be translated into neutral equivalents without incurring significant loss from Spinoza's philosophical standpoint. This warning should apply above all to the word *God* and some of its derivatives, but also to such terms as "piety," "beatitude," "love," and the like, which maintain the affinity of rational philosophy with religious sensibilities and concerns. Although Spinoza secularizes religion, he also creates a system of naturalist rationalism which preserves some of the supreme goals of the historical religions it rejects. It is therefore essential to Spinoza that the semireligious dimension of philosophy not be shed along with the many errors and superstitions that have governed it in the past. Spinoza's philosophy is also concerned with God, or the absolute, and the soul's identification with it; and ultimately it aspires to wisdom and a new form of salvation. This is a major difference between Spinoza and naturalist philosophers after him, most of whom renounced such exalted aspirations and made do with more modest spiritual results. (Freud, in certain ways a modern Spinozist, is an interesting case in point.)[8]

In Spinoza, although the life and ethics of reason are marked by naturalism, this does not make them banal and prosaic. On the contrary, some of the major drives that had in the past animated religion and even mysticism are still partly at work within Spinoza's naturalist rationalism; and, to preserve this essential feature, it is indispensable to continue using some of the old vocabulary, above all the word *God* in its new and daring association with "nature." Neither of these two terms can be abandoned, since it is their conjunction in *deus seu natura* which transmits Spinoza's actual message—both naturalizing God and sacralizing nature.

Hence the need not only for the word *God* but for other charged terms, whose redefinition transports their high spiritual tension to the correct object. From a strictly formal or "geometrical" viewpoint, the terms *deus* and *natura* are interchangeable; yet *natura* alone, because of its historical connotations, cannot express the immanence and inherence of the divine in everything natural. The semantic halo of this term, as used for centuries and as ingrained in every European mind since childhood, has negative shades which suggest something quite antithetical to the divine and inherently devoid of it. Spinoza, however, seeks to attach the elevated states of mind which traditionally have been associated with God and with things divine to their true, natural objects; hence he must employ select theological terms even within his strictly philosophical discourse, while giving them revolutionary new interpretations. (This, as we have seen in another context, is also a reason why a fully transparent and synchronic language is impossible in Spinoza.)

Like God, the terms *piety* and *religion* have a similar function. But let me consider another example which is not directly connected with theology. In discussing natural right, Spinoza uses the term *jus* as interchangeable with *potentia* (power or capacity). However, only power is the strictly adequate term; in the state of nature, before any political authority has been constituted, the concept of right is meaningless under any interpretation. Man's so-called natural right extends to anything that his passions covet and his power can attain, and he will seize this by natural necessity alone: no normative concept whatsoever is or can be involved here. Yet Spinoza, who insists upon calling this natural power by the name of "right," performs thereby another rhetorical exercise. He exploits the dignified sense which *jus* has in traditional, non-Spinozistic discourse (as something transcendental and higher than mere nature), in order to attach this dignity to the natural power itself. Strictly speaking, however, no right can yet be involved here, and the term *jus* is used parasitically to convey a halo of favorable connotations to something other than itself.[9]

Conclusion   The constructive role of hermeneutics is seen in broad perspective as Spinoza turns traditional terms into building-blocks of his own innovative system. While this often produces semantic revolutions, Spinoza always preserves certain elements of the reinterpreted historical term, which he draws from its kernel or its semantic margins and halo; and by means of this term he always addressed himself to some real philosophical issue or object that the historical word had always referred to and vaguely envisaged, but had always missed because of false or prejudiced definition.*

---

* Applying to Spinoza a distinction made current by the philosopher Frege it might

In this sense Spinoza, the official proponent of the geometrical method, is more historically oriented than meets the eye. Writing as he does within a given set of convictions and vocabularies that have long articulated the philosophical concerns of his culture, Spinoza cannot start philosophizing from the linguistic tabula rasa that Descartes' method may seem to suggest. Actually, even in his "geometrical" train of reasoning Spinoza performs a good deal of hermeneutical work, using traditional concepts to reinterpret others, while preserving some of their denotative and much of their connotative import. In general, he remains within the broad confines of a philosophical quest which former philosophers had both delineated and misconstrued.

Of course, the task of redefining the true objects of this quest amounts in Spinoza to no less than a momentous revolution. His departure from the dominant trends in philosophy and theology is most radical. Yet even this revolution is inevitably articulated by means of the historic and linguistic context which at the same time it transforms. It also has other social and strategic aims which require that language be used in a versatile manner, adapted to its various functions as we have examined them in this chapter. Historical terms, metaphor, and equivocation all have their indispensable place within this scheme. We have seen how they are used defensively as a means of prudence; offensively as a weapon to subvert superstition; and constructively, as a hermeneutical tool that helps set up the reformed, semi-rational imagination, which is Spinoza's positive program for the multitude. In addition, a constructive hermeneutical function applies to the level of rational discourse proper, where historical terms and/or their connotative halo are used to draw some vital elements from the old philosophy and theology, especially to maintain an affective and semireligious dimension in Spinoza's philosophy or reason, which does not seek knowledge only but a change of heart and mind and, eventually, a new form of salvation.

A Note on Strauss's Insight and Its Limits

Since the publication of Strauss's *Persecution and the Art of Writing*, his ideas on esoteric writing have provoked exaggerated reactions, both of devotion and (even more so) of hostility. This may be due to other reasons than pure methodology, perhaps to aggravated religious feelings or to Strauss's penchant for elitist esoterism. Clearly a more bal-

---

be said, for example, that God has always been the *reference* (*Bedeutung*) of the historical word *God*, though its *meaning* (*Sinn*) had never been adequately conveyed because of theological prejudice or philosophical confusion.

anced (and impassionate) view is necessary. Such a view, I think, will need to recognize the soundness of Strauss's basic point while indicating its limits and the sometimes unnuanced interpretation that Strauss himself seems to give it. In addition, one can without contradiction be a "Straussian" of sort in textual hermeneutics without taking a position on the rest of his philosophy. (In chapter 4 I made a similar point about Americo Castro.)

Almost by definition, equivocation must lend itself also to strict literal reading. This limits the force of particular textual items in deciding whether an equivocation has been intended;[10] more weight must be placed on the overall coherence and plausibility of the suggested interpretation, and also on external evidence concerning the author, his situation, the linguistic tradition he inherited, and so on. In the final analysis, however—and unavoidably—some element of direct recognition must come into play, whereby equivocative language is identified simply by encountering it in the text.

This calls for sensitivity and moderation, an openness toward this phenomenon along with a healthy critical reserve to keep it in check. It is as absurd to deny the existence of equivocal language as it is to hunt for it under every phrase. At the same time, no pious adherence to literal reading can do. The familiar slogan "let's be faithful to what the author himself said" will hardly get us out of the equivocational circle, for if the author had intended an equivocation, then our literal reading will be *unfaithful* to him or her.

Literary equivocation has existed since ancient times, the Bible not excepted. Heterodox authors in the early Enlightenment—Hobbes, Spinoza, and Bayle, among others—have practiced it, as do some contemporary Soviet writers and Western satirists. Yet Strauss tends to put excessive weight on the notion of "persecution" and on the function of prudence and dissimulation. Games of language have served many other purposes as well, including seduction, entertainment, diplomacy, or self-deception. Even Spinoza and Maimonides, Strauss's main examples, use this genre for other purposes. Maimonides recognizes that every human group must be addressed according to its level of comprehension—not as manipulation merely but in order to provide it with some *positive* metaphysico-religious substance and with a semblance of truth. Later, Hegel put forward a historicized version of the same theory, where truth is clothed in a hierarchy of lower images, including especially those of religion, from which it explicates itself in successive historical phases.

Although Spinoza opposes an allegorical reading of the Bible, he nevertheless accepts a protohistorical view, in which traditional terms are maintained and reinterpreted according to their true rational concept. This "constructive" hermeneutical function, and the positive role it gives to metaphor and equivocation, has not been sufficiently appreciated by Strauss and his followers. In addition, because he tends to dismiss most of Spinoza's theological idiom as dissimulation, Strauss fails to do full justice to the religious intent and substrate behind Spinoza's endeavor. Perhaps this is because Strauss in general did not recognize the import of Spinoza's Marrano background—which, nevertheless, would supply Strauss with a *proximate cause* in support of his famous thesis.

A Marrano of reason, Spinoza was not only a master of multiple language but also a seeker of salvation in a new way. This puts a limit to dissimilation in his use of religious terms. The word *God* and its derivatives, and also such terms as "religion" or "salvation" are not intended as an atheist's mask merely but also, and primarily, as a means for preserving essential elements of religion within Spinoza's new philosophy of reason, so as to make it a *religion* of reason. Knowledge is not bare science but, in its higher form intuitive reason; it is meant to assume the spiritual roles of religion—all the way to the highest religious achievement, salvation. This will occupy us in the next chapter, both as a systematic problem in Spinoza and as another illustration of his being a Marrano of reason.[12]

Knowledge as Alternative Salvation

Salvation is not found in Jesus, but in the Law of Moses: this, as the files of the Inquisition attest, was the invariable claim of Judaizing Marranos, the common secret that made them an esoteric fraternity holding in its possession no less than the greatest treasure their culture can offer. Only they, a persecuted minority, possessed the key to salvation; they alone could attain what others, the ruling Christian establishment, had invariably distorted, misrepresented, and therefore missed.

As Georg Simmel suggests, the sharing of such a hidden and exclusive possession can foster a secret group's identity and reinforce the individual's devotion to it even where other sociological indicators may show dispersion, discord, or poor communication. Marranos, however, not only shared a metaphysical secret but also "impure blood." This is what made them a "nation" (as indeed they were called) rather than merely a secret sect. But the Judaizers among this "nation" also had the traits of a secret religious fraternity, neither Christian nor actually Jewish, and bound by a road to salvation that defied that of the established tradition around them.

Spinoza, too, as we have seen in chapter 2, retained an analogous Marrano feature, translated into rational and secular terms. He, too, believed he held the key to true salvation which only a select group might attain, and which challenged that of the established tradition. But whereas Judaizing Marranos replaced Christ by Moses within historical religion, Spinoza rejected all historical religions and cults as superstitions. Salvation lies neither in Christ nor in the Law of Moses, but in the laws of reason leading to the third kind of knowledge. Reason thereby yields the same elevated results that traditional religion and mysticism have claimed to attain, but have always distorted because of the irrational ways they followed. Spinoza thus offers a religion of reason over and above ordinary rationality, one which expresses itself in science and in practical ethics. Rationality has two forms, discursive and intuitive, fragmentary and synoptic, emotionally dull and emotionally explosive; and through the higher form of rationality—which, as we shall see, presupposes the former and cannot be attained by a direct leap—reason alone can lead to an immanent, this-worldly form of salvation, in which eternity penetrates temporal life, finitude is redeemed, the passions are turned into free, positive emotions as the inner quality of one's whole life is transformed to the point of a "new birth," and the individual realizes his or her unity with God (= the deified universe) through knowledge and intellectual love.

The vehicle of this salvation is the third kind of knowledge, one of the most difficult and controversial aspects of Spinoza's system. My aim in this chapter is (1) to offer a new interpretation of the third kind of knowledge as it stands in the *Ethics* (Spinoza's mature position); and thereby also (2) to illustrate the "Marrano of reason" dimension in Spinoza and how it can illuminate and provide a context for understanding systematic problems as well.

I do not insist that the interpretation I shall offer was held by Spinoza clearly and explicitly (although I think this probable), but that his texts suggest it as a plausible reconstruction. Since my reconstruction depends in large measure on the way I interpret other issues in Spinoza's system, I shall have to mention them, too, in brief.

The Third Kind of Knowledge: An Outline

The *Ethics* is notoriously parsimonious in speaking of the third kind of knowledge. Furthermore, part of what it does say on this subject is confusing, if not blatantly wrong from Spinoza's mature standpoint. I refer particularly to a famous example, carried over from Spinoza's earliest and less mature works (the *Treatise on the Intellect* and the *Short Treatise*), where Spinoza explains intuitive knowledge by invoking the way in which a mathematician may grasp the nature of proportion in a single flash. If all there is to the third kind of knowledge is an ordinary mathematical intuition which, as Spinoza adds, no one (*nemo*) would fail to achieve, then we may wonder how such a banality became so prominent in the system. Who would dream of using this commonplace kind of knowledge as a lever for mental emancipation—let alone salvation?[1]

The third kind of knowledge, however, is clearly a matter for the happy few. It is the road Spinoza shows to secular salvation—a rational road, unmediated by any historical creed, to the same exalted goal that

Spinoza believes, traditional religion and mysticism have sought in vain to achieve through irrational faith and acts. That Spinoza's philosophical effort was ultimately aimed at this goal is made unmistakably clear throughout his work, from the first lines of the *Treatise on the Intellect* to the conclusion of the *Ethics*.

In the former, his first philosophical work,* Spinoza sets up an ethical goal, the "highest good" to which philosophy and all human endeavor should be directed. He seeks a radically new kind of life, in which one seeks and tries to attach to what is permanent and eternal. The same perspective later dominates Spinoza's mature thought, and also explains why he chose to entitle his major work the *Ethics*, even though the book deals mainly with metaphysics, the theory of knowledge, and the psychology of the emotions. These branches of knowledge, along with the physical sciences, are to serve an ethical goal, first on the lower level of *ratio* (discursive rationality) and then, for the select few, leading to salvation through the third kind of knowledge.

Some modern readers may find this pervasive goal annoying or its elaboration incoherent; but one dismisses this dimension of Spinoza's thought only at the risk of losing much of his philosophical meaning.[2] Without the third kind of knowledge, Spinoza would be as crippled throughout as Plato would be without the Ideas. In both cases we shall be unable to form an adequate notion of the *rest* of the system without considering where it is meant (and construed) to lead.

The scant information that the *Ethics* supplies about the third kind of knowledge revolves around the following definition, which occurs twice in the book:

> The third kind of knowledge proceeds from an adequate idea of [the formal essence of] certain attributes of God to an adequate knowledge of the essence of things. (Pt. 2, prop. 40; pt. 5, prop. 25, dem; in the latter the bracketed phrase is omitted.)

Adding the idea of "one glance" or synopsis, we understand that the third kind of knowledge grasps a multiple chain of derivations at a single glance, by which the essence of a particular thing follows from God through one of his attributes. The latter part is crucial, since the third kind of knowledge is defined not only by its mode of cognition but also by the kind of object which is thereby formed and revealed. When the third kind of knowledge takes place, a plurality of items of

* I follow here the judgment of Filippo Mignini (see his "Per la datazione e l'interpretazione del *Tractatus de Intellectus Emendatione* di B. Spinoza," *La Cultura* 17 [1979]: 87–160).

knowledge is synthesized in a new way, so as to form a new cognitive object proper to this mode of cognition. What is this object, and what further knowledge or insight do we gain by it?

For the moment I set aside the moral and existential gains which the third kind of knowledge is said to produce. My first question is whether it is supposed to add anything new to our *knowledge*. Does it represent a net cognitive advance over the second kind of knowledge? Is it meant to enrich us cognitively even before it produces its alleged salutary effects?

To anticipate my answer to these questions, it is both No and Yes. No, there is no additional information gained through the third kind of knowledge. All the information we need and can possess of the object of our inquiry has already been supplied by *ratio*, the scientific investigation which subjects the object to a network of mechanistic natural laws. But Yes, there is a distinct cognitive gain involved, because what we already know of the object by external causality is now interiorized[3] to produce a grasp of its particular essence and, thereby, also of the immanent-logical way in which it derives from the nature-God and inheres in it.

This is a change of perspective which, without addition or subtraction, provides us with a deeper insight of the same thing through a new processing, or synthesis, of the same informative ingredients. Before there were only external causes and universal laws by which to understand the particular thing, or rather, the way this thing instantiates a set of abstract common properties. Now, however, all previous information coalesces to produce a singular item, the particular essence of this thing as it follows immanently from one of God's attributes according to a logical principle of particularization.

Spinoza characteristically sees both approaches as expressing the same fundamental information and as having a single ontological reference. The higher form of rationality (*scientia intuitiva*) does not abolish its ordinary form (*ratio*) but is taken to express the same metaphysical truth in a complementary and deeper way. Moreover, according to Spinoza's mature position, the internal viewpoint depends upon the external as a necessary condition. This is a crucial novelty introduced in the *Ethics*. There is no direct access to immanent essences. First we must explicate the object externally, by the intersection of mechanistic causal laws, and only when a point of saturation has been achieved, when a network of lawlike explanations has, so to speak, closed in on the object from all relevant angles, can we expect the third kind of knowledge to take place. By an intuitive flash, all the causal information is now reprocessed in a new synthesis that lays bare the particular essence of the thing and the inherent way in which it flows by logical necessity from one of nature's attributes.[4]

This account of the third kind of knowledge is far less mystical than the one given in the *Short Treatise*. Insofar as a semimystical element remains, it is reminiscent of Plato's passage from *dianoia* to *nous*, from the account of the world through the discursive sciences to the vision of eternal essences. And for Spinoza as for Plato, intuitive reason presupposes scientific knowledge as a necessary condition.

Needless to say, this interpretation of the third kind of knowledge depends on Spinoza's metaphysics, which views all things as immanently derived from the divine substance according to a logical principle (*Ethics*, pt. 1, props. 16, 18, 25, and C), and which, as I see it, admits particular essences in addition to natural laws as to adequate ways of explaining the same entity.

The Third Kind of Knowledge: The Context

There are further background issues which provide the context for my reading of the third kind of knowledge. I refer specifically to what Spinoza scholars (following Curley and others) call "vertical" and "horizontal" causation; to the logic of complementarity which dominates Spinoza's system; and to his view of natural laws and of particular essences. I shall briefly discuss each of these matters before summarizing the cognitive import of the third kind of knowledge. Then, in the last part of this chapter, I shall consider its role as secular salvation.

Vertical and Horizontal
(Immanent and Transitive) Causality

Given a particular thing, there are two ways Spinoza accounts for it. According to *Ethics*, pt. 1, prop. 28, a thing is produced by other finite things in an endless chain of external causation. This is the "horizontal" line, expressing the universe from the viewpoint of mechanism and finitude. However far we may regress or progress in the line of causes, we shall always remain in the realm of finite modes and external determination.

On the other hand, according to *Ethics*, pt. 1, prop. 16 (and its extensions in propositions 18 through 25), particular things are derived from God as their immanent cause, following a *logical* principle of particularization. This is the "vertical" line of causation. It goes from the substance through an attribute to a series of infinite modes (direct and mediated), until it is said to reach and determine the particular individual.

I interpret the infinite modes as the locus of natural laws in Spinoza. Natural laws are individual entities transmitting the power and necessity of God through one of his attributes. They thereby serve as intermediary agents in engendering particulars. Spinoza conceives of natural laws as real powers, the actual causes of the particular things falling under them. Laws do not merely describe how a finite thing will behave but *make* it behave in that way.

Spinoza evidently sees the horizontal and the vertical lines of causation as expressing the same process—that of cosmic particularization. But how is their relation to be constructed?

The answer, I think, is that horizontal causality realizes vertical causality by translating its inner logical character into external mechanistic terms. This realization applies especially to the crucial last step in the vertical line, when passing from the narrowest law or infinite mode to the finite particular. How does a law determine particular things? Not directly, Spinoza answers, but in that it determines how *other* particular things will act and affect it. Suppose that A is determined by B, C, and D as its mechanistic causes, and that these causes operate in accordance with law L. We may say that L determines A in that it determines how B, C, and D will act upon A. And if we are ready, as Spinoza is, to view as equivalent the following two statements:

1. A is determined by the logical necessity of the law L
2. A is determined by the mechanistic causes B, C, and D whose action obeys and instantiates the law L

then we have acknowledged the equivalence, or complementarity, or the vertical and horizontal views of causation.

This dual perspective implies that we must distinguish between what causes a law to exist, and what causes a particular thing to exist under that law. The law is generated in nature by immanent logical derivation. But the particular thing is produced under that law by other particular things, transmitting external causality to each other in endless chains.

Let us elaborate on the former example. When a car is moving on the road, it is vertically determined by a system of mechanical laws anchored in the supreme law of motion and rest. This law is the "infinite mode" in the world of extension, which assigns a fixed proportion of movement and rest to the universe at large; thereby it determines the rule which binds all changes in the universe and it shapes the universe itself as a single individual. The laws of nature are the permanent features of this global individual; their network is, so to speak, inscribed upon the universe as its immutable "face" (*facies totius universi*, "the face of the whole universe").[5]

These laws, or a cross-section of them, also determine the car moving on the road. But how? In that they determine, both generally and with reference to this particular instance, how gasoline burns, gears are shifted, power is transmitted, and metals resist pressure—in short, how the horizontal factors that actually engender the car and produce its movement will behave.

Thus the laws determine the particular thing vertically by the mediation of other particulars that affect it horizontally. And this is how Spinoza supposes prop. 28 to translate and realize the logical principle implied in prop. 16, and why he thinks of the vertical and horizontal systems as equivalent.

The Logic of Complementary Systems

This complementarity is no ad hoc device, but Spinoza's characteristic way of handling dualities. In order to maintain his radical monism while avoiding Parmenides' results or Hegelian-like dialectics, Spinoza handles the fundamental dualities in the universe by declaring them to be complementary aspects of the same. This logic of equivalence is more prevalent in Spinoza than first meets the eye. Officially it is said to obtain between extension and thought, body and mind, and the order and connection of things and the order and connection of ideas; but it also applies in the relation of *natura naturans* to *natura naturata* (i.e., of the infinite and finite aspects of nature, nature as totality and nature as a plurality of finite things): this distinction replaces the traditional dualism of the Creator and the things he creates; of perceptions to their accompanying affects; of God's "intellect" to his "will"— and also to the relation between logical derivation and mechanistic causation. These are two parallel, or equivalent, ways of construing the same universe and the same process of particularization within it.

A similar logic had been used before Spinoza—but with reference to God alone, not to nature and finite things. God was so different from the world that he had an ontology of his own, and it has been frequently said that knowledge, will, and creation are in God one and the same. Spinoza eliminates God's transcendence and transfers to nature the radical unity of God—and the special ontology which accompanies it.

Several points should be underscored to avoid misunderstanding. First, equivalences in Spinoza are not necessarily dualities. They do not always work in pairs, as we see in the case of the attributes, which are numerous. Even the pair we discussed, logical derivation and mechanistic causation, may well have a third and somewhat more obscure member—the cosmic love that unites all things (*Ethics*, pt. 5, prop. 35–37).

Also, I admit the analogy with the attributes is incomplete.[6] But what counts more than the differences in detail is the common methodological thrust, the logic of complementarity which marks Spinoza's thinking throughout.

Finally—and at some greater length—let me point out that finite modes in Spinoza are as eternal as the substance from which they derive. The vertical line of causality should be understood not as a process of "creation" or "emanation" but as ontological dependence or support. Seen *sub specie aeternitatis* (through their essences), finite things are just as eternal and primordial as their sustaining substance. The difference is that the essence of finite things does not imply existence but requires the essence of the substance in order to exist. Yet this dependence is eternal; it is a logical, timeless relation by which the modes, seen as particular essences, presuppose God. They inhere in God as their ontological support and are implications of God's essence, but they are there eternally like God himself.

Generation and destruction occur in Spinoza as particular essences are translated into concrete things in the domain of duration and external causality. Here horizontal causality takes over from the vertical, and a time-dimension is added to being. This is *natura naturata*, the world of dependent things, seen (and existing) *sub specie durationis*. But the same system of finitude exists and can be seen also *sub specie aeternitatis*, and in this case the particular things in it are grasped as having neither beginning nor end.

Thus the eternity (and sempiternity: existence in all times) of the world of particulars can be interpreted in two ways: (1) the subsystem of *natura naturata* is eternal, though particular modes within it are generated and destroyed; (2) particular things, too, are eternal when seen through their essences, though their span within *duratio* is necessarily limited.

In conclusion, *natura naturans* and *natura naturata* are simultaneously eternal systems, existing irrespective of beginning or end. The system comprising the substance, the attributes, and the infinite modes, provides finite things with ontological support and with their nature and laws; it does not so much engender them (in time) as it constitutes them (timelessly). For such a thing, entering into time translates the vertical relation into a horizontal one which is conceived as another facet of the same system. Thus eternity and duration are also, eventually, a dual pair understood in terms of the logic of equivalence.

This interpretation is made both possible and inevitable by the fact that particular things have eternal essences which are logically (and thus simultaneously) implied in God's essence.

Infinite Modes, Laws, and Particular Essences

To complete this picture we must consider the status of natural laws and essences in Spinoza. Earlier I interpreted natural laws as infinite modes and as the causes of the particulars which they govern. In Spinoza's metaphoric language, the laws of nature embody God's immutable "will" or "decrees"[7]—that is, they express his necessity to be and to operate in certain modes. If by inner necessity God must particularize himself, then the immutable patterns in which this particularization takes place mediate between God as One and God as Many, between *natura naturans* and *natura naturata*. They express the unity and infinity of God in a variety of hierarchically ordered patterns, and transmit his power and necessity downward to the world of finite modes.

In calling laws "infinite," Spinoza means that, like the attribute, laws are uniformly present in an infinite range of phenomena falling within their domain. Just as the attribute of extension is present in all extended bodies, so these bodies are all uniformly subject to the laws of motion, from the supreme law (the direct infinite mode) to the more specific laws that derive from it.

Infinity also has a second sense, in which laws are distinguished from the attribute. Laws are permanent and immutable in the sense of duration. They are sempiternal and belong to *natura naturata*, the world seen as a plurality of modes. The attribute is eternal in the sense of timelessness and belongs to *natura naturans*, the world seen from the standpoint of totality.

The use of natural laws instead of genus and species is one of the characteristics of the new science of Spinoza's day. Scientific explanation since ancient times typically had been understood as requiring the subsumption of a particular item under some principle of universality. Plato had spoken of independent universal essences, whereas Aristotelian science placed these essences in the actual individuals as their inherent generic forms. Explanation was by and large a matter of essential classification, the referring of a particular thing to its genus and species, understood also as the thing's ideal perfection. This gave science a teleological orientation and a marked qualitative character.

The scientific revolution of the seventeenth century replaced species with natural laws as the universal principle by which science proceeds. Laws are indifferent to genus and species; they cut through qualitatively different domains and allow only unilateral effective causes as valid. Hence they lend themselves to a mechanistic and quantifiable explanation of nature, barring purposes, ideal models, and universal essences.

Spinoza was a proponent of the new science in that in his thought too, the causal, mechanistic laws of nature have replaced genus and species as the universal principles by which science proceeds. This abolishes universal essences—but not the concept of essence as such. Along with the modern category of natural law Spinoza adheres to the older category of essence as a valid, even as a deeper scientific category—but he substitutes particular essences for the universal ones.

Universal essence is a fiction, an empty word. But essences do exist—as *particular* essences. Each individual thing in the universe has its own essence, by which its specificity is constituted. The essence of a particular thing is the unique place it occupies in reality; it is, so to speak, the logical or metaphysical "point" which belongs exclusively to it in the overall map of being. Of course, this specific point is determined by the other items and coordinates of the map—that is, by everything which determines the thing to exist and to act in the way proper to it. And this establishes a logical link—even an equivalence—between what the thing is and the causal network which makes it be what it is. In other words, a thing's particular essence is ontologically equivalent to the process of its determination (an idea which Spinoza has conceived and was groping for already in the *Treatise on the Intellect*).[8]

Particular essences exist actually (*formaliter*) in God and are presented as ideas in the "infinite intellect." According to pt. 1, prop. 16 and its corollaries (including a distant but crucial corollary in pt. 5, prop. 29S), God particularizes himself into an infinitely diverse system of particular things, or existing ("formal," in seventeenth century jargon) essences, each of which, when seen vertically, is as eternal and necessary as God himself. In this sense, Spinoza's particular essences assume a status somewhat similar to that of the Platonic Ideas. They are pure and immutable, even eternal in a supratemporal sense, yet each refers to only one particular thing. Existing as separate items in the attribute of thought (or in God's infinite intellect), they are objective metaphysical definitions that assign to each thing its specific place in being or, what amounts to the same, by which the uniqueness of each thing is immanently constituted and engendered in God. (This uniqueness may imply the career or biography peculiar to it: essences are generic in nature and may involve complex stories and processes; but each of these will amount to the necessary and sufficient account of one single entity, and all will be a priori, contained timelessly in one of God's attributes [or in God's infinite intellect] from which they derive.)

As Spinoza says:

> If God had created all men like Adam . . . then he would have created only Adam, and not Peter and Paul. But God's true perfection is that he gives all [individual] things their essence, from the last to the greatest. . . . (*Short Treatise*, 1, vi [p. 87])

> Things must agree with their particular ideas, whose being must be a perfect essence, and not with universal ones, because then they would not exist. (Ibid., 1, x [p. 92])

> Peter must agree with the idea of Peter . . . and not with the idea of Man. (Ibid., 1, vi [p. 87])

The same view recurs in *Metaphysical Thoughts*[9] and the *Ethics*. In the *Ethics*, particular essence is defined (pt. 2, def. 2) as what constitutes a thing's individuality, and the definition lends itself to explication both in terms of logical essences and of complete mechanistic determination.[10]

Since essences lay bare the internal design of nature and its occupants, they offer, on the basis of the same body of information, a more profound view of the world. Herein lies the cognitive advantage of the third kind of knowledge. We can also see from this that Spinoza, though a nominalist of sorts, is not a positivist, since he attributes a metaphysical interior to things and makes it accessible through the third kind of knowledge. Grasping this interior is not a direct mystical revelation. It is based upon a discursive, mechanistic science which it supplements not with new informative ingredients, but with a new synthesis of the old ones.

A final remark concerning essences is in order here. Spinoza's adherence both to essences and to mechanistic causality may indicate his position between two distinct scientific cultures, the ancient and the modern, a position which his theory of wisdom and intellectual salvation highlights even more. On the matter of essences, however, Spinoza has not gone beyond the frontiers of his Zeitgeist. Other philosophers made an attempt to reconcile a mechanistic science with entities having an interior essence (Leibniz) or residing eternally in God (Malebranche). They, too, described the eternal essences as unfolding themselves in their things' career (Leibniz). And yet, contrary to Leibniz, Spinoza refuses to see these essences as substances; to him they are individual crystallizations of the causal processes themselves. In that he comes closer, I think, to the modern outlook. In addition, there may be a certain affinity between Spinoza's way of thinking and some contemporary theories about how things can be individuated by means of the causal processes that lead to (or from) them. In Spinoza, however, this takes place in a single world—the idea of many possible worlds being self-contradictory.

The Third Kind of Knowledge Reconsidered

In principle the third kind of knowledge can apply to any particular thing; but because he offers this kind of knowledge as an alternative salvation, Spinoza makes no secret that he has a privileged object for it: the philosopher himself, his body, mind, and environment. The third kind of knowledge is preferably, though not exclusively, a form of self-knowledge. But it is the opposite of direct self-awareness. It is not a subjective mode of *cognitio*, not an immediate grasp of ourselves, but a most elaborate form of mediated self-knowledge. The intuitive element is added only at the end, to crown the process of scientific objectivation.

What in direct awareness I feel to be my "innermost self" is but a distorted idea of my body affected by external causes. Therefore, to achieve self-knowledge of the third kind I must not develop my direct self-awareness (as in yoga and mystical experiences), but rather expel it as a form of *imaginatio*. True self-knowledge starts with overcoming the illusion of pure subjectivity and objectivizing the *cogito*, by referring it to the body and by referring them both to the causal order of nature at large. To do this I have to engage in an arduous scientific investigation (of my body, my mind, my situation) in which I approach myself "from the outside," through the mechanistic laws of nature and other natural entities that determine my own being in the world.

This may seem to entail a form of self-alienation, but only apparently so. Objectivation may often be painful and hard to perform, but it is not necessarily alienation, because what I actually approach in this objectivized way is my true being rather than a feigned, illusory self. For in Spinoza's ontology I am, in both body and mind, the product of an impersonal substance-God which has no humanlike features and may not be anthropomorphized. In other words, the natural processes that produce me bear no resemblance to my own subjectivity: they do not work by intention and purpose, have no privileged affinity to human affairs, and allow no room or special laws for history as distinguished from the rest of nature. Recognizing this, I may well become emancipated from religious and metaphysical illusions, but also lose their soothing comforts.[11] This "hard" element in liberation (I call it "dark enlightenment") is what attracted Nietzsche to Spinoza and invoked Hegel's criticism.[12] It is also part of the reason why true philosophy—even at the level of *ratio*—is never for Spinoza a matter for the multitude.

Equally painful to accept is the idea that one's dear and most intimately felt self is but a confused idea. Yet as long as nothing makes people objectivize and externalize their view of themselves, they will not be able to attain true self-knowledge, neither in the external mode of *ratio* nor in the intuitive mode that recurs in the third kind of knowledge; for the latter is based upon the former as a necessary prerequisite.

In the ordinary rational mode (*ratio*), the philosopher studies himself through the general, mechanistic processes of nature. He understands his bodily existence as determined by all the causal processes explained by physics and its corollaries—chemistry, biology, medicine (and, as we may add today: genetics, neurophysiology, biochemistry, etc.). Equally, he studies his mind by the help of psychology and its various derivatives, including sociology, linguistics, and politics (today we may add psychotherapy and the study of the unconscious). Each of the two branches of study is independent and irreducible to the other, yet both express one and the same ontological entity. Moreover, investigations in both branches of knowledge are conducted in conformity with the mechanistic paradigm of explanation which Spinoza believes applies to all sciences. Everything occurs by external, transitive causes obeying the laws of nature.

This scientific knowledge is supplemented, or rather undergirded, by a basic metaphysical framework. The philosopher understands nature as a single substance equivalent to God, in which we all inhere as modes. This is, roughly speaking, the contents of part 1 of the *Ethics*, which is here grasped in the second mode of knowledge. It already gives metaphysical (and even a semitheological) interpretation to the body of scientific knowledge, but it fails to turn this interpretation into a living experience.

However, as I gather more scientific knowledge of my body and of my mind, as I close in, so to speak, on myself from all relevant causal angles, the ground is set for the third kind of knowledge. The network of transitive causes has placed and defined my body as it stands uniquely within nature at large. Now, in a flash of intuition, all this causal information is synthesized in a new way, which produces its epistemic counterpart: my particular essence. Nothing new is added to the scientific information already possessed, yet all its ingredients co-

alesce in the formation (or reproduction) of this essence as a new synthesis, a synthesis which lays bare the metaphysical "interior" of the
thing I am and the way in which I derive immediately (or vertically)
from God as my immanent logical cause.

Therefore, the third kind of knowledge represents a net cognitive
gain over the second kind, since it gives me a new and deeper perspective on myself and the world, though it uses exactly the same materials
as before.

The second kind of knowledge gives me only a partial account of
reality. It draws the lawlike ways in which transitive causes produce
their effects in an endless chain. Thereby it serves as an adequate explication of pt. 1, prop. 28, but not of the crucial pt. 1, prop. 16. What it
lacks, and the third kind of knowledge supplies, is the grasp of things
according to their particular essences as they immanently issue from
God. This changes not only the mental quality of our perception but
the categories embedded in it. Things are understood by their particular essences, not merely by their universal laws, and the causes which
determine them are understood as logical and immanent, not as mechanical and transitive. This now allows the philosopher to penetrate
into nature's interior design where formerly he had its external facet
only.

It is essential to see that the same thing occurs in the other direction
as well. I do not only grasp myself now as I exist in and through God;
I also grasp God, the totality, through some concrete particular (myself) and no longer as an abstract concept or entity. This is a crucial
change with respect to my former metaphysical knowledge. I had an
adequate idea of God, or the totality of nature, before as well; but it
was general and abstract. I knew that individuals are, in principle, in
God and that God, in principle, must be expressed as particulars. But
all this knowledge remained abstract for me; I did not realize it as an
actual awareness. Now, in *scientia intuitiva*, direct awareness comes
back to the fore, no longer a first and overall stage but the last stage in
a long rational and demonstrative process. It is only after I have investigated how exactly my particular essence is determined by the universe at large that I can also interiorize this knowledge and become
aware in one grasp that, and how, I exist in God just as God necessarily
exists and expresses himself in me. This is a powerful realization, redeeming, liberating, and engulfing all, not in the diffuse manner of
romantic pantheism but controlled by rational comprehension (which
is why the love for the universe which flows from here is described as
"intellectual love"). And it is the content of this realization, not only

its intuitive manner, which gives it the powerful affective response it has.

It is through part 5 of the *Ethics* that the student comes back again to part 1 and understands it in its true and deeper light. Our metaphysical comprehension, too, has passed into the phase of *scientia intuitiva*. What we had known before as an external abstraction we now experience as a full realization. Again, nothing has changed in the material ingredients of this knowledge; if we were to verbalize them, they would yield exactly the same statements. But it is not any more the same cognitive object and experience.[13]

This deeper insight into the totality (and the place of the actual particular within it) cannot be attained in the merely discursive stage of *ratio*. This is why part 1 of the *Ethics* is only grasped in full when approached from the standpoint of part 5. Spinoza's book, no less than his system, has this tacit circular (or spiral) form which overshadows its apparent linearity. The linear progression is a necessary condition for attaining the third kind of knowledge, but is transformed and superseded in its new, holistic, and intuitive grasp.

THE THIRD KIND OF KNOWLEDGE AS SECULAR SALVATION

Thus far I have concentrated on the cognitive gain involved in the third kind of knowledge. Let me now refer in brief to the ethical effects which make it count as salvation.

These salvational effects are of two kinds, psychological and metaphysical. Psychologically, the third kind of knowledge is supposed to produce vigor, joy, love, and an intense sense of liberation capable of transforming the whole personality to the point of "rebirth"; metaphysically, it is said to overcome the mind's finitude and endow it with immortality—or rather (to express Spinoza's meaning more accurately), with eternity. Let me comment briefly on these two aspects.

Salvation as Mental Transformation

Cognitions are affective events in Spinoza. Every idea has a corresponding affective response, and the two are not separate entities but the same thing seen from different angles. (This is another of Spinoza's equivalences.) The claim that the third kind of knowledge provokes, or comes along with, the most potent affect which has power to overcome all the others, is made plausible by Spinoza both by the mode of this experience and by its content (though primarily, I think, by the latter).

In this mode, the third kind of knowledge is an intensive intuition, in which a great many items of discursive knowledge are compressed into a single cognitive object and grasped at one glance. Such concentration has the potential to make the experience highly potent and intense, regardless of what it contains.

And yet, the content of the third kind of knowledge plays a relatively much larger role than its mode in producing its beneficial effects. The intuition only compounds what in itself already has immense psychological power. For what the intuition compressed is no less than my detailed and concrete realization that I exist in God and that God exists through me, a unity which rivals (and in its way, usurps) the most exalted states envisaged by mystics and great religious figures. It is a rational translation of the ideal of *unio mystica*, in which the individual both actualizes his or her unity with God and becomes powerfully aware of it.

At this point I should like to pause and consider how Spinoza's Marrano background is here translated into his revolutionary new context, that of immanent reason. Like the Marranos, Spinoza was looking for an alternative road to salvation, in defiance of the one traditionally accepted in his established culture. But whereas Marranos sought it in a substitute historical religion (the Law of Moses replacing Christ's), Spinoza looked for it beyond all historical religions. It is by the third kind of knowledge, a rational-intuitive procedure bound by no historical cult, revelation, election, covenant, and the like, that philosophers are eventually supposed to be able to attain what the great mystics and religious aspirants have always been seeking and inevitably failed to find, because they relied on superstitious beliefs and practices. As in their conceptions of God, they were aiming at something true and real but missing the actual reference of their concepts.

I think this dimension is crucial when trying to interpret the moral and metaphysical effects attributed to the third kind of knowledge. Spinoza was not a mystic, but he recognized in mysticism a misguided form of yearning and endeavor which, correctly transformed by reason and the third kind of knowledge, would become the rational philosopher's way of salvation, a reward as rare and high in achievement as that which mystics have been striving to attain by irrational means. In other words, it will be a secular and truly universal form of salvation.

This secular salvation also has a metaphysical dimension, associated by Spinoza with eternity and immortality. Without removing all the difficulties involved in this theory, I think an adequate interpretation should distinguish between the two concepts, eternity and immortality, and view salvation, or the overcoming of finitude, as a state achieved *within this life* rather than after it. Whatever else it is, it enriches the philosopher's immanent, this-worldly existence and has no important meaning beyond it.

Salvation and Immortality

Particular essences are eternal in the sense of supratemporality. But in their case (unlike God), essence does not involve existence. This means that they can either exist in a definite time and place, or not. In the latter case they exist logically as implied in God's attributes (*Ethics*, pt. 2, prop. 8), and their ideas are contained in God's infinite idea,[14] but they do not have *duratio*. An essence will enter into the realm of duration when there are specific mechanistic (external) causes that will produce the thing of which it is the essence. The existence in duration of an essence is expressed in all the attributes simultaneously, as does its ceasing to endure. Hence the duration of the mind must end with that of the body. Minds cannot endure as separate entities.[15]

How then is immortality possible? To answer in a word: it is not possible. When the third kind of knowledge takes place, I know myself through my particular essence as it inheres in God. This essence is eternal, as is the idea by which I know it; and in the act of knowledge the eternal idea by which I know myself becomes identical with part of the complex idea which is my mind, so to this extent my mind gains eternity. But it gains this eternity within this life and not beyond it. Eternity is not sempiternity; it is a metaphysical state or quality, which does not signify indefinite existence, and which is here seen as penetrating into duration and as being attained and realized within it. In other words, the mind attains a form of eternity within this life and while the body, too, endures.

This entails a distinction between eternity, salvation, and immortality in Spinoza. While every finite thing has an eternal side, nothing is immortal and only a small group of humans can attain salvation.

Every finite thing has eternity by virtue of having an eternal essence and an idea reflecting it in the infinite intellect of God. But no finite thing is immortal, if by this we understand that it endures indefinitely in the realm of duration and external causes. No finite thing which comes into existence in duration can sustain this kind of existence indefinitely; at a certain point the external causes will overcome its conatus and destroy it.[16] This destruction will affect both body and mind, since a mind (*mens*) is constituted by the ideas of its body (and reflexively also of itself) as they, the body and the mind, exist in duration, not as they are from the standpoint of eternity. Therefore minds die with their bodies; what remains is the eternal essence which was there all along.[17]

We may say that particular essences are eternal while minds are perishable. Salvation consists in uniting the two, the perishable mind and the eternal essence, so that they become identical over a significant range. According to Spinoza, the mind does not "have" ideas but *is* the complex of its ideas. A true idea, however, is timeless and unique and is the same in all its occurrences; therefore, the more true ideas I know, a larger part of my actual or existential mind is constituted of timeless ingredients. This is the cognitive basis of salvation in Spinoza, on which all the rest hinges; and it is an occurrence within this life and world, as eternity penetrates my actual existence and transforms its quality and direction.

Sometimes Spinoza is understood as saying that my eternal essence is modified by the knowledge I have gained during life—I enter life with one essence and exit with another. But such a reading of Spinoza is incoherent. Nothing, by definition, can affect an eternal essence. What can be affected by the third kind of knowledge is my actual existential mind, when larger parts of it become identical with eternal ideas; but this achievement is attained within life and can in no way affect the way "I" shall exist after death, since without my body there will be no "I"—no individual *ego cogito* and no *conatus* to sustain. There will only be an eternal particular essence existing regardless of time (as it did even before my birth).

Thus Spinoza keeps to his strict immanent philosophy even when offering a theory of salvation. The transcendent-religious idea of an afterlife, in which our existence will be modified in proportion to what we have done in this life, is foreign to him. His famous statement, that virtue is its own reward, implies the same. A Marrano of reason, Spinoza unites this-worldliness with a new way to salvation, one which not only relies upon reason and knowledge rather than on religious cult, but also makes salvation an immanent affair, consummated within this world and life.

It is therefore not in immortality that metaphysical salvation consists, but in the realization of eternity within time. The third kind of knowledge helps me overcome my finitude, not my mortality. I am saved as long as I live. I enjoy a state of timeless necessity in the midst of my duration, but when I die all will be over, except for an impersonal essence, or idea, existing in God's infinite intellect. The mere existence of this idea is no comfort to me and does not signify my salvation; it is only a metaphysical prerequisite for it. All things in the universe have such ideas, my dog, Emperor Caligula, his horse, the bomb in Hiroshima. What if I knew that my idea, like that of Caligula's horse, is timeless? Neither of us is thereby saved. Salvation means that a timeless idea has become part of my actual, enduring mind. And this can happen only while I endure.

Eternity in itself has no salvational significance. What makes eternity count as salvation is its incursion into the individual's life as a mortal and enduring thing. It is the eternal affecting the temporal, or realized in its domain. This alone, Spinoza believes, can make an existential difference and plausibly count as a secular mode of salvation, that "rare and difficult" reward Spinoza was seeking as philosopher and as the Marrano of Reason.

CHAPTER 7

Epilogue
Spinoza and His People:
The First Secular Jew?

Seldom, if ever, was a philosopher so lonely as was Baruch Spinoza. Romantic legend notwithstanding, his solitude was not of a social nature. On the contrary, Spinoza had a gift for friendship and was surrounded by loyal friends, as well as by inquisitive intellectuals. Some of his friends even saw to his livelihood, thus refuting yet another legend: that the lonely and ostracized Spinoza, on the brink of starvation, was forced to grind lenses for a living, an occupation which hastened his death. As a matter of fact, Spinoza did earn a supplementary income through the practice of this highly demanding art but he engaged in it primarily because of his interest in optics, a science that was then undergoing vigorous development. Since Galileo, the science of optics had attracted many scholars both theoretically and practically. Christian Huygens, the great Dutch scientist (who subsequently became secretary of the French Scientific Society established by Louis XIV) also ground lenses, together with his brother Constantijn. Indeed, their own scientific investigations prompted their great interest in Spinoza's method, which they knew to be different from their own. "How goes it with our Jew from Voorburg?" Huygens asks his brother in a letter from France, referring to the latest advances of their competitor in lens-grinding. By posing this question, Huygens not only throws light on Spinoza's preoccupation with avant-garde technological research but, indirectly, on Spinoza's existential situation as a Jew. Banned from the Jewish community, indifferent to Jewish law, and abjuring the God of Israel—along with the gods of every other historical religion—Spinoza nonetheless is regarded as "our Jew from Voorburg," even after he had joined the international community of scholars.

Spinoza thus exemplifies and adumbrates the situation of the modern Jew—secular, assimilationist, or national—without himself falling neatly into any of these categories. Countless Jews in the coming centuries were to find themselves in a similar predicament. The secular Jews tried to define their Jewishness in terms of the Jewish people (or nation); and the assimilationists tried to leave the people and merge into gentile society. Most often, however, they were thrust by the attitude of the gentiles (or by what Sartre calls their "look") back into the existential Jewish situation they tried to escape. Spinoza himself perceived the Jew's inability to escape his condition, but was unable to offer an alternative.

That the world regarded him as a Jew was one of the hallmarks of Spinoza's loneliness, which was not social, but existential. He refused to identify with any of the cultural or religious associations of his day. He was a loner, the individual par excellence, who demands to be defined solely in terms of his private being and beliefs, not in terms of any social or historical framework supposed to provide him with the essential ingredients of his identity. The only affiliation Spinoza accepted, at least theoretically, was political. He regarded himself as a citizen of the Netherlands Republic, to which he even referred as his "homeland." Nevertheless, in several respects (ethnic, linguistic, and partly also political), he lived as an alien in that country. The son of recent immigrants, his family had its origins in Spain and Portugal, the arch-enemy of the Netherlands. In terms of religion, his family was originally Catholic (ostensibly at least), and subsequently Jewish. Both faiths were at variance with the dominant Calvinist culture of the young Netherlands Republic.

Nor did Spinoza enjoy the full civil status that was accorded to Christians from birth. Born into the relatively foreign milieu of the Jewish-Portuguese quarter of Amsterdam he was probably not entirely fluent in the language of the country. In fact, it is unclear which, if any, of the languages he knew was predominantly his own. As a child, he evidently spoke Portuguese at home; at the same time he learned Spanish, which as an adult he liked to use for his casual reading (travels, drama, history, etc.). He later learned Latin, which he adopted for his philosophical studies. He knew Hebrew from an early age, but as the scholarly language of the classroom and the *Yeshiva*, not as a living tongue; and he seems to have picked up Dutch "by osmosis," enough for all practical purposes but without making it his truly active language. Only one of his essays—*The Short Treatise*, discovered some two hundred years after his death—is in Dutch; but some scholars believe that it is actually someone else's translation of Spinoza's Latin.

What, then, was Spinoza's language? In a word: he had none. Like many Jews, he was a polyglot, lacking a single language in which he was exclusively and genuinely at home and which dominated his life and semantic universe. Nor was there a single society to which he belonged. Having left the Jewish congregation, he was never fully integrated within the Dutch republic. His belonging to it was more an abstract political stance than a real living experiernce. Spinoza regarded the state as the individual's direct frame of reference without the mediation of religion, church, corporation, or any other body which claims to be "a kingdom within a kingdom." Yet such an intellectual position is remarkably different from an existential sense of belonging.

This difference evolved into a real breach with the overthrow of the government in 1672 and the murder of Johan de Witt, leader of the republic and its ruling oligarchy, whom Spinoza had supported and perhaps befriended (though not as closely as legend would have it). "*Ultima barbarorum!*" ("the height of barbarism") Spinoza cried out when de Witt and his brother were butchered and dissected by a mob in the center of the Hague, just a few blocks from where Spinoza lived, while the guardians of law and order looked on. Spinoza's reaction was not just a momentary one. The knife that dissected the murdered republican ruler also lacerated Spinoza's body politic. The return of the monarchy was accompanied by an increase in mob rule, as the House of Orange owed its strength to the popular masses who supported it against the liberal bourgeoisie. Monarchy and mob—these were two closely related political forces of which Spinoza had been apprehensive all his life. With the liquidation of the republican regime, Spinoza's attachment to his homeland was presumably attenuated not only (or not necessarily) because of his origins or his nonconformist thinking, but also because of his inability to rediscover himself and acquiesce in the country's prevailing political practices and values.

In an era when it was virtually impossible for anyone to exist and find his identity other than from within a recognized religious framework, Spinoza, the typical individual, left the Jewish congregation but did not enter the church. He refused to be baptized, nor did he join any of the radical sects that flourished in the Netherlands: neither the Mennonites nor the Remonstrants, though he agreed with some of their political positions; neither the Quakers, in whose service he earned his living for a time following his excommunication; nor the Collegiants, among whom he resided for a period in Rijnsburg, finding among them friends and disciples. The term "disciples" also requires severe qualification, as it illuminates further the nature of Spinoza's isolation. The new doctrine that Spinoza taught was not properly understood even by most of those who considered themselves his disciples. They entertained him, accorded him friendship, and some of them even supported him financially and helped him publish his works. Yet, in the final analysis he was lonely, since they failed to grasp his meaning. They could not fathom the radical, yet rich and nuanced nature of his position.

Even among rationalist philosophers, Spinoza was unique to the point of solitariness. He transcended the conceptual universe of Descartes and of Leibniz, and also of skeptical deism, no less than the world of traditional faith. These other thinkers postulated a "God of the philosophers" as part of their rational systems, but preserved his extraworldly role as Creator and First Cause. Spinoza alone refused to assign God such a role. Rather, he identified God with the totality of the universe itself. His conception, indeed, remained *sui generis* in the annals of philosophy.[1] As a result, Spinoza was rejected and despised not only by the traditional philososphical establishment but also by the Cartesian innovators and revolutionaries.

The identification of God with the world implies a more profound rejection of Judaism and Christianity than ordinary atheism. Spinoza does not contend that there is no God, only the inferior natural world. Such a contention is itself steeped in a Christian world view. Spinoza contends, on the contrary, that by virtue of identifying the world with God, immanent reality itself acquires divine status. Only Christianity considers the world of the here-and-now so base and so insignificant in and of itself, that denial of the transcendent divinity who gives it meaning robs the world of any significance whatsoever. The problem and anxiety of modern skeptics and atheists is usually Christian at root and subject to the categories of Christianity. Spinoza is far more radical in rejecting Christian (and Judaic) categories than the ordinary atheists—and as such is exceptional even among them.

Spinoza himself points at the rarity of true philosophical wisdom, at its singular and difficult nature. Very few can attain the intellectual love of God and be initiated into its insights. The multitude will respond to philosophical truth with fury and intolerance, not only because it lies beyond their grasp, but because it threatens their prejudices and undermines the sacrosanct images inculcated in them by "superstition," that is, by the different varieties of historical religion. Hence Spinoza's motto, to be prudent; hence the ambivalent, at times dissembling, style he employs in his more open writings, particularly his correspondence and *Theologico-Political Treatise*; and hence, more generally, the special strategy he adopts in dealing with the problem of the multitude, which he considers of prime importance and to which he devotes his reflections on politics and popular religion. Spinoza was among the first, if not the very first, to treat the problem of the multitude as a philosophical issue per se.

Spinoza's teachings, then, are highly esoteric, of the kind propounded by a philosopher who knows that only a few can share his knowledge. Such esotericism has usually been the province of secret sects and of mystics. In Spinoza, the "mystic of reason," it becomes an esotericism of the third kind of knowledge. Certainly, universal reason (*ratio*), dealing with scientific laws and logical inferences, is accessible to many (and, in time, perhaps, to the majority). But *ratio* is only the lower degree of reason, as yet incapable of transforming one's personality or of generating a revolution in the inner quality of life. *Ratio* provides no basis for the intellectual love of God, and no key to redemption and the eternity of the soul. As for the synoptic and intuitive degree of reason (which Spinoza terms simply "knowledge of the third kind," and which contains the key to all these changes of personality), it is seen by Spinoza as attainable only by rare individuals. "All things excellent are as difficult as they are rare": these simple and lofty words conclude Spinoza's chief work, the *Ethics*. In this sentence reverberate not only his lifelong efforts to attain his own ideal, not only his solitude and esotericism, but also, perhaps, echoes of the experience of his Marrano forefathers. Like Spinoza, they steadfastly adhered to a secret truth that was theirs alone: they and not the Christian multitude around them possessed the true key to salvation. They alone knew that salvation would come through the Law of Moses, and not through Christ. Spinoza, the "Marrano of reason" (as we saw in chapter 2) preserved patterns of life and experience whose roots lay with his Marrano-Judaizing forefathers.

Indeed, we have seen that Spinoza was the "Marrano of reason" during the two principal periods of his life: as a member of the Jewish congregation where he displayed signs of heresy long before the formal breach between him and the community; and later, as a member of Dutch society, keeping most of his thoughts to himself, preferring to divulge them parsimoniously to his friends and "disciples," writing in an equivocal style, publishing anonymous texts addressed to large audiences, and keeping locked away to his last days his own true philosophical treatise, the *Ethics*. Thus Spinoza lived in a dual tension between the external and the internal, between his thoughts and the inner workings of his mind, on the one hand, and his conformity to society on the other.

During his youth and early manhood, it was Spinoza's consideration for his father that led him to keep his skeptical thoughts from bursting out in open rebellion. He officially broke with Judaism only after his father's death. Yet even after Spinoza left the Jewish quarter and lived among the Dutch, he remained a "Marrano of reason"—not because his life was in jeopardy, but because of the disjunction between his inner self-knowledge and what he thought could be given social and verbal expression. Holland was a Christian land, fired by a vigorous Calvinist fervor, whereas Spinoza had disavowed all religions and their attendant organizational and conceptual extensions.

Spinoza's espousal of secularity makes him, indeed, a true harbinger of modernity. Yet the new principle he enunciated could not change his own life as an individual, because that principle was as yet untenable in the social reality. A single individual exemplifying it was fated, in a crucial sense, to suffer an alienated existence. Religious affiliation was the individual's passport to social acceptance. It was possible to abandon Catholicism, but only by taking up Protestantism (Lutheranism, Calvinism, etc.), or, in exceptional instances, Islam or Judaism. But to renounce all historical religions was tantamount to opting for social and existential isolation. Membership in the secular body politic alone was not yet a viable form of social identity, as Spinoza was bound to discover. Nevertheless, he articulated and exemplified in his person what was to emerge in time as the overriding principle of modern life.

The same may be said with regard to Spinoza's relation to his own people and what we may term the secularization of Jewish life. Alone and alienated, he prefigured what later generations would call "Jewish secularism." So Spinoza contributed to the emergence of a phenomenon which was neither viable nor possible during his own lifetime.

Spinoza and the Jews

We must distinguish between what Spinoza himself thought or wrote about Judaism, and the significance of his peculiar existence as a Jew, something of which he himself could not be fully aware. First, I will elaborate upon Spinoza's image of Judaism and its attendant implications, including certain Jewish motifs in the deep structure of his thinking. Then I will discuss the relevance of his life for our times.

At the core of our discussion lies the notion of secularity. Spinoza attempts to secularize Jewish history in order to secularize history in general, and then goes on to reinvest certain implicit Jewish values with universal significance for the modern secular world. In both instances, Spinoza continues to make Jewish history the model and lever of world history—albeit without divine providence and without election.

Spinoza's approach to Judaism rests on a strictly philosophical basis, vividly colored by his own emotional history. His philososphical position is consistent with his doctrine as a whole in that he attempts to examine the peculiar destiny of the Jewish people in the light of natural causes, uninformed by divine-transcendental meaning. In other words, he continues to use the immanent approach also with regard to the history of the Jews. The Jewish people is traditionally considered to be the bearer of historical meaning in general. As it happens, it is also Spinoza's own people and community, in which he was unable to express himself as a free thinker, but was rather castigated and inexorably driven from the fold.

The Rhetorical Context

The traces of this bitter experience are quite perceptible in Spinoza's language. When it comes to his fellow Jews, Spinoza loses his philosophical cool. His writings betray his rancor toward the adversaries of his youth, the rabbis, who sanctioned or actually initiated his ban. Yet here and there one also hears a *cri du coeur*, the cry of a Jew struggling with his brethren over the paradoxical nature of Jewish existence, in which faith and reason are implacably pitched against each other. Here there are no easy answers. Moreover, as we shall see, Spinoza's writings betray a personal, even intimate, feeling of kinship with Jewish destiny—despite his disavowal of Jewish *religion*—and, subsequently, a strong sense of alienation.[2]

In order to understand the context, we must also bear in mind that Spinoza was writing largely for a Christian audience in an attempt to discredit their superstitions. To this end he employs a rhetorical language adapted to his readers and to his purposes (see chapter 5, above). Spinoza rejects Christianity as a *vana religio* no less than he rejects Judaism. But to achieve his ends he must ostensibly accept the principles of Christianity and argue from its point of view. This is a kind of Marranesque technique which, however difficult it might have been for him to apply, was rhetorically necessary.

For this reason, inter alia, Spinoza accords Jesus pride of place among the prophets—but only as a human being, not as a divine being. Jesus' divinity for Spinoza is an irrational notion.[3] Spinoza employs here an old Jewish argument against Christianity, but cautiously couched in ambiguity: when he writes that he "does not understand" the notion of Jesus' divinity, he clearly intends that it be understood as: "the notion is absurd and meaningless *in itself*." But, of course, it could be read as: "The notion is so profound that it lies beyond my intellectual powers," thus providing an alternate option for certain readers.[4]

Spinoza's rhetorical needs vis-à-vis his Christian audience effectively accommodate his antirabbinical rancor as well. This is done when he refers to the rabbis as Pharisees, a strongly perjorative term to Christian ears.

We should, however, recall that Da Costa had already employed the same term in his polemic against the rabbinical establishment, and that sarcasm and virulent invective were fairly typical of the intramural criticism leveled at the orthodox by later opponents. Generations after Da Costa and Spinoza, the rhetoric of enlightened Jews (*maskilim*), nationalists, heretics, and Zionists makes Spinoza's abuse pale in comparison.

There is of course a difference; the latter critics, or most of them, sought some sort of Jewish alternative. Spinoza, two centuries earlier and lacking any alternative, abandoned Jewish society altogether. Nevertheless, a reminder of this sort helps place Spinoza's aspersions in their proper rhetorical perspective.

Judaism—A Political Religion and Historical Anachronism

Spinoza's image of Judaism is anchored in a thesis which proved useful to later Jewish reformers and anti-Semites alike. For Spinoza, Judaism is fundamentally a political religion that was designed specifically for the ancient Hebrews as the basis for a theological regime. When the temple was destroyed and the Jews were deprived of their political existence, their religion also lost its meaning, and Judaism became historically obsolete and self-contradictory.

This view would appear to smack of Christian logic. After all, the Christians were the first to claim that since Jesus had redeemed the world, Judaism had been superseded: God's "chosen people" were now those who adhered to the Christian church. But this is mere rhetoric. Spinoza does not consider Judaism anachronistic because God's elect are now the Christians: Spinoza rejects the very notion of election. What makes Judaism obsolete is not a theological argument but a purely profane analysis, which treats history as a natural causal system, uninformed by divine providence.

Judaism lost its historical rationale, according to Spinoza, because the political nature of the Jewish religion no longer corresponded to the nonpolitical existence of the Jews in the Diaspora. In the absence of a Jewish body politic, Jewish religion is superfluous. To sustain this view Spinoza must turn to a sociohistorical analysis, showing that the essence of the ancient Jewish religion was theocratic, that is, a political regime where the laws of God are also the supreme civil authority. Crucial sections of chapters 3 and 17 of the *Theologico-Political Treatise* are given over to this analysis, which is Spinoza's alternative to traditional theological interpretations of Judaism.

While his methodological principle is sound, Spinoza's detailed explanation is imprecise. As we know, the ancient Jewish state was racked throughout its existence by a relentless struggle to convert it into a theocracy. That struggle, however, was never quite resolved. Even if, as Spinoza contends, the Jewish religion projected the ideal of a theocratic state, it was never strong enough to impose it on concrete reality. Prior to the destruction of the second temple, the influence of the Pharisees (which came closest to the theorcratic model) considerably increased, but its great achievement came, paradoxically, after the destruction of the second temple. Then Rabban Yochanan Ben-Zakkai requested and received from the Roman emperor authority over "Yavneh and its provinces," in order to establish there a center of Jewish culture and law. Rabban Yochanan, with whom Spinoza is quite familiar, is thus considered to have laid the cornerstone for autonomous Jewish life in the Diaspora as well. Such autonomy is based on the sanction of the gentile government and the voluntary development of a system of rabbinical commandments as a substitute for the Jewish body politic. This development is also seen, to a certain extent, as a triumph of the Pharisaic approach.[5]

From Spinoza's point of view, it is an absurd and incongruous state of affairs when the laws of a religion, whose entire purpose is the political constitution of some concrete and actual theocratic state, succeed in gaining ascendancy over reality only *after* the state itself is annihilated. Henceforth, the Pharisees are able to dictate the shape of future Jewish history. Yet, under these circumstances, the theocratic laws have taken over in a distorted and absurd manner. In the absence of a concrete state, a phantom substitute has been created by the imagination, nourished by piety and a hatred of other nations, and this phantom "homeland" is carried by the Jews everywhere in their exile. The Jews continue to regard themselves not only as a separate nation but even a separate polity, however bizarre and incongruous in reality.

Of course, Spinoza's main interest is in the present—with his analysis of Jewish existence in the exile, from which he also projects back into the Jewish past. The Jews in Palestine never lived under an absolute theocracy. The almost full coalescence of law and religion emerges only in the phantom state Spinoza criticizes—and with which, we may add, he had an existential clash. Only in the exile is it possible to say as Spinoza says in painful reproach that "everyone who fell away from religion ceased to be a citizen, and was, on that ground alone, accounted an enemy" (*Theologico-Political Treatise*, chap. 17, pp. 219-20). In this type of reality, a critic of religion like Spinoza was forced to relinquish his membership in the Jewish community. In the ancient Jewish states, however, both in the first and the second temple periods, there were many Jews who disavowed religious authority or transgressed against its laws without being considered enemies; or who took issue (like the Sadducees) with the Oral Law and with the very principle of theocracy, and yet were legitimate, even influential, citizens of the polity. A person like Da Costa or Spinoza would conceivably have been better off, certainly less alienated, in ancient Israel. And it is quite probable that in depicting the idealized and somewhat imaginary theocracy of the ancient Israelites, Spinoza is projecting a negative print of what he considers the distorted life of the Jewish exile.

The Survival of the Jews

Even if Judaism has lost its raison d'être with the destruction of the temple, the Jewish people continue to survive. For centuries they zealously preserve their phantom "homeland," rooted, as it is, in religious superstition. Moreover, like Spinoza's own parents and fellow Marranos, they prevail even in the face of forced conversion and cruel persecution, returning openly to Judaism after generations of secret practice. From a logical point of view, there is something incomprehensible in all this, a kind of theoretical scandal; and empirically, at least prima facie, this poses a riddle.

Thus Spinoza, in his own way, faces the same problem that has perplexed Jews and Christians alike: the amazing survival of the Jewish people. The Jews maintain that they are God's chosen people who, even though sinners, yearn for redemption. Christians, on the other hand, maintain that the Jews *were* God's chosen people who, because they rejected Jesus as the Messiah, are themselves rejected by God.

Spinoza of course, must dismiss both explanations as transcendent. What is demanded is a purely natural explanation, based upon social and psychological causes. Significantly, the twofold explanation Spinoza offers is drawn in part from his Marrrano background. What preserved the Jews, he says, was gentile hatred of the Jews from without and the power of their religious faith ("superstition") from within.

Gentile hatred of the Jews, in Spinoza's view, enhances their survival. So intensely do the Jews differentiate themselves from other peoples, that they cannot help but arouse animosity and revulsion. As a result, even if many individuals are ostracized and lost to their people, the external pressure reinforces the Jews' survival as a group. This is a modern, essentially secular, explanation which has by now become banal (the last important writer to use it was Sartre).[6] Spinoza, however, was among the first, if not actually the first, to express it so succinctly.[7] Spinoza's outlook derives from the accumulated experience of the Jewish people in general, and from his own Marrano forefathers in particular.

> At the present time, therefore, there is absolutely nothing which the Jews can arrogate to themselves beyond other people.
>
> As to their continuance so long after dispersion and the loss of empire, there is nothing marvellous in it, for they so separated themselves from every other nation as to draw down upon themselves universal hate, not only by their outward rites, rites conflicting with those of other nations, but also by the sign of circumcision which they most scrupulously observe. (*Theologico-Political Treatise*, 3:55)

After citing an example from the history of the Marranos (to which we shall refer separately), Spinoza continues:

> The sign of circumcision is, as I think, so important that I could persuade myself that it alone would preserve the nation for ever. Nay, I would go so far as to believe that if the foundations of their religion have not emasculated their minds they may even, if occasion offers, so changeable are human affairs, raise up their empire afresh, and that God may a second time elect them. (Ibid., p. 56)

Since Spinoza aspires to an objective, scientific posture, even when dealing with such highly emotional matters, he postulates an analogy between the Jews and the Chinese with respect to this same anthropological process.

> Of such a possibility we have a very famous example in the Chinese. They, too, have some distinctive mark on their heads which they most scrupulously observe, and by which they keep themselves apart from everyone else, and have thus kept themselves during so many thousand years that they far surpass all other nations in antiquity. They have not always retained empire, but they have recovered it when lost, and doubtless will do so again after the spirit of the Tartars becomes relaxed through the luxury of riches and pride. (Ibid.)

This discussion of the Jewish people should be read in conjunction with chapter 17. There Spinoza asserts that gentile hatred of the Jews is psychologically motivated by the Jews' own xenophobia toward the gentiles, which in turn derives from the Jews' sense of the superiority of their unique religious faith. However, Spinoza again underscores the solidarity generated by external pressure, and cites another example from the annals of his Marrano brethren:

> That they have been preserved in great measure by Gentile hatred, experience demonstrates. When the king of Spain formerly compelled the Jews to embrace the State religion or to go into exile, a large number of Jews accepted Catholicisms. Now, as these renegades were admitted to all the native privileges of Spaniards, and deemed worthy of filling all honourable offices, it came to pass that they straightway became so intermingled with the Spaniards as to leave of themselves no relic or remembrance. But exactly the opposite happened to those whom the king of Portugal compelled to become Christians, for they always, though converted, lived apart, inasmuch as they were considered unworthy of any civic honours. (Ibid.)

A number of scholars have justly contested Spinoza's historical account.[8] When he speaks of the exclusion of the conversos from "all honourable offices," he is referring to the so-called "statutes of blood purity" (*limpieza de sangre*). Yet, oddly enough, he refers only to the Portuguese statutes, ignoring those of Spain. It is true that by the end of the sixteenth century most of the original Spanish Marranos were close to assimilation, whereas the Portuguese Marranos persevered for many generations. Furthermore, the Marrano reawakening that occurred in Spain at the end of the sixteenth century was a result of the immigration of Portuguese Marranos to Spain. With regard to the restrictions imposed on the Marranos, as Yerushalmi notes, the situation was more or less identical in both countries; in Portugal it merely came later.[9] Yet by the time the blood purity regulations were effectively enforced, the assimilation of the Marranos of Spain had already reached its zenith. In fact, by the time the regulations were institutionalized by royal decree, over 170 years of Marrano life in Spain had already passed (1391–1566), and seven decades elapsed since the expulsion, the date from which Spinoza begins his reckoning. While these data do not expunge Spinoza's error, they do perhaps mitigate his critics' charges of tendentious, even unbridled, disregard of the facts.[10]

The above-quoted passage provides us with a rather interesting glimpse into the recesses of Spinoza's consciousness as well a view of his self-image. To illustrate his thesis, Spinoza selects not ordinary Jews but Marranos, and not only Judaizing Marranos but all conversos, even those who willfully assimilated. To all of them he assigns the universal name "Jew." (The importance of such a *nomen universalis* will presently become apparent.) Here Spinoza reveals that, to his mind, even those who have disavowed the Jewish religion have not, ipso facto, been severed from the "nation" or from Jewish destiny—if only because of the hostile attitude of the gentiles toward them. Spinoza, no doubt, is converting his own personal experience into a prodigious generalization. He, Baruch Spinoza, continues to be seen by others as a Jew in the empirical-historical sense of the word and, as a consequence, implicitly sees himself in the same way.

Yet Spinoza's implicit image is that of a lost and alienated Jew, locked in a paradox, unable either to live positively as a Jew or to shed his basic Jewish identification.

Jewish and Marrano Experience as Reflected in the Ethics

Spinoza's preoccupation with this issue resonates quite powerfully—and surprisingly—in his purely systematic work, the *Ethics*. I refer to part 3 of the book, which is devoted primarily to the psychology of the emotions. Throughout the discussion, Spinoza concerns himself with individuals rather than social or group psychology. He deals with joy and grief, love and hate, hope and fear, and the like, all on the personal, individual level. And then, abruptly, without warning, we find ourselves in the realm of social psychology. This occurs when Spinoza is discussing hatred—that same variety of hatred which is so decisive in preserving the Jewish people. In terms of style, this proposition is, like the rest of the book, dry and scientific, yet attesting to such intense emotions within its geometrical form of discourse that at times it seems to explode from the weight of its excessive scientific neutrality.

> Prop. 46. If someone has been affected with joy or sadness by someone of *a class or nation different from his own*, and his joy or sadness is accompanied by the idea of that person as its cause, under the universal name of the class or nation, he will feel love or hate not only to that person, but everyone of the same class or nation. Demonstration: The demonstration of this matter is evident from prop. 16. (Emphasis added)

A puzzling proposition: How and why does Spinoza suddenly plunge from individual psychology into this sociological theory? On the face of it, this is a purely scientific proposition, the forty-sixth in a deductive chain, that dissects the most powerful emotions "as though they were points, surfaces and bodies." Similarly, the content of the proposition would apply in principle to any "foreign class or nation" that became the object of either love or, more probably and closer to the author's intention, hatred, by dint of such association as described in the text. Yet what erupts from beneath that dry sociological generalization and its irregular position within the text, is the singular fate of the Jewish people, and within it, the Marranos. Who more than members of that "nation" (*natio; nação*), as they were commonly called, had collectively suffered from hatred and prejudice nourished by invidious individual-collective stereotypes? Moreover, this is Spinoza's own "nation," subsumed under the same "universal name" (*nomen universalis*),[11] on behalf of which he continues to suffer even after he has withdrawn from the community. Evidently, this tacit reference to the "nation" of the Marranos and the Jewish people as a whole accounts for the appearance of this extraordinary proposition within the deductive chain of the *Ethics*.

No less remarkable than the proposition itself is its demonstration. By way of proof, Spinoza merely cites a corroborating proposition, some thirty propositional steps away. This underscores the status of prop. 46 as a formalized "passing remark" which could just as well have been inserted anywhere else. Spinoza chooses to include it here precisely because his present context is hatred: that same hatred that has preserved the Jews and the Marranos, and of which, perforce, Spinoza himself is an object.

Thus a perceptive reader might complete this dry laconic proof—so joltingly trenchant in its simplicity—and write it thus:

Demonstration: The demonstration of this matter is evident from prop. 16—*and from the entire history of the Jews and the Marranos.*

Spinoza did not actually write this but it must have hovered over his pen.

The Power of Superstitious Faith

Gentile hatred is not the only explanation Spinoza provides for the astounding survival of the Jews. He posits an "internal" explanation as well, inherent in Jewish life itself: the unique power of the Jewish faith. Spinoza as a philosopher rejects this faith as "superstition," yet he is bound to recognize its power as a natural phenomenon, toward which he betrays ambivalent feelings of empathy and admiration. As we shall presently see, the Marrano experience once again speaks through Spinoza, coloring his thesis.

This complementary explanation is mentioned in chapter 17 of the *Theologico-Political Treatise* but is more evident in Spinoza's correspondence. Spinoza writes to a pious, ungifted young man named Albert Burgh who went to Rome and became a Catholic. He had written to Spinoza, seeking to convince him of the truth of the Catholic faith. Spinoza, unforbearingly, replies in a tone he does not often employ:

> O youth deprived of understanding, who had bewitched you into believing that the Supreme and Eternal is eaten by you, and held in your intestines? (tr. Elwes, p. 416)

Such mockery of the Eucharist was common among Jews in the Middle Ages and Judaizing Marranos in Iberia (as well as among radical Protestants). The rest of the letter also oozes with anti-Catholic sarcasm. It is against this background that we must read what Spinoza says about the Jews.

Burgh had justified his new Catholicism by the uninterrupted ecclesiastical successison through which generation upon generation have accepted its message of Catholicism. Spinoza, the former *yeshiva* student, familiar with Rabbi Yehuda Halevi and others, replies: "This is the very catch-word of the Pharisees" (i.e., the rabbis), who "as pertinaciously as the Roman witnesses repeat what they have heard as though it were their personal experience." The indignant Spinoza does not realize that within a few lines he himself will fall into the same trap. In the meantime he adds, thinking no doubt of himself, and not only of Jesus:

> That all heretics have left them, and that they [the Pharisees] have remained constant through thousands of years under the constraint of no government, but by the sole efficacy of their superstition, no one can deny. (Ibid., p. 417; Elwes tr. modified)

Once more we are confronted with the miracle, the scandal, the anachronism: how do the Jewish people exist apolitically, without a state and a government? This time Spinoza's answer does not invoke the hatred of the gentiles but "superstition," a term he uses to denote all historical religions alike, both Jewish and non-Jewish. What sets the Jews apart—and invests their faith with such "efficacy"—is their peculiar (and counterrational) success in converting patriotism (i.e., fidelity to the homeland) into fidelity to their religious superstition. This engenders manifestations of heroism and self-sacrifice which Spinoza, the rationalist philosopher, but also the son of the Marranos, views with irritated awe and a mixture of repulsion and fascination. In speaking of Jewish martyrdom, his Marrano background surfaces again. Without mitigating his revulsion of religious fanaticism, it heightens the sense of affinity and empathy which Spinoza would share with anyone who can recognize sublimity even while rejecting its wellsprings.

> But their chief boast is, that they count a far greater number of martyrs than any other nation, a number which is daily increased by those who suffer with singular constancy for the faith they profess; nor is their boasting false. I myself knew among others [of] a certain Judah called the faithful, who in the midst of the flames, when he was already thought to be dead, lifted his voice to sing the hymn beginning, "To Thee, O God, I offer up my soul," and so singing perished. (Ibid., pp. 417–18)

What Spinoza fails to discern is that he, like the Pharisees he deplores, is quite close to "repeating what he has heard as though it were his personal experience." Spinoza could not possibly have witnessed these acts. The Inquisition did its work in the Iberian Peninsula (and America); Spinoza never left the Low Countries. His childhood, however, was rife with reports and stories of the Inquisition and its *autos-da-fé*, and they may have branded themselves so deeply on the boy's mind that he later remembered them as vividly as if he had actually experienced them.[12]

Who was "Judah the faithful"? He was "Judah the *Believer*" of whom the reconverted Marrano, Isaac Cardoso, speaks in his book *Las excelencias y calumnias de los Hebreos* (1679). This Judah (whose original name was Don Lope de Vera y Alarcon) was not a Marrano but a Christian who had converted, circumcised himself, and studied Hebrew. Imprisoned by the Inquisition, he refused to recant, and went to the stake chanting psalms. That Spinoza calls him "the faithful" and not "the believer" demonstrates, in my view, that Spinoza's thinking here operates through the mediation of the Hebrew language and its associations. For the words *creyente* and *fidus* have no common root, neither in Spanish nor in Latin. In Hebrew, however, the two words (*ma'amin, ne'eman*) have the same root (*amn*) and are closely related; and if Spinoza erred here inadvertently, it shows how deeply engrained the Hebrew language was in his mind.

This may, however, be a Freudian slip, a symptom of Spinoza's profound ambiguity in the face of martyrdom. As a rationalist philosopher, he was not only repulsed by religious fanaticism but was unable, as he avowed, to fathom suicide and self-denial. This is a general philosophical problem in Spinoza (as in Hobbes) with no special bearing on his Jewishness. In addition, as a critic of Judaism, Spinoza should have rejected martyrdom as fanaticism and madness. Yet not only is he powerfully attracted by the sublimity of the phenomenon; the subject also plays a painful and ambivalent role in his own life. After all, from a Jewish standpoint, was not he, Spinoza, the very antithesis of martyrdom? Shortly before Spinoza's ban, the Amsterdam congregation was shocked by yet another case of Marrano martyrdom, when Abraham Nuñez Bernal was burnt at the stake in Spain (see chapter 1). The contrast was manifest to everyone—not in the least to Spinoza himself. He, the heretic, must leave the congregation as a traitor; the other gives his life for his faith and is hailed as a hero. Etching itself deeply in Spinoza's mind, this contrast suddenly reappears in a key passage in the *Theologico-Political Treatise*:

> Thus in the Hebrew state, the civil and religious authority . . . were one and the same. The dogmas of religion were not precepts, but laws and ordinances; piety was regarded as the same as loyalty, impiety the same as disaffection. *Everyone who fell away from religion ceased to be a citizen and was, on that ground alone, accounted an enemy; those who died for the sake of religion were held to have died for their country.* (*Theologico-Political Treatise*, 17: 219–20; emphasis added)

A most telling passage, encapsulating at once Spinoza's general thesis regarding Judaism and his most personal experience. The characters mentioned at the end of the quote are not just abstract types but have proper names: one is Spinoza, the other Nuñez Bernal. In a painful effort of self-understanding, as he reflects upon his personal situation, Spinoza is able to see through it into a general structure of Judaism as a whole. Herein lies the existential source of his thesis regarding the political nature of the Jewish religion. This nature forced him to abandon his "citizenship" in the Jewish fold when he became a nonbeliever; and the same political nature raises martyrdom to prestigious heights in Judaism as a defense of the phantom "homeland" that the Jews carry in their superstitious imagination wherever they go, and for which they are prepared to perform acts of fanatical daring and sublimity.

The connection between the hatred of the gentiles and superstitious faith, the two elements that have preserved the Jews, is explicated in chapter 17 of the *Theologico-Political Treatise*, which should be read as complementary to chapter 3. Yet several new points emerge in chapter 17. It turns out, for example, that the unique fusion of patriotism and religious piety existed already in the ancient kingdom and was merely emulated in the exile. Further, we find that the gentiles' hatred of the Jews is the result of the Jews' hatred of the gentiles, fed by their superstitious faith and their sense of uniqueness and superiority. "Of all hatreds, none is more deep and tenacious than that which springs from extreme devoutness or piety" (17: 229), and, in reaction to such feelings, the nations rewarded the Jews with "a hatred just as intense." All of this, Spinoza adds, "strengthened the heart of the Jews to bear all things for their country with extraordinary constancy and valor" (ibid.). Chapter 17 complements Spinoza's remarks about Jewish survival which appear at the end of chapter 3. When the two sections are read as one substantive unit, we find that Spinoza adduces both reasons for the survival of the Jews, and not just the gentiles' hatred (as Yerushalmi seems to believe).[13] Religious superstition leads the Jews to disdain and hate the gentiles. This in turn feeds the gentiles' hatred of them, which further forges their internal solidarity and power of resistance. Thus the reciprocal interaction of both factors, the internal and the external, explains the phenomenon.

The Marranos and Existential Anti-Semitism

As Spinoza knew from his own experience and from Marrano history, the external factor may remain effective long after the internal factor has lost its validity. For this reason, apparently, Spinoza believed that even if the Jews became wholly secularized individually, they would still exist as Jews (and be called by that name) collectively; from that point of view, gentile hatred would preserve them *in perpetuo*.

It was, therefore, particularly ingenious of Spinoza to choose the Marranos, rather than ordinary Jews, to illustrate his theses. The Marranos suffered from a unique brand of anti-Semitism several hundred years before the onset of modern anti-Semitism. For the first time in Jewish history, anti-Semitism stemmed not from opposition to the Jewish religion but from a hostility to Jewish existence itself: it was existential anti-Semitism. The converso who disavowed the Jewish religion and sincerely sought to assimilate into Christian society, found that he was still discriminated against because of his ancestry and his blood. This existential anti-Semitism reemerged in the nineteenth and twentieth centuries, and was given its most inexorable expression in the crematoria of Auschwitz; but the earlier version is to be found in Iberia in the waning days of the Renaissance. The concept of "racial purity" adduced by modern anti-Semites, and that of "blood purity" propounded by their Iberian predecessors, are two sides of the same coin: hatred of the Jew no longer depended on his religion but was anchored in his very being. There is something tainted, contemptible, and abhorrent in the mere existence of the Jew per se. The Jew can convert to Christianity or (like Spinoza) disavow all religion; yet, willy-nilly, he will continue to be subsumed under that "universal name" referred to in proposition 46, and remain, thereby, an object of loathing.

Auschwitz is the logical conclusion of this type of anti-Semitism; for if the stigma inheres in the Jew's very existence, it can only be expunged by physical extermination. But the Iberian Inquisition never dreamed of going as far as that. During the Middle Ages and the Renaissance, exile was the common practice for getting rid of the Jews. Only the "enlightened" modern era actually made physical extermination possible. Yet through Marrano history Spinoza could have peered into a deep structure of Jewish existence: he made the discovery—to which he was still unable to give conceptual articulation—that Jewish existence was broader in scope than Jewish religion, and the two could not simply be identified.

Spinoza's "Zionism"

Was Spinoza a "closet Zionist"? Perhaps he saw in the renewal of Jewish sovereignty an answer to the anomaly of Jewish existence in the exile. After all, Zionists of three generations regarded him as their forerunner—all on the basis of his somewhat obscure, though moving, remarks at the end of the third chapter of the *Theologico-Political Treatise*. After explaining that the hostility of the gentiles is what preserves the Jews, Spinoza goes on to say:

> The sign of circumcision is, I think, so important that I could persuade myself that it alone would preserve the nation forever. Nay, I would go so far as to believe that if the foundations of their religion have not emasculated their minds, they may even, if occasion offers, so changeable are human affairs, raise up their empire afresh and that God may a second time elect them. (3: 56)

This passage appears in the chapter entitled "Of the Vocation of the Hebrews," which is designed to demolish the entire concept of election. Spinoza's use of the term *God's election* is actually metaphorical and means "successful political existence."[14] He argues that even from the viewpoint of the Bible (a viewpoint he adopts for rhetorical purposes), the election of the Hebrews refers solely to "dominion and physical advantages" (p. 56). This also implies that the election is temporal, not eternal; and while Spinoza as a philosopher recognizes neither, he uses the Bible's own language and authority as a weapon against itself. If the "election" of the Hebrews is a mere temporal, earthly (in fact, empirical) event, nothing will remain of the idea of eternal, transcendent election. Thus Spinoza discredits the idea of "sacred history" altogether, secularizing Jewish history and, consequently, all human history. All things happen in accordance with the laws of nature—and this is the meaning (and part of the intent) of Spinoza's remarks about the return to Zion.

Although Spinoza's point is strictly philosophical, it has a particular bearing upon current issues of his time. Spinoza is writing only a few years after the upheaval fomented by Sabbetai Zevi, the false messiah who unleashed a wave of mystical enthusiasm throughout the Jewish Diaspora, from Marakesh to Vilno, and from Thessaloniki to Hamburg. The effect was particularly fierce in Amsterdam, probably due to the Marrano background of its Jews.[15] Spinoza, though no longer of the community, must have been relatively well informed. This was, at least, the view of Oldenburg, secretary of the Royal Society in London (where millennarian sentiment was also prevalent). In a letter to Spinoza he writes:

> Everyone here is talking of a report that the Jews, after remaining scattered for more than two thousand years, are about to return to their country. Few here believe in it, but many desire it. Please tell your friend what you hear and think of the matter. . . . I should like to know what the Jews of Amsterdam have heard about the matter, and how they are affected by such important tidings which, if true, would assuredly seem to harbinger the end of the world.[16] (Letter 33)

We do not have Spinoza's reply. Perhaps he never made one; perhaps his letter was lost or destroyed. However, chapter 3 of the *Theologico-Political Treatise* offers an indirect answer, not only to Oldenburg and his friends but to the Sabbatians themselves (and also to Spinoza's old friend and adversary, Isaac La Peyrère, author of *The Recall of the Jews*). It presents an antithesis to the Sabbatian torment and madness (as Spinoza was bound to view it), and at the same time a different version— rational and secular—of the messianic longing that beat confusedly in Sabbatian hearts. Since all human affairs are transient, Spinoza says, the renewal of the Jewish kingdom is not inevitable;[17] but if the return to Zion should take place, it will be because of the immanent laws of nature and not by providence, divine reelection, or messianism. For Spinoza, the Jewish vision of redemption (traditionally understood as "liberation from the dominion of the nations") is thus not devoid of sense, but its content is entirely historical and secular.[18]

This then is the import of Spinoza's "Zionist" dictum, to which later Zionists clung. They failed to see that Spinoza does not recommend the establishment of a Jewish state; he merely posits it as one of the possibilities offered by secular history. Moreover, the logic of his position theoretically precludes such a recommendation. True, a Jewish state would remedy one major distortion of Jewish life, namely, the gap between the political essence of Judaism and the apolitical character of Jewish existence in the Diaspora. Yet this would entail the renewal of the ancient theocratic regime, a solution Spinoza cannot possibly accept, for as a political philosopher, he favors religious tolerance and the separation of church and state.

Would not then a secular Jewish state provide a solution? Presumably it would restore to the Jews a tangible homeland, revoke the alienation inherent in their present situation, and enable a person like Spinoza to live in a Jewish milieu as a full "citizen." From this point of view, the contemporary State of Israel (as long as it remains secular) would seem to suggest a solution for several of the basic problems tackled by Spinoza.

But this is an anachronistic solution, anchored in an altogether different situation. In Spinoza's time, it had no social basis and was not even a glimmer on the horizon of consciousness. To Spinoza, of course, every state should be secular: that is his ground-breaking message to the era which he was ushering in. But a secular Jewish state was still inconceivable to him.

From his own experience and from Marrano history, Spinoza pinpoints the gap between Jewish religion and Jewish existence, but gives it no theoretical underpinnings. He neither defines the gap positively nor develops from it the concept of Jewish "destiny" or "nation" as separate from religion. Spinoza, we could say, lacks the theoretical tools with which to articulate what he has experienced existentially. From this point of view, he was not only ahead of his time but actually ahead of himself: his life preceded the state of his own consciousness.

Still, Spinoza clings to several of the deepest motifs in Jewish consciousness—the eternity of Israel, the vision of redemption (understood as political liberation), and the covenant with God as symbolized by circumcision. But true to himself he submits them all to an utterly prosaic, natural, and secular interpretation. The eternity of Israel, for example, is contingent upon causes similar to those relating to the Chinese. A Jewish ear may be offended by the comparison, but this is how Spinoza, the Jewish heretic, paraphrases the words of the prophet

Amos on behalf of his new God, Nature: "Are you not like the Ethiopians to me, O people of Israel?" (Amos 9:7). In other words, like the other nations, you too are subordinated to the laws of nature, which are the sole expression of God's "will" and "decrees." You too are subject to the same causal system of secular history, which is all there is. It does not follow that there is nothing unique about Jewish history; on the contrary, there definitely is, and who can know this better than the son of reconverted Marranos, who thus fulfilled the quasi messianic hope, *esperanza*, which attended their "exile" in Iberia? Nonetheless, even the uniqueness of Judaism is the result of natural causes; and if the hope of return is ever realized, it will take place only through the agency of secular history.

This may entail a significant message for modern Zionism—which, indeed, chose not to wait for transcendent or messianic redemption but to work for Jewish redemption within the course of secular history. Spinoza may not have defined Zionism as a goal but he pointed out the methodological approach. Zionism can be meaningful only if accepted as a development within secular history—and not as a mystical doctrine about an elect people led by God to its sacred land to the beat of the Messiah's drum. Everything Spinoza said about *vana religio* is true of the false messianism and religious fanaticism which today endanger the State of Israel. Spinoza, the errant Jew, the heretic, the premature secularist, who responded to the insanities of Sabbatian messianism, by asserting that only secular history exists and must be respected if Jews are to fulfill their age-old aspirations, may in this respect still offer his people timely advice.

ELEMENTS OF SPINOZA'S JEWISH SELF-IMAGE

To what extent did Spinoza remain Jewish in a subjective sense? I shall now recapitulate the evidence (part of which has already been mentioned) for the Jewish self-image that continues to dwell in various layers of Spinoza's consciousness.

CONVERSOS AS PARADIGMATIC OF JEWS   By his choice of the Marranos as paradigmatic of Jewish history, Spinoza discloses that at some level of consciousness he views himself, too, as a Jew—perhaps by deterministic necessity. The Marranos he cites were not only Judaizers but the whole converso "nation," including those who tried unsuccessfully to assimilate into Christianity—and all of them he calls "Jews" in a straightforward and bona fide manner. Hence, this name will apply to him as well. True, Spinoza was a Marrano of reason and not of Christianity, but the same pattern recurs in his case—and whatever his views, his belonging to the same group or "nation" was, as he knew, irradicable.

THE DESTINY OF "THE NATION"   Similarly, proposition 46, part 3 of the *Ethics*, implies: (1) the structural homology of Jews and Marranos; (2) Spinoza's affiliation by means of the "universal name" to both of them, and consequently, to the common destiny of the members of that "class or nation."

ACCEPTING THE JEWISH CONDITION   Generalizing further, we may say that Spinoza remains "our Jew from Voorburg," not only in the eyes of the gentiles, but in his own eyes as well. His refusal to become a Christian, even for appearance sake, reflects this special awareness as well and not just his abstract intellectual integrity. It indicates that Spinoza has comprehended and internalized the necessity of his destiny and made it part of his effective consciousness—as implied, indeed, by the Spinozistic theory of ethics. The Jewish "class or nation" includes Spinoza, too, under its "universal name" and, therefore, by natural necessity he is subject to the same common destiny. Accepting as he does the laws of nature as the salient and exclusive expression of "God's decrees" (or, in nonmetaphorical language, as an immanent rational necessity stemming from God as the totality of being), Spinoza accepts the condition of his Jewishness and does not attempt to escape it. Yet, as an individual, he cannot find a positive expression for his heterodox Jewishness, and remains alienated, the victim of a double rejection. In the words of the highly perceptive Heine: "The gentiles were generous enough to grant him the title of Jew of which the Jews had deprived him."[19]

Incidentally, double rejection was also the lot of the Iberian Marranos. The gentiles rejected the Christian converts among them as Jews, and the rabbis (or at least most of them) rejected the Judaizers among them as idolators. There too Spinoza conforms to a long-established Marrano pattern, albeit in another context.

PRESERVING JEWISH MOTIFS IN A SECULAR FORM   Spinoza's Jewishness also crops up through his use of a series of classical Jewish motifs which he secularizes, severing them from their original context. As we have noted before, Spinoza preserves such notions as the eternity of Israel, the redemption, and the covenant with God. True, he invests each of these concepts with a new heterodox meaning, prosaic and subject to natural laws; yet the fact remains that he does preserve them in his new, secularized universe. It is still a Jew who is writing these things, even if he is already a heretic or quasi secular. With regard to the reestablishment of the kingdom of Israel, we have seen that while Spinoza does not explicitly recommend the idea, he certainly is ambivalent about it. Oldenburg was not entirely off the mark when he assumed that Spinoza the Jew would welcome such an eventuality. Even with regard to martyrdom—an agonizing issue for him—Spinoza has mixed feelings: as a rationalist he cannot justify the act of suicide and he deplores the "obstinacy of superstition," but as one brought up on these values, he also cannot cast off the sense of sublimity, and perhaps even pride, that martyrdom evokes in him.

Even certain variants of the idea of the "chosen people" are preserved by Spinoza. Implicitly, Judaism plays a special role in the shaping of a new secular world, for it is both an object of paradigmatic criticism and the source from which a new universal message is extracted.

SECULARIZING JEWISH HISTORY AS A NEW MESSAGE TO THE WORLD   The critique of Judaism is, first of all, meant to be the lever for the general secularization and modernization of civilization through the negation of its religious-transcendental foundations. Spinoza aims to accomplish this by specifically undercutting the principles of election and theocracy inherent in Judaism and thus, dialectically, he retains for Judaism a central role in shaping the new world.

Again, it is no accident that a Jew revises the history of his own people as a means of presenting a revolutionary message to the rest of the world. Allowing for differences in content, this resembles the work of the first Jewish Christians, particularly Paul and his disciples, only this time the pattern occurs in a secular version that repudiates Christianity and Judaism alike.

The early Jewish Christians saw the fulfillment of the Judaic message in its metamorphosis into a "universal" church under the aegis of the Savior, the Son of God. In practice, however, they did not accomplish genuine universality, but produced yet another historical creed. Christianity became a particular religion in competition with other religions, and primarily with Judaism itself—which the Christians persecuted by means of the law and by force of arms. For Spinoza, however, the universalization of Judaism must result in the rule of reason, that will displace *all* historical religions, those of persecutors and persecuted alike, and will abolish religious persecution altogether by granting equality and tolerance to all (including Jews who wish to remain as such).

Spinoza's position implies, moreover, that the secularization of Judaism, as a message for all of humanity, will succeed in undermining Christianity more than in destroying Judaism—for which Spinoza prophesies, as we have noted, eternality. Thus, in generalizing his critique of Jewish history into a message for humanity Spinoza does not commit the kind of "apostasy" or "defection to the enemy" that Jews had seen in converts to Christianity. From that standpoint, too, it is significant that Spinoza refused to convert even while following the Pauline pattern—which he reenacted, in contrast to Paul, on the level of universal reason, transcending all religious particularity and negating religious persecution of any kind.

MODERNIZING POLITICS THROUGH A CRITIQUE OF JEWISH THEOCRACY

More particularly, the critique of Judaism is to be a lever for the modernization of politics (and of political theory). Here Spinoza criticizes both forms of Jewish theocracy: that which he believes existed in ancient times, and that which developed in the exile into a "state within a state."

When Spinoza describes the political rule of God through his priestly representatives, he thinks more of the rabbis in the Diaspora than of Moses and the Levites. But his chief targets lie in the Christian world. He aims at the political claims of the pope and the Catholic establishment; at the demands of the Dutch Calvinist *predikanten*; at the Iberian Inquisition; and at the ostensibly modern principle which emerged from the wars of religion (*cuius regio eius religio* [religion in the state goes by its ruler]). Rather than truly modern, this principle was to Spinoza a culmination of the system we now call medieval, for it endorses the concept while allowing for a plurality of state religions. Spinoza, in contrast, demands to sever the states, as such, from all confessional links and other varieties of creed and ideology. This lays down the modern principle of the separation of state and religion (and, concomitantly, contra Hobbes, the principle of the liberal state). And all this Spinoza serves up to his audience of "theologians" and lay intellectuals via a critique of Jewish theocracy.

Jewish life in the Diaspora is another example of the medieval conception of polity that Spinoza seeks to expunge. Following Hobbes, Spinoza's ideal state is a single, all-embracing sovereign body, independent of any prescriptive authority, in which the citizen or subject is recognized by virtue of his individual identity rather than any collective quality vested in him. The medieval polity was based upon the mediation of autonomous groups—corporation, class, feudal lord, church, guild, and the like—to which the individual belonged and owed allegiance, and through which he related to the broader political entity (the kingdom or state). The Diaspora Jews embody this medieval principle in owing their allegiance to the phantom "state" they carry with them over and above the laws of the earthly state. And though Spinoza does not say so explicitly, the gentiles, in granting the Jews communal autonomy, were legally sanctioning the Jewish "state within a state" and its authority over its own "citizens." In the modern state, founded on the universality of reason, such authority would have no place.

While Spinoza's critique of Judaism was intended as a lever for modernizing of politics and heralded the secular, egalitarian state that came into being later, it was also fraught with implications for Jewish life itself. Implicit in it was the demand for religious tolerance and equal civil rights for the Jews, but also for the abolition of their communal autonomy and for the direct affiliation of the individual Jew to the state as a citizen. Spinoza thus adumbrates the two distinguishing features of the political condition of the Jew in the modern era, which was to emerge in the West after the French Revolution. This ties up with a third development that Spinoza foresaw: the new, existential kind of anti-Semitism, no longer contingent upon religious belief but upon the person of the Jew as such. These three developments have produced the typical situation of the modern Jew, who cannot (or does not wish to) escape his Jewish identity. As his traditional "ghetto" community has disintegrated, is he now to express his Jewish affiliation within the confines of his individuality, or within a voluntary group, or in a sovereign state of his own, or in some other way?

The logic of Spinoza's analysis seems to favor a quasi-Zionist solution. As modern politics can no longer admit the "kingdom within a kingdom" that marked Jewish life in the Diaspora, the Jews must either relinquish all self-rule and disperse as individuals among the gentiles, or establish their own political state. From a Spinozistic point of view, then, the only valid way for Jewish self-rule to continue in the modern era would be within a sovereign Jewish state. This implication (which Spinoza did not draw explicitly) may well have attracted Zionists like David Ben-Gurion, Nachum Sokolov, and Joseph Klausner to Spinoza even more than his famous remark in the *Theologico-Political Treatise*.

THE JEWISH RELIGION OF PRACTICE AS A MODEL OF UNIVERSAL RELIGION
Spinoza suggests a "universal religion" for the masses, based not on beliefs or opinions, but only on obedience to rules of action consistent with the demands of a universal practical intelligence. This is how Spi-

noza as philosopher addresses the problem of creating an enlightened society even while most persons do not attain true rationality. And as the model for the popular "universal religion," Spinoza uses the basic feature of Judaism, which, he believes, is founded on practical commands and not upon cognitive beliefs. In claiming that *all* true religion prescribes only actions and no opinions (following an entire Jewish school of thought), Spinoza's theological-political program takes its clue from its picture of Judaism, whose fundamental character it generalizes into a message for all of humanity. In other words, although Spinoza rejects Judaism as a particular historical religion, he employs one of its fundamental tenets as the underlying principle of the universal religion he hopes will supersede all historical religions.[20]

In depicting Judaism as merely practical, Spinoza follows a trend in medieval Judaism itself. And in calling it political, he does not mean to disparage or belittle Judaism (as Kant or Hegel did later). On the contrary, according to Spinoza (following Machiavelli and Hobbes) the proper role of religion *is* political. It is subservient to the state and should foster its basic goals (security and liberty, in Spinoza's view) by educating the people to a life of justice and solidarity; and these values can receive their content only from the civil government in its ordinary, secular legislation.

In this respect, the universal religion would be a political religion, its functions united in the indivisibility of the sovereign authority. This is a fundamentally "Jewish" model with its theocratic principle reversed. Yet even ancient Hebrew theocracy is preferable to regimes where the political authority is distinct from the religious, yet obeys its dictates. In ancient Israel, at least, religion was inherently political and functioned as the expression of the state. Spinoza wishes to restore this "Jewish" principle while reversing its inner balance: within their unity, the religious function should yield to the political and not vice versa.[21]

In its deep structure, then, the program of the *Theologico-Political Treatise* entails a kind of universalization of Judaism. Judaism as a "political" religion and as a religion of "commandments only," becomes the paradigm for what must take place in the world as a condition for rational progress. The message of Judaism is extended into a universal system in which historical Judaism, though abolished as a particular religion, fundamentally informs the system that replaces it.[22] Universalist Jews in the coming centuries, whether they were Spinozists or not (an outstanding example is Moses Hess), may well have viewed this as Spinoza's principal message for them.

Judaism thus continues to be the bearer of human progress, and the critique of Judaism, in both its negative and its positive aspects, is the lever of that evolution. Even if Spinoza did not pronounce this idea consciously, it certainly informs his consciousness and constitutes a distinct undercurrent of his thought.

THE FIRST SECULAR JEW?

Was Spinoza then the first secular Jew? What can be said confidently is that Spinoza took the first step in the eventual secularization of Jewish life by examining it empirically as a natural phenomenon subject solely to the forces of secular history. In doing so he opened a breach between the Jewish religion and traditional community, on the one hand, and the broader totality of Jewish life on the other. Yet the question remains of how to interpret this new Judaism. A multiplicity of alternatives, some (but not all) of them contradictory, present themselves, all contained as logical possibilities in Spinoza's position though he himself was historically unable to choose from among them.

1. *Assimilation*, which would place the individual directly within the universal dimension of society; and his link to the state, as the political sovereign, would then be his only binding affiliative relationship.
2. *Religious reform*, which would sever Jewish attachment to an autonomous political authority and make of its believers German, French, U.S., etc., citizens "of the Mosaic faith."
3. *Secular nationalism*, stressing the concept of the Jewish people (independently of religion and of political citizenship), as the basic existential and collective dimension of Jewish identity.
4. *Zionism*, entailing the renewal of Jewish political existence within an independent state.

These alternatives are neither exhaustive nor mutually exclusive, and each entails several nuances. Nor are they equally inferable from Spinoza's position. Assimilation, on Spinoza's theory, may solve the problem for individuals but not for the entire people, since gentile hostility alone will preserve the Jewish people forever. Religious reform within Judaism, though not incompatible with his views, was not on Spinoza's agenda; the only reform he envisaged went in the direction of a popular universal religion. As for the renewal of the Jewish state, Spinoza could not recommend its theocratic form, and its secular variety was still devoid of meaning for him. Although he knew that Jews, Marranos, and a nonbeliever like himself, were referred to as belonging to the same nation (and suffered similar conditions), the concept of Jewish national existence, as separate from religion, did not yet exist for him as a defined theoretical concept. Existentially, in his singular life and experience, Spinoza was indeed the harbinger of this idea but he did not articulate it consciously, not even as a personal demand. Had Spinoza claimed for himself the right to disavow religion yet remain within the congregation, we might have been able to view him as, consciously, the "first secular Jew." But as we saw in chapter 3, that title belongs, if at all, to his less gifted friend, Dr. Daniel De Prado, who insisted on his right to remain within the Jewish congregation while disputing the rabbinical commandments.[23]

Prado himself was not aware of the far-reaching significance of his demand. His approach was more personal and self-interested. Still, Prado, even more than Spinoza, embodies in his confused personality the emerging phenomenon of secular Judaism. He firmly resisted the principle before which Spinoza yielded, that only religion accords "citizenship" in the Jewish community. He insisted—in vain—on his right to belong to the congregation and to the Jewish people even after he had ceased to believe in the Torah and to observe its commandments.

Spinoza made no such claims. Imbued with broader intellectual interests, his message of secularity was meant for the world as a whole. He evidently assumed (correctly, at the time) that within Judaism this struggle was hopeless, and he was certainly affected by Da Costa's experience. What trapped him tragically at the personal level was this lack of perspective for change within Judaism. On the one hand, he knew he could not escape his Jewish condition, nor did he seek to do so; yet neither did he attempt to rehabilitate himself as a Jew (not even in the explicit direction of secular Judaism). Thus he was caught up in a double negation, rejected by the gentiles as a Jew and by the Jews as a heretic. Spinoza lived in this situation without being able to suggest any way to remedy it. Nonetheless, his life itself presaged possibilities that assumed historic importance in subsequent generations.

Secularization and the New Jewish "Citizenship"

Because the concept of secular Judaism is a modern one, and has an inevitable social dimension, it cannot be realized by the traditional congregation. The Jewish body to which the secular Jew wishes to go on belonging as a "citizen" is no longer the autonomous medieval congregation but the Jewish people. In Spinoza's time, however, only the medieval community structure could offer an expression of Jewish affiliation. From this perspective, too, what befell Prado and Spinoza must be considered anachronistic in terms of "Jewish secularism," even though it certainly anticipates it.

I use the word *anachronistic* descriptively, with no pejorative connotation. In the same anachronistic sense, Spinoza could be called, "the first assimilated Jew," albeit with less justification. It was one of the abstract possibilities in his case—and the distinction between mere possibilities and their actualization is crucial. None of these concepts—secular Judaism, Jewish nationalism, Zionism, even assimilation—has an a priori or supratemporal definition; their meaning emerges only in a historical context. In the absence of a historical reality to rely upon, they appear abstract and in certain cases absurd. The very concept of secularity was not yet established in Spinoza's time, let alone the more complex idea of Jewish secularism. People were identified above all by their religion—and this applies especially to the Jews. To belong to a particular society, one had to belong to the religion it confessed. True, Spinoza used his critique of Judaism to fight against this linkage of "citizenship" and religion. Yet whereas he offered a clear secular message to society at large, he had no solution for Judaism as such. Spinoza fought for the secularization of *individuals* and of *states*, but he lacked the modern concept of a nonpolitical secular Jewish nation. Marrano history and his own fate as a "Marrano of reason" provided him with an optic fiber, penetrating into the depth of the Jewish situation and distinguishing between the religion of the Jews and their actual, more fundamental existence. But Spinoza did not develop this insight beyond the theory that gentile hostility preserves the Jews and will do so forever. While offering Western society a clear, positive doctrine of secularity, for his own people Spinoza had only a cry of protest. He could neither accept nor find a way to sever the link in Judaism between "citizenship" and religious observance. Thus, in his time, even if he had wished to remain a part of his people he possessed neither the theoretical nor sociological means to do so.

At this juncture an immense existential difference is apparent between Spinoza and the contemporary Jewish situation. Today a Jew can become non-observant and deny the divine origin of his religion without losing his Jewish "citizenship" either in the eyes of non-Jews or in the eyes of his own people. Not only atheist Jews exist today but, in rare cases, even atheist rabbis as well. In the State of Israel the majority of Jewish citizens define themselves as non-observant or down right secular. Jewish identity is unquestioned, even if its content is debated. While the problems that Jewish secularism entails have not been resolved, it is today a living, historically resonant concept, for Jews both in the Diaspora and especially in the State of Israel. Spinoza helped set this revolution in motion—not because he explicitly enunciated it but because it was the foremost challenge that his case posited for the generations to come.

In the past two hundred years, following the emancipation which undermined the traditional Jewish congregations from within and the Holocaust which destroyed them from without, new forms of Jewish existence have emerged. Some of them are still in the formative stage, some already moribund, but all seeking historical legitimacy. They encompass a multiplicity of approaches, some deriving from the pluralism that informed Jewish civilization even in the past, others superseding it. But Spinoza himself, who presaged these developments, could not have benefited from its results, but was forced to live as a lost and alienated Jew, caught between two negations and two false identities, neither of which was necessarily consistent with his own self-consciousness. Even had he wished to remain a loyal "citizen" of his people (and we have no proof of this, beyond a few textual ambiguities) he would not have been able to do so, not only because the Jews rejected him, but also because Christian society was yet undisposed to recognize persons independently of their religious affiliation. At the same time, Spinoza was instrumental in the emergence of European secularism and through it, indirectly also contributed to the secularization of Judaism, which his own life foretold. Therefore, when this process finally penetrated Jewish society as well, it evoked the name of one Baruch Benedictus de Spinoza—Jewish heretic, lost and alienated, but Jew nevertheless, whose personal fate embodied and presaged the fate of his people in later generations and the multiplicity of ways in which they tried to cope with modernity.

Lifting the Ban

From time to time, petitions are made to have Spinoza's ban revoked. In 1925, the late Israeli historian, Joseph Klausner, stood on Mount Scopus, Jerusalem, and proclaimed: "Baruch Spinoza, you are our brother." In the early 1950s, Israel's prime minister, David Ben-Gurion, conducted a campaign to have the ban lifted. And in 1953, the then Chief Rabbi of Israel, Yizhak (Isaac) Halevi Herzog, replied to an application from the late G. Herz Shikmoni, director of the "Spinozaeum" in Haifa, asking him if the excommunication was still in force from the point of view of the *halakhah*. In reply to the question of whether the excommunication was intended to apply only to Spinoza's lifetime or also to future generations, Rabbi Herzog did not rule, leaving the matter open to further consideration. But with regard to the ban on Spinoza's works, the rabbinical ruling was clear:

> I have examined the text of the proclamation [the writ of excommunication quoted at the beginning of chapter 1] and I have found: (a) at the end in regard to his books and composition it is written only "we warn" and not "we warn to excommunicate"; (b) even if we say that we can deduce the end from the beginning, it is shown by the language of the above sentence that the intention is not specified for future generations, but only for the period of Spinoza's lifetime. It is possible that it was thought unnecessary to prolong the period of the ban, and it is possible that due to modesty the authorities did not wish to rule for future generations. Be this as it may, it seems that the ban on the reading of Spinoza's books and compositions no longer stands.[24]

A legalistic quibble, in other words, enabled the chief rabbi to rule that there was no longer a ban on the reading of Spinoza. And one gains the impression from the beginning of the letter that Rabbi Herzog was also seeking a loophole that would have enabled him to rule that the excommunication, too, was no longer in force.

Yet all these attempts to have the ban revoked are really beside the point. Spinoza does not need certification by any authorities, whoever they may be, and one cannot but be struck by the astonishing discrepancy between his actual impact on intellectual history and the attempts to grant him belated institutional legitimization. The significance of the ban was in isolating Spinoza from the actual Jewish community of his day, and whoever wishes to revoke it today is late by three hundred years. The demand to revoke the ban would not sound anachronistic only if it were to have some symbolic meaning—national, perhaps, or ideological—rather than being purely religious; such a case, however, would entail the contradiction of both adopting the religious concept of the ban (as implied in the demand to revoke Spinoza's) and at the same time rejecting it (by changing its meaning).

Lastly, and this is perhaps the crux of the matter, who in the Jewish world today might be authorized to accept Spinoza back into the Jewish fold? The Lubavitcher Rebbe? The prime minister of Israel? The board of the Jewish Theological Seminary? The B'nai B'rith? There is no longer a single normative Judaism today—a development of which Spinoza himself was a harbinger.

In abandoning the observant Judaism of his day, but refusing to convert to Christianity, Spinoza unwittingly embodied the alternatives which lay in wait for Jews of later generations following the encounter of Judaism with the modern world. As a result of this encounter, there is no longer one norm of Jewish existence today. There are Orthodox and secular Jews, Conservative and Reform Jews, Zionist and anti-Zionist Jews, and nuances and subcategories within all of these; in fact, Judaism today is determined by the way actual Jews live it, and not by any one compulsory model. This being the case, there is no longer an institution or an individual with the authority to include or exclude, to excommunicate or bring back to the fold (even symbolically). Since Spinoza himself foretold this development (less in his philososphy than in his biography), he has once more become central to contemporary thinking about Judaism and the complexities of its existence and survival.

Postscript

As this book was going to the publisher, I was interested to note on a visit to the newly reopened Jewish Museum in Amsterdam, that without fanfare, Spinoza has been readmitted by his erstwhile community. In a section devoted to "Jewish Identity," the museum has a text explaining that for many centuries, being Jewish had entailed belonging to the orthodox Jewish community; but ever since the Act of Civil Equality (1796), granting political emancipation to the Dutch Jews, "every Jewish person could decide what expression to give to his or her Jewishness" and how to relate to the Jewish community. On this new description Spinoza will certainly count as Jewish—as indeed he does in this museum. The text is illustrated by an impressive gallery of Jewish characters, all unnamed but some easily identifiable. There is an orthodox Jew, a secular intellectual, a reform cantor, a coquette nineteenth-century matron, a modern woman wrapped in a prayer shawl, two orthodox boys with ritual curls (*peot*), a medieval Jew in oriental cap, a Jew in Nazi Europe wearing a yellow David's Star, an Israeli baby in woolen *yarmulka* (Zionist-orthodox), a contemporary young man in loosened tie—and the familiar features of Baruch Spinoza and, at the very end, the severe and distinguished face of the great Amsterdam Rabbi Isaac Aboab, one of the signatories of Spinoza's ban. So finally the banned dissenter and the banning rabbi end up together in this minor pantheon of Jewish diversity. What better way for the Amsterdam Jewish community to readmit Spinoza, not by a declamatory gesture like lifting the ban, but by recognizing, with good historical sense, the new Jewish situation which Spinoza's own case had anticipated and tragically embodied.

Notes

1. Spinoza does speak at the end of *Ethics* of a kind of immortality of the soul, but not in any individual sense; the individual perishes and what remains is a kind of eternal truth. See also chapter 6 below.

2. Quoted in the French edition of Spinoza's works (Paris: Flammarion, 1969).

3. Richard Popkin, "Epicureanism and Scepticism in the Early Seventeenth Century," in *Philomathes*, ed. R. B. Palmey and R. Hamerton-Kelly (The Hague: Nijhoff, 1971).

4. Yosef Yerushalmi, "Marranos Returning to Judaism in the 17th Century: Their Jewish Knowledge and Psychological Readiness," in *Proceedings of the Fifth World Congress of Jewish Studies* [Heb.] (Jerusalem: World Union of Jewish Studies, 1969), 2:202.

5. *Treatise on the Intellect* §17.

6. Jean M. Lucas, *The Oldest Biography of Spinoza*, ed. A. Wolf (London: Allen and Unwin, 1927).

7. See A. Wiznitzer, "The Merger Agreement and Regulations of Congregation Talmud Torah of Amsterdam, 1638–39," *Historia Judaica* 20 (1958): 48. Between 1623 and 1677 there were thirty-five excommunications recorded in the records of the congregation (mainly the book of *Ascamot*) of which five, including Spinoza's, have not been revoked, but the number of actual bans probably exceeded those on record; see Y. Kaplan, "The Social Functions of the *Herem* in the Portuguese Jewish Community of Amsterdam in the Seventeenth Century," in *Dutch Jewish History: Proceedings of the Symposium on the History of the Jews in the Netherlands*, ed. Jozeph Michman (Jerusalem: Institute for Research on Dutch Jewry, 1984), pp. 111–55, esp. appendix.

8. The text was published and introduced by Jacob Meijer, *Hugo de Groot: Remonstrantie nopende de ordre dije in de landen van Hollandt ende Westvrieslandt dijent gestelt op de Joden* [. . .] (Amsterdam, 1949). He also published a shorter English essay, "Hugo Grotius' *Remonstrantie*," *Jewish Social Studies* 17 (1955): 91–103. See also A. K. Kuhn, "Hugo Grotius and the Emancipation of the Jews in Holland," *Publications of the American Jewish Historical Society* 31 (1928):

173–80; and Salo W. Baron, *A Social and Religious History of the Jews*, 2d ed., 18 vols. (New York: Columbia University Press, 1973), 16: 310–13. Baron's account has been severely criticized by Jozeph Michman, "Historiography of the Jews in the Netherlands," in *Dutch Jewish History*, pp. 16–22. Michman takes issue with Baron's claims that Grotius was more liberal toward the Jews than Pauw was and that eventually the regulations passed were in fact more restrictive on paper than in practice. He also cites various minor mistakes in Baron. What makes a decision difficult is that Pauw's original text has been lost and there is no reliable comparative analysis of Grotius, Pauw, and the actual regulations passed by various cities afterward.

9. J. L. Teicher, "Why Was Spinoza Banned?" *Menorah Journal* 45 (1957): 41–60.

CHAPTER 2

1. This had been noted by contemporary witnesses like Hugo Grotius, who, in his *Jaerboeken en Historïen* (1598), remarked that many Marranos arrived to flee the Inquisition "and others with a view to greater gain" (quoted by Jacob Meijer, "Hugo Grotius' *Remonstrantie*," *Jewish Social Studies* 17 [1955]: 91).

2. See Samuel Schwarz, *Os Christãos novos em Portugal no século XX* (Lisboa: Empresa Portuguesa de Livros, 1925), p. 99.

3. See Fritz Baer, *Die Juden in christlichen Spanien* (Berlin: Schocken, 1936), Vol. 1, Pt. 2: Inquisitionsakten, no. 423.

4. See Y. Baer, *History of the Jews in Christian Spain*, 2 vols. (Philadelphia: Jewish Publication Society of America, 1961), 2: 276–77.

5. References to Rojas, as well as to other names and places mentioned in this chapter, are given in the notes of the following chapters where these topics are expanded.

6. There are three kinds of knowledge in Spinoza:
   1. *Imaginatio* (Imagination). This is confused knowledge (i.e., error or accidental truth) gained from crude sense perception, association, hearsay (including authority), and the like.
   2. *Ratio* (Reason). This is knowledge of the universal laws of nature and reason, both in themselves and as applied in particular causal explanations.
   3. *Scientia intuitiva* (Intuitive Knowledge). This is a synoptic grasp of some particular thing as it inheres in God-nature: essence through an immanent chain of causes. (This is a rational intuition explained in chapter 6.)

7. Yosef Yerushalmi, *From Spanish Court to Italian Ghetto* (Seattle: University of Washington Press, 1981).

8. Violated only by Hegel and the Hegelian offshoots in nineteenth-century ideologies. See Yirmiyahu Yovel, *Spinoza and Other Heretics: The Adventures of Immanence* (Princeton: Princeton University Press, 1989), chap. 2.

9. See M. Bataillon, *Érasme et l'Espagne* (Paris: E. Dros, 1937); enl. Spanish

ed.: *Erasmo y España*, 2 vols. (México: Fondo de Cultura Económica, 1950, 1966).

CHAPTER 3

1. The literature on the Amsterdam Jewish community is rich and growing. See Salo W. Baron, *A Social and Religious History of the Jews*, 2d ed., 18 vols. (New York: Columbia University Press, 1973), vol. 15, chap. 9, "Dutch Jerusalem," pp. 3–37, the notes of which (pp. 379–411) contain a rich bibliography. For further references, see H. Méchoulan and G. Nahon, "Amsterdam, des Marranes à la communauté juive portugaise," introduction to *Espérance d'Israel*, by Menasseh ben Israel (Paris: Vrin, 1979), pp. 15–34, which also contains many bibliographical notes; Cecil Roth, *A History of the Marranos* (Philadelphia: Jewish Publication Society of America, 1941), esp. chap. 9; G. Nahon, "Amsterdam, métropole occidentale des *Sefarades* au XVIIe siècle," *Cahiers Spinoza* 3 (1980): 15–50, also with references. For a recent bibliographical survey, see also idem, "Les Marranes espagnols et portugais et les communautés juives issues du Marranisme dans l'historiographie récente (1960–1975)," *Revue des Etudes Juives* 136 (1977): 297–367. Some of the older sources and many specialized studies are included in Baron and the other bibliographies.

Most of the hitherto-published documents on Spinoza's Jewish-Marrano links (including those found by Revah) along with less reliable accounts and chronicles are contained in Gabriel Albiac's recent work, *La Sinagoga Vacía* (Madrid: Hiperion, 1987), which reached me after my manuscript had gone to the publisher.

2. Carl Gebhardt, *Die Schriften des Uriel da Costa* (Amsterdam: Curis Societatis Spinozanae, 1922), p. xix.

3. The *Exemplar humanae vitae* was first published in 1687, almost half a century after Da Costa's suicide, by the Remonstrant (liberal Calvinist of the Arminian School) theologian Philip van Limborch (1633–1712) as an appendix to his "friendly debate" with the former Marrano scholar and Jewish apologist, Isaac Orobio de Castro (see below), entitled *De Veritate Religionis Christianae amica collatio cum erudito Judeo* (Gouda, 1687), reissued in facsimile by Gregg International, Farnborough, Hampshire, in 1969. Limborch claims to have found his copy of the text among the papers of his great-uncle, Simon Episcopius (1583–1643), a leading Remonstrant theologian of tolerant leanings, to whom it had presumably been given "by an outstanding man of this town [Amsterdam]." Limborch himself polemicized against Da Costa's deism but deemed it important to publish and confront his challenge.

Da Costa reportedly had written other tracts that were banned and probably even destroyed during his lifetime, but that can, perhaps, be partly reconstructed from polemical responses written against them. Gebhardt (in *Schriften d. da Costa*) published, along with the *Exemplar*, a reconstruction of the two texts he attributed to Da Costa: first, *Sobre a Mortalidade da Alma do Homem* (On the mortality of the human soul), an attack on the belief in the afterlife, to which the former Marrano doctor, Samuel da Silva, wrote a strong polemical reply while quoting several sections from Da Costa's own argument; and second, *Propostas contra a Tradição* (Propositions Against Tradition), to which the Venetian rabbi Leon Modena may have responded in his Hebrew *Magen ve-Tsina*, written to refute an unnamed heretic in Hamburg and paraphrasing that heretic's objections in some detail. The identification of the Hamburg heretic with Da Costa, first suggested by S. Seeligman in 1911 and S. Porges in 1918 (see Gebhardt, *Schriften d. da Costa*, p. 233), has some plausibility but cannot be taken as conclusive. Gebhardt thought he had made this identification conclusive by finding a Portuguese manuscript in the hand of Raphaël Mosé d'Aguilar that contained a shorter version of the same heretical objections, along with d'Aguilar's presumably independent responses to them. Gebhardt concluded that what he had was a copy of Da Costa's *original* Portuguese *Propostas* (hence Da Costa and the Hamburg heretic are one and the same). Recent examination, however (by J. P. Osier), has shown that d'Aguilar's text was simply an unpublished Portuguese translation (which did not mention the author's name) of Modena's *Magen ve-Tsina*. This undermines Gebhardt's "independent corroboration" of Da Costa's identity with the Hamburg heretic to whom Modena responded, although it does not, as Osier believes, exclude this identity altogether.

Osier's reasons for excluding the *Propostas* are given in *Avant-propos* and *Annexe* (pp. 249–51) of his recent French Da Costa anthology, *D'Uriel da Costa à Spinoza* (Paris: Berg International, 1983). On the other hand, Osier accepts the authenticity of the *Exemplar* almost *in toto* and without reservations (pp. 59–61, 73–74). See also idem, "Un aspect du judaisme individualiste d'Uriel da Costa," *Cahiers Spinoza* 3 (1980): 101–15. For a new Spanish translation (with notes and references), see Uriel Da Costa, *Espejo de una vida humana*, ed. Gabriel Albiac (Madrid: Hiperion, 1985).

The history of Da Costa literature (and legend) up to 1922 is given in Gebhardt, *Schriften d. da Costa*, pp. 225–33, and enriched in Osier, *D'Uriel da Costa à Spinoza*. Documentary research into Da Costa's life was begun in 1877 by J. Perles, and it continued with J. Mendes dos Remedios—who found the text of Da Costa's Amsterdam ban (1911), S. Seeligman (1911), and S. Porges (1918). After Gebhardt, significant findings about Da Costa's life and family in Porto, based upon the records of the Portuguese Inquisition, were made by Artur de Magalhães Basto (1930–1931) and especially by Israel S. Revah (1962–1973). Of particular interest is Revah's article, "La religion d'Uriel da Costa, Marrane de Porto, d'après des documents inédits," *Revue de l'Histoire des Religions* 161 (1962): 45–76. This work significantly modifies the picture of Da Costa's background and state of knowledge as drawn in the *Exemplar*. For Revah's genealogical research into Da Costa's family, see his reports in the *Annuaire du Collège de France* (1969–1970), pp. 325–26; (1970–1971), pp. 569–78; (1972–1973), pp. 653–63—all entitled "Du marranisme au judaisme et au déisme: Uriel da Costa et sa famille." Also by Revah are "Uriel da Costa," *Annuaire de l'Ecole Pratique des Hautes Etudes* (1962–1963), pp. 46–47; and "Les écrits portugais d'Uriel da Costa," *Annuaire de l'Ecole Pratique des Hautes Etudes* (1963–1965), pp. 265–74.

4. Or at least, the version of the author of the *Exemplar*. Whether this work is truly autobiographical or a biography written by someone else in an assumed autobiographical genre is, for present purposes, of secondary importance; what counts is Da Costa's portrait as such. On this I follow Revah, who accepted the text in principle while recognizing—as did Gebhardt (see *Schriften d. da Costa*, p. 105)—interpolations by foreign hands.

5. *Exemplar humanae vitae*, ibid., p. 122.

6. Cf. note 3 above.

7. In his "La religion d'Uriel da Costa," see esp. p. 73. Methodologically, there are two different questions: First, who wrote the bulk of the *Exemplar*? And second, how accurate is it? For my purposes, the second question is by far the more important; Revah, in confirming parts of the *Exemplar's* account while disproving or correcting others, helps give a more accurate picture of the historical Da Costa—a picture that reinforces the thesis about Marrano religious ambiguities and split identities. Even if, hypothetically, the *Exemplar* should be proven to be not really autobiographical but a biography of Da Costa written in the assumed first person (as in a picaresque novel, which the *Exemplar* sometimes resembles in reverse; see Osier, *D'Uriel da Costa à Spinoza*, pp. 65–68), the consequence for my purposes may well remain the same.

8. Quoted in ibid., p. 60. Osier, however, seems to revert to the other extreme in accepting the *Exemplar* in one piece, as one accepts a work of art, and in paying little heed to the serious critical points raised by Revah and by Gebhardt (see *Schriften d. da Costa*, p. 260).

9. For example lighting candles on Saturday night; fasting on Mondays and Thursdays; fasting on 17 Tamuz and 9 Ab (two anniversaries of the destruction of Jerusalem); a longer fast of Esther (before Purim).

10. For example incorporating Christian Sunday prayers into Marrano liturgy, or abstaining from eating meat during Easter or at meals terminating a fast (Revah, "La Religion d'Uriel da Costa," pp. 74–75).

11. Ibid., p. 74.

12. Yosef Yerushalmi, "Marranos Returning to Judaism in the Seventeenth Century: Their Jewish Knowledge and Psychological Readiness" (in Hebrew), in *Proceedings of the Fifth World Congress of Jewish Studies* (Jerusalem, 1969), 2: 201–9. A similar point is made in idem, *From Spanish Court to Italian Ghetto* (Seattle: University of Washington Press, 1981).

13. Yerushalmi, "Marranos Returning to Judaism," p. 208.

14. On this point I fully concur with Yerushalmi's interesting suggestion (*From Court to Ghetto*, p. 209). Da Costa's presumed Erasmian leaning is discussed in another context by Osier (*D'Uriel da Costa à Spinoza*, p. 74), to explain why Da Costa expected to find sympathetic hearing among the Dutch liberal Calvinists—who in their way have "prolonged an Erasmian strand within Erasmus' own fatherland." Osier speculates that this is why Da Costa

sent, or "addressed," the *Examplar* to the Remonstrant leader Simon Episcopius.

15. Of the extensive literature on these issues, Marcel Bataillon, *Erasmo y España*, 2 vols. (Mexico: Fondo de Cultura Económica, 1966). See also Antonio Márquez, *Los Alumbrados*, 2d rev. ed. (Madrid: Taurus, 1980).

16. I hope to elaborate on this issue in a forthcoming work on Marranism.

17. Richard Popkin, "Epicureanism and Scepticism in the Early Seventeenth Century," in *Philomathes*, ed. R. B. Palmey and R. Hamerton-Kelly (The Hague: Nijhoff, 1971), p. 353.

18. Da Costa's case calls to mind Hegel's arguments against the Stoics and other subjectivist philosophers (*The Phenomenology of Mind*, tr. J. B. Baillie [New York: Harper Torchbooks, 1967], p. 244) who claim that a person, due to his inner consciousness, can be free of all circumstances, "on the throne as well as in fetters"; which implies that a person can live without alienation—or can live at all—even when the reality he faces in his life embodies a principle that is utterly opposed to his inner consciousness, for it will allow of no legitimate expression or social externalization of subjective feelings and beliefs.

19. Da Costa himself complains of harassment by the children (*Exemplar*, p. 109).

20. Carl Gebhardt, *Spinoza* (Leipzig: Reclam, 1932), p. 15.

21. Da Costa's *Exemplar* was unavailable to Spinoza, and Da Costa's refutation of the immortality of the soul was banned and its copies lost or destroyed. However, Da Costa's views were fairly well known from secondary sources and from polemics against them. Harry A. Wolfson, *The Philosophy of Spinoza*, 2 vols. (Cambridge: Harvard University Press, 1948), 2: 324–25, and Revah have even suggested that Spinoza (*Ethics*, pt. 5, prop. 36), uses Da Costa's own words when opposing the latter's doctrine of the soul and trying to maintain some version of immortality; in Revah's opinion, this wording is an explicit gesture to "poor Uriel"; see Israel S. Revah, *Spinoza et Juan de Prado* (Paris: Mouton, 1959), p. 37.

22. Gebhardt, *Schriften d. da Costa*, pp. xxxiii–xxxix.

23. See Israel S. Revah's report in *Annuaire du Collège de France* (1967), p. 519.

24. Besides his findings about Da Costa and his family, Revah made also outstanding findings about other intellectuals active in Jewish Amsterdam. See, esp., the documents appended in Revah, *Spinoza et Prado*, and idem, "Aux origines de la rupture spinozienne," *Revue des Etudes Juives* 123 (1964): 359–429; and in his reports in the *Annuaire de l'Ecole Pratique des Hautes Etudes and the Annuaire du Collège de France*; see also idem, "Spinoza et les hérétiques de la communauté judéo-portugaise d'Amsterdam," *Revue de l'Histoire des Religions* 154 (1958): 173–218; and idem, "L'hérésie marrane dans l'Europe catholique du 15e au 18e siècle," in *Hérésies et sociétés dans l'Europe preindustrielle*, ed. J. Le Goff (Paris: Mouton, 1968), pp. 327–37. Among other things, Revah tries to eliminate the possibility that Spinoza's heresies were induced by external, non-Jewish factors. Dutch biographers, notably Meinsma, tend to picture

Spinoza as influenced mainly by the Collegiant sect. This view is refuted by Madeleine Francès, who, in *Spinoza dans les pays néerlandais de la seconde moitié du XVIIe siècle* (Paris: Alcan, 1937), points out the incompatibility of the relevant dates. Francès stresses the influence of Spinoza's libertine teacher, Van den Enden, as decisive in his intellectual development; Revah, however, with some success, again by analyzing dates and again by using calendary arguments, tends to minimize the role of Van den Enden, adding also that the freethinker had actually retained his Catholic identity. Having presumably eliminated external influences, Revah turns to undermining the testimony of Spinoza's early biographers—Lucas and Colerus—who lacked firsthand information, and gives credence to the testimony of the New Jews—Orobio de Castro and Daniel Levi de Barrios—who saw the Spinoza affair as a joint Prado-Spinoza affair and (on Revah's reading) believed that Prado was responsible for Spinoza's heresies.

Revah's findings, however, only reinforce Gebhardt's original intuition about the split Marrano mind. As for Spinoza's heresy, Revah tends to interpret it as a personal event or as the result of a chain of several people's leading one another to heresy; he sees the chain as triggered not so much by the Marrano situation as by rationalist tendencies that had been prevalent in Jewish Spain even before the expulsion. In this chapter, however, I interpret Revah's findings in terms of a specific psychocultural structure which the Marrano experience produced and by which, as Gebhardt claimed, Spinoza's heresy, too, must be explained.

25. Superficially, it may seem that concreteness demands indication of an influence exercised by one particular individual on some other particular individual and thus provide a proximate cause. Yet in fact, in taking each individual and every event in its separateness, one disjoins and therefore abstracts them from the context in which they acquire their meaning—a context which, indeed, cannot be understood without them (or without their similars), but which in turn is equally indispensable for understanding them. Using such holistic explanatory structures—and as many particular facts reinforcing them as possible—is a necessary condition for the concreteness of the explanation. The use of such structures is not of itself committed to any ontological position: Do they have independent existence in the sense one attributes to persons or to facts in any other sense? Or are these only methodological ideal types? One need not decide these matters, while recognizing the methodological indispensability of the universal structures as such.

26. On Orobio, see Y. Kaplan, *From Christianity to Judaism: The Life and Work of the Marrano Isaac Orobio de Castro*, in Hebrew (Jerusalem: Magnes Press, 1982); on the Orobio-Prado conflict, see especially pp. 128–40. Earlier discussions of Orobio are mentioned in the bibliography, and also in Revah, *Spinoza et Prado*; and Yerushalmi, *From Court to Ghetto*, p. 325n. The first to quote Orobio's manuscript testimony and point out its significance for Spinoza's background was Carl Gebhardt. Of the three texts Orobio wrote against Prado, Gebhardt knew only the major one, the *Epistola Invectiva contra*

Prado: Un Philósopho Médico que dudava o no creía la verdad de la divina escriptura y pretendió encubrir su malicia con la afectada confession de Dios y Ley de Naturaleza. For other titles and a list of extant transcripts see Kaplan, *From Christianity to Judaism,* app. d. The first version of this tract was entitled *Tratado contra la ympiedad de los deistas;* Orobio wrote a personalized preface against Prado (see Revah, "Origines de la rupture," p. 427); later Orobio dropped this direct address to the excommunicated Prado and wrote a new *Prologo* from which his remarks on the former Marranos are excerpted. In addition to the *Epistola Invectiva,* Orobio wrote two other works against Prado: *Carta Apologética del Doctor Ishack Orobio de Castro al Doctor Prado* and *Carta al hijo de el Doctor Prado.* The latter two texts and most of the *Epistola invectiva* were published by Revah, *Spinoza et Prado,* "Textes et Documents," pp. 84–163.

For an interesting—and ironic—use which the French libertines made of Orobio's polemics, see Miguel Benitez, "Orobio de Castro et la littérature clandestine," in Oliver Bloch (ed.), *Le matérialisme du XVIIIᵉ siècle et la littérature clandestine* (Paris: Vrin, 1982), pp. 219–26. Although Orobio had opposed the libertines and passionately defended the religious outlook, his being a Jew (and a former Marrano) in polemics against the ruling Christian religion (for example, his argument that the Bible nowhere demands belief in the Messiah as a condition for salvation), served the libertines themselves as a weapon. As Benitez says: "Under the pretext of refuting Spinoza's atheism, this literary genre usually served to propagate his ideas" (ibid., p. 220, my tr.). So Orobio, we might add, remained a Marrano even after his death.

27. From Orobio's first *Prologo* to his *Epistola Invectiva,* p. 687, published by Revah, *Spinoza et Prado,* "Textes et Documents," p. 90. An earlier German quotation appears in Gebhardt's, *Schriften d. da Costa,* p. xx.

28. Ibid., p. 694; Revah, *Spinoza et Prado,* p. 93.

29. Gebhardt, *Schriften d. da Costa,* pp. xixff. Revah maintained that Orobio had Prado specifically in mind, but this does not lessen the broader significance of this text and of the target audience of the invective letter it prefaces. Indeed, the work argues separately against different kinds of New Jewish skeptics and heretics, who must have existed if Orobio thought it worthwhile to combat them in such detail.

30. Yerushalmi, "Marranos Returning to Judaism," p. 202.

31. Orobio, *Epistola Invectiva,* discurso 3, cap. 1, pp. 775–77; Revah, *Spinoza et Prado,* "Textes et Documents," pp. 126–27.

32. Yerushalmi to author; Cardoso's words in Yerushalmi's rendering (*From Court to Ghetto,* p. 325).

33. On the semi-Christian motifs in the Sabbatian movement, see Gershom Scholem, *Sabbatai Sevi: The Mystical Messiah,* 1626–1676 (Princeton: Princeton University Press, 1973). Sabbatai Ṣevi calls himself "the only-begotten and first-born Son of God" (p. 616); he fixes his mother's tomb as a place of worship (pp. 613–14); he addresses the Jews as "Lord your God Sabbatai Ṣevi" (p. 247); his soul is mystically rooted in Jesus as its demonic "shell" and he is to redeem Jesus' soul (pp. 285–86). Another important motif is the deprecation

of external practice and the crucial importance placed on faith in the Messiah, which becomes a major religious value in itself. Scholem (pp. 795–97) calls this a "Christian" element generally; in addition to its special place in reformed Christianity, the emphasis on inner religious consciousness as opposed to external cult also has specific affinities with the Marrano experience and was launched within Catholic Iberia by religious reformers and mystics, many of whom were of converso origin. That Saint Teresa and Abraham Cardoso may both on both sides of the Jewish-Christian barrier, have drawn part of their mystical nonconformity from a similar Marrano-like structure may be a surprising, but certainly not wild, conjecture.

34. For this reason, Yerushalmi classifies Abraham Cardoso himself within a fourth group of New Jews, whose Marrano background shows in their attachment to the "heretical mysticism of the Sabbatian movement" (*From Court to Ghetto*, pp. 46–47). On Marrano elements in Sabbatianism, see also Gershom Scholem, "Redemption through Sin," in his *Messianic Idea in Judaism* (New York: Schocken, 1971).

35. It was equally expressed in religious unrest, dissent, and reform within the Catholic fold itself, accounting as we saw at the end of the previous chapter, in part for Erasmianism, the Illuminati, and Sebastianism in Catholic Ibera.

36. See L. Alvares Vega, *Het Beth Haim van Ouderkerk* (Amsterdam: Van Gorcum, 1975). I am grateful to the author for his guidance and instruction during my 1978 visit to the cemetery.

37. See I. S. Emmanuel, *Precious Stones of the Jews of Curaçao* (New York: Bloch, 1957). An exhibition of photographs of this cemetery by Micha Baram was shown at the Museum of the Jewish Diaspora in Tel Aviv, Winter 1981.

38. See Heinrich Graetz, *History of the Jews* (1891–98), 6 vols. (Philadelphia: Jewish Publication Society of America, 1967), 4: 535.

39. Only Rabbi Isaac Aboab's tombstone is ornamented, but not with animal or human figures.

40. Revah, "Origines de la rupture," p. 367.

41. Although Gebhardt stresses the milieu (*Umwelt*) in which Spinoza developed rather than the unidirectional influence of any single person who corrupted him, he does attribute a special role to Prado as the person through whom Spinoza became acquainted with the extant naturalist views; see "Juan de Prado," *Chronicon Spinozanum* 3 (1923): 273. Gebhardt, who first discovered the testimony of Orobio and de Barrios and established its relevance, was, however, somewhat carried away by what he thought were their views; he goes as far as seeing Spinoza's *deus sive natura* contained *in nuce* in Prado's views (when the latter were actually of the more ordinary transcendent kind of deism and thus worlds apart from Spinoza's immanent nature God). However, even when he exaggerates, there is nothing in Gebhardt's position to suggest a rigid, unidirectional corruption as Revah seems to uphold. On the contrary, it is Gebhardt's profound and fruitful intuition about the Marrano split mind

that helps correct both Revah's approach and, when necessary, Gebhardt's own occasional exaggerations.

42. Kaplan (*From Judaism to Christianity*, p. 111n) conjectures that Prado helped in Orobio's admission by election to the theological school where Prado studied. But Orobio speaks of several and continuous favors that Prado extended to him (*Carta Apologética*, p. 876).

43. Israel S. Revah, "Du marranisme au judaisme et au déisme: Uriel da Costa et sa famille," *Annuaire du Collège de France* (1972–1973), pp. 650–53.

44. Revah, ibid., p. 650. Prado uses a motif that became prevalent in the hybrid religion of the Judaizing Marranos: salvation (a Christian theme) can be attained only by the Law of Moses and not by Christianity.

45. Ibid.

46. It also provides an interesting corroboration of Yerushalmi's thesis about the possible sources of the Marrano's Jewish knowledge; see above, note 12.

47. This phenomenon is not known from Marrano life; Romano may be exaggerating and ornamenting his testimony. However, it may also be the case that Prado on his own initiative had instituted such an oath. This would reinforce his image as a person particularly bent upon the brotherhood aspect of the Judaizing Marrano's existence.

48. Revah, "Du marranisme au judaism," *Annuaire du Collège de France* (1972), pp. 651–52.

49. See Revah, "Origins de la rupture," pp. 366ff; documents et textes, pp. 402–8.

50. Don Juan Pinhero (or Pinheyro or Piñero), a physician whom Orobio knew personally. Cf. Kaplan, *From Christianity to Judaism*, p. 112n.

51. He clearly was not a simple informer or adventurer, but a complex person, either an utter skeptic or a confused religious seeker, but above all and fundamentally a *Marrano*, someone for whom religious duplicity has almost become a way of life.

52. Revah, "Du marranisme au judaisme," *Annuaire du College de France* (1972), pp. 650–51.

53. Orobio, *Carta Apologética*, p. 881 (my translation of quotation in Revah, *Spinoza et Prado*, p. 133).

54. Ibid.

55. The preface to the first version of the *Epistola Invectiva*.

56. I use the adjectives *doctrinal* and *theoretical* to denote a theory that contains not only beliefs but also rules of conduct and a prescribed way of life. These rules and prescriptions constitute the theory, or the doctrine, behind the daily acts.

57. Revah, *Spinoza et Prado*, p. 22.

58. The version used by Gebhardt reads "student physician" (*estudiante medico*). Gebhardt rightly parallels this with the term *philosopho medico* by which Orobio explicitly refers to Prado in one of the early titles of the *Epistola Invectiva* (Gebhardt, "Juan de Prado," p. 280). The term *medico* connotes knowledge of natural science in general.

59. Revah, *Spinoza et Prado*, p. 22.

60. Revah, "Du marranisme au judaisme" *Annuaire du Collège de France* (1970), pp. 563–64. Kaplan, ibid., p. 132n, reports having seen the different version: 327v, MS 48 D 6, Montesinos Ets-Haim Library, formerly in Amsterdam, now in Jerusalem at the Jewish National and University Library.

61. Revah himself rejects this suggestion and calls the occurrences of *este* "errors." And indeed, if there was a joint Prado-Spinoza affair, as is commonly believed—and the above description fits Spinoza too—then it is implausible that the writer had only Prado in mind. Kaplan (*From Christianity to Judaism*, p. 132) argues that in 1663 Spinoza's philosophy was not yet known to Orobio; but in order to refer to Spinoza as the subject of great scandal and heresy, and as one who gained recognition outside Judaism, one need not be familiar with his mature thought. The very memory of the scandal, the trauma and harshly worded herem of 1656, are more than sufficient. It is rather the overlooking of Spinoza that must seem strange. In addition, Spinoza's philosophical ideas were no secret by 1663. The *Short Treatise* and the *Treatise on the Intellect* were surely written no later than 1661, as was, in all probability, the first version of book 1 of the *Ethics*; and Spinoza's metaphysical texts started circulating and being discussed among a small group of Christian friends, as we know from his correspondence with Oldenburg (Letters 7, 13) and Simon de Vries (Letters 8–9), and from remarks in the *Short Treatise*. This in itself indicates the recognition and following he had outside Judaism, as does the publication in 1663 of his *Principles of Cartesian Philosophy* with the appended *Metaphysical Thoughts* (1663). Kaplan doubts whether Orobio had time to read these works before writing the *Epistola Invectiva*; but Orobio did not have to actually study Spinoza's works in order to be aware of his scholarly recognition, or of the general tenor of his "scandalous" ideas. Moreover, as Gebhardt reminds his readers ("Juan de Prado," p. 291), the Jewish community already possessed the no longer extant apology Spinoza had composed to defend himself during the *herem* proceedings. Gebhardt's other arguments, too, make it highly improbable that Orobio should write a description that fits Spinoza even more than Prado (who did not have such impressive recognition outside Judaism), and yet have in mind only Prado and not Spinoza at all, when their cases and scandal were so tightly linked. It is therefore impossible to decide with certainty which version to accept, the one with *uno* or the one with *este*; the latter does shed doubt on Gebhardt's early assurance, but is far from deciding the question.

62. In his *Carta Apologética* to Prado, Orobio speaks of Piñero as "the cursed and detestable Pinheyro" (*el maldito y detestable Pinheyro*); see p. 879 in Revah's publication of this text (*Spinoza et Prado*, p. 132).

63. "Hebreo de nacion, primero Christiano, despues Judio, despues ni Judio, ni Christiano, hombre de cortissimo juizio, poco Philosopho, y menos Medico, loco en su discurrir, intrepido en su hablar, amigo de novedades, solicitador de paradoxas, y lo peor abominabile en sus costumbres" (Gebhardt, "Juan de Prado," p. 285n.).

64. See Revah, *Annuaire du Collège de France* (1972), pp. 643–44.

65. From folio 407 of *Livro dos Acordos da Naçam* A[nn]o 5398–5440 (see also my reference to the text of Spinoza's ban, beginning of chap. 1), first transcribed by Carl Gebhardt (*Chronicon Spinozanum* 3: 273) and later published by Revah in *Spinoza et Prado*, Documents, p. 57. The English translation is mine.

66. *Spinoza et Prado*, Documents, p. 59.

67. For a while, the congregation extended financial help to the banned Prado by the intermediacy of his wife; but the latter soon died ("Origines de la rupture," p. 389).

68. *Spinoza et Prado*, Documents, p. 59.

69. Latin was, of course, the scholarly language of the time, and it could be presumed that the young man, Spinoza, studied it in order to read scientific and secular works, thus risking skepticism and heresy.

70. "Origines de la rupture," Documents et textes, pp. 394–95.

71. Especially by R. Popkin, who quotes a letter by a Quaker working in Holland, reporting his meeting with a Jew (possibly Spinoza), and a second letter, also mentioning a Jew, who had agreed to translate into Hebrew a pamphlet by the Quaker leader Margaret Fell. Popkin identifies the two Jews and concludes that Spinoza did the translation; but there is no evidence for this identification. (Spinoza, incidentally, did not know English). However, if the Jew mentioned in the first letter was Spinoza (and this is probable), then we have a record of the ties he had with the Quakers, as with other Protestant radical sects. For Popkin's hypothesis, see Richard Popkin and Michael A. Signer, *Spinoza's Earliest Publication?* (Assen: Van Gorcum, 1987).

72. *Spinoza et Prado*, Documents, p. 64.

73. In fact, Spinoza was by then a little over twenty-six, and Prado about forty years old.

74. See "Origines de la rupture," Documents et textes, pp. 384ff.

75. The exact date of the ban has been, however, a matter of debate. See A. Kasher and S. Biderman, "When was Spinoza Banned?" *Studia Rosenthaliana* 12 (1978): 108–10.

76. R. Popkin, "The Marrano Theology of Isaac La Peyrère," *Studi Internazionali di Filosofia* 5 (1973): 97. Popkin's long work and many papers on La Peyrère have recently led to a book-size study: *Isaac La Peyrère 1596–1676* (Leiden: Brill, 1987). For other works on La Peyrère see Miriam Yardeni, "La religion de la Peyrère et *Le Rappel des Juifs*," *Revue d'Histoire et de Philosophie religieuse* 51 (1971): 245–59; Hans Joachim Schoeps, "Der Praeadamit Isaak de la Peyrère," *Der Weg* 51 (1947): 5–6; Ira Robinson, "Isaac de la Peyrère and the Recall of the Jews," *Jewish Social Studies* 40 (1978): 117–30.

77. S. Pines, "The Renewal of the Jewish State According to Ibn-Caspi and Spinoza," *Iyyun, A Hebrew Philosophical Quarterly* 14–15 (1963–1964): 289–317.

78. At one point Orobio speaks in the same breath against "Pre-Adamites, atheists and Theologico-Politicists," thus combining all three into a single group. (See Kaplan, *From Christianity to Judaism*, p. 118).

79. See e.g., his paper "Spinoza and La Peyrère" in *The Southwestern Journal of Philosophy* 8 (1977): 177–95, in which Popkin states: "I suggest that he [La Peyrère] was a major source of the development of Spinoza's religious scepticism and helped to force Spinoza to find a nontheological base for his theory of God" (p. 182). I have expressed my criticism of this view in talks with Professor Popkin and in my paper (in French) "Marranisme et dissidence: Spinoza et quelques prédécesseur," *Cahiers Spinoza* 3 (1979–80): 67–99, see especially pp. 92–98. Recently, in his book-length study, *Isaac La Peyrère* (Leiden: Brill, 1987), Popkin has revised his position and now sees La Peyrère's relation to Spinoza as more reciprocal and mediated by the cultural milieu. (Incidentally, Popkin also modified his earlier insistence on ancestry, which in the seventies he had regarded as established; see, e.g., his "The Pre-Adamite Theory in the Renaissance" in Edward P. Mahoney (ed.), *Philosophy and Humanism* [Leiden: Brill, 1976], p. 65.)

80. The experience of Marranism has expressed itself in a plurality of modes—including devout Catholicism in Iberia. Even in the narrower type of New Jewish experience we have been analyzing, there is no sense in speaking of a cultural structure or a former Marrano "ideal type" existing in and of itself, independently of the variety of singular cases in which it was expressed. Nor is there any singular case that can be held as pradigmatic of the Marrano or the New Jewish state, as if embodying the whole universal structure in its singularity. At the same time, we must avoid a purely nominalistic approach, as if we encounter but atomic and disconnected items (persons, acts, biographies), with no unifying general structure beyond them. On the contrary, we cannot properly understand these cases without perceiving a universal structure by which their particular meaning and destiny is at least partly constituted, and which in turn is constituted by their diversity.

81. *The Philosophy of Spinoza* (Cambridge, Mass.: Harvard University Press, 1948).

CHAPTER 4

1. The terms *conversos, Marranos,* and *New Christians* are sometimes given special definitions, which prove to be imprecise. To simplify I shall use all of them in the same general sense, to denote Iberian Christians of Jewish descent of any generation, whether they were sincere Catholics or hidden Judaizers. When required, I shall add such qualifiers as "*Judaizing* Marrano" or "*first-generation* converso" or "*former* Marrano" (for Marranos returning officially to Judaism).

2. *La Celestina,* in its full name: *Comedia* (in later versions *Tragicomedia*) *de Calisto y Melibea* (*The Comedy/Tragi-comedy of Calisto and Melibea*). *La Celestina* appears in various editions. I used G. D. Trotter and M. Criado de Val (eds.), *Tragicomedia de Calixto y Melibea* (Madrid: CSIS, 1958, 1970). The English quotations are based upon the English translation of L. B. Simpson, *The Celestina* (Berkeley, Los Angeles, London: University of California Press, 1971).

Incidentally, Simpson's edition contains only the sixteen-act version of *La Celestina*. For the publication history, see note 7.

3. E.g., Lesley B. Simpson, in the preface to his English translation of *La Celestina*. W. Byron in *Cervantes: A Biography* (New York: Doubleday, 1978), p. 19, says that *La Celestina* "ranked just behind *Don Quixote* as the period's most brilliant prose masterpiece." See also M. Bataillon, *"La Célestine" selon Fernando de Rojas* (Paris: Didier, 1961), p. 13; and Stephen Gilman, *The Spain of Fernando de Rojas* (Princeton, N.J.: Princeton University Press, 1972), p. 357, who compares Rojas to Shakespeare.

4. L. B. Simpson, *Celestina*. Gerald Brenan calls it "one of the most vivid and splendid creations of all literature" (*The Literature of the Spanish People* [Cambridge, England: Cambridge University Press, 1951], p. 133); The *Diccionario de Literatura Española* (Madrid: Ediciones Boris Bureba, 1949) attaches to it "an extraordinary importance in the history of [Spanish] national art" (p. 121); the editors of the French edition, Haldas and Herrera Petere see it as a "strange and genial work," "the source of all the Spanish Threatre" and also of the picaresque literary genre, Spain's unique contribution to world literature (*Sommets de la littérature espagnole* [Lausanne: Editions rencontre, 1961], pp. 12, 14, 15); whereas to Brennan it is the first European novel. Menéndez y Pelayo, too, includes it in his *Orígenes de la Novela* (Santander, 1947). To McPheeters it is "the greatest modern story of star-crossed lovers before Romeo and Juliet" ("The Present Status of *Celestina* Studies," *Symposium* 12 [1958]: 196–205).

5. See Americo Castro, *La realidad historica de España* (Mexico: Editorial Porrua, 1954), pp. 18, 536, 537. Castro's dictum is also quoted by Gilman as the theme of *The Spain*. Castro, one of the most important and controversial Hispanists of this century, has dealt with *La Celestina* from early on, starting with an essay on "El problema histórico de la *La Celestina*" (in his *Santa Teresa y otros ensayos*, Madrid, 1929), through various references and discussions in his other works, to *La Celestina como contienda literaria* (Madrid: Revista de Occidente, 1965). His views have greatly changed over the decades, and in his mature thought he regards the birth of the modern drama and novel in the Spanish "tragic sentiment of life" and the special group or "caste" of "Hispano-Jewry" represented by the conversos, whose sense of life *La Celestina* is supposed to have expressed. Castro makes this assessment part of a speculative, global picture of Spanish history, culture, and national characteristics—indeed of a whole metaphysics and metahistory—which one need not endorse in order to recognize the traits of the converso experience in *La Celestina*. These traits can (and should) be identified wherever this is called for by the particular text and context—without thereby accepting Castro's ambitious generalizations. Uncovering the converso layer of *La Celestina* is thus logically independent of Castro's historiosophy. (See also note 34 below.)

6. María Rosa Lida de Malkiel, *La originalidad artística de "La Celestina"* (Buenos Aires: Eudeba, 1963).

7. It was first published in Burgos in 1499, a quarter-century after the invention of print had penetrated Spain (Barcelona, 1475). The first edition appeared

in Burgos anonymously; it was called a comedy and had sixteen acts. After several other editions had appeared (mainly Toledo, 1500; Seville, 1501), an enlarged version was published (Salamanca, 1502); the work was now called a "tragi-comedy" and five more acts were added, bringing the total number of acts to twenty-one. Between the two versions, in the second edition of the sixteen-act "comedy," Rojas added verses in acrostics revealing his name and birthplace. He also added a "letter from the author to his friend" in which he claimed (whether he did so in earnest or as a matter of literary stratagem is still a subject of debate) to have found the text of the first act which he then "completed" during a fortnight. There were other, more doubtful editions of *La Celestina*, among them Medina del Campo (1499) and Seville (1500). Some scholars date the alleged 1502 editions of the twenty-one act tragi-comedy much later. On the whole issue of *La Celestina* editions, consult the study by Clara L. Penney, *The Book Called "Celestina,"* in the Library of the Hispanic Society of America (New York: Hispanic Society, 1954). The modern Spanish editors of the work, G. D. Trotter and M. Criado de Val (Madrid, 1958; henceforth Trotter-Criado) divided the various editions into three groups: (1) the first Burgos edition of 1499; (2) the "comedy" editions of Toledo and Seville (1500–1501); and (3) the twenty-one-act versions. I shall follow this division. (Incidentally, the twenty-one-act edition once appeared in Seville also under the title of *The Book of Calisto and Melibea and the Old Whore Celestina.*) Simpson did not translate the additional acts since they seemed to him inferior—a curious policy.

8. Thus according to Haldas and Herrera Petere (p. 14); Simpson (*Celestina*, p. v) gives the number as eighty by the end of the sixteenth century (and 119 by the middle of the twentieth century). He adds that by the middle of the sixteenth century, eighteen Italian editions had appeared, and fourteen French editions were issued by the end of that century. The Latin edition was published in Frankfurt in 1624 by Gaspard Barthias. The Hebrew translation, now lost, was made before 1527 by the Renaissance Hebrew poet Yosef ben Shmuel Sarfati. The translation itself is no longer extant, but Cassuto published the opening poem, in which Sarfati apologizes for introducing such daring novelties into Hebrew as the art of the theater and, especially, a morally dubious subject; and he, too, defends himself by saying his intention was moral education—just as Rojas himself had claimed. The sincerity of both men may well have been the same. Sarfati, in any case, is certainly interested in the secular artistic values of the work. For moral education there were better-known methods in Jewish tradition. See M. D. Cassuto, "The First Comedy in Hebrew," *Jewish Studies in Memory of George A. Kohut* (New York, 1935), pp. 121–28. (Gilman [*The Spain*, p. 366n.] quotes this essay by its English title, given in the book's table of contents as "The First *Hebrew* Comedy"; but its title actually reads "The First Comedy *in* Hebrew"; Sarfati, indeed, only translated Rojas.)

9. I hope to include an analysis of the seduction scene in an expanded essay on *La Celestina*, to be published separately.

10. Rojas himself seems to hint at this excess in a moment of self-irony.

11. Manuel Serrano y Sanz, "Noticias biográficas de Fernando de Rojas, autor de *La Celestina* y del impresor Juan de Lucena," *Revista de Archivos, Bibliotecas y Museos* 6 (1902): 245ff. These documents are complemented by others, published by Valle Lersundi, probably a descendent of Rojas; see Fernando del Valle Lersundi, "Documentos referentes a Fernando de Rojas," *Revista de Filología Española* 12 (1925): 385–96; idem., "Testamento de Fernando de Rojas," *Revista de Filología Española* 16 (1929): 367–88. These documents are part of the Valle Lersundi archive which Gilman (in *The Spain*) has investigated in more depth.

12. Americo Castro, for one, has emphasized this. At times, however, Castro overrates this fact, or is too liberal in admitting evidence for it; he also uses it to construct a whole metaphysics of Spanish history, based upon the notion of the three "castes" and on ideas inspired by German philosophers of history, like Dilthey. In particular, he adopts and evolves such notions as a "consciousness of belonging" and "collective sense of life." One need not, however, subscribe to Castro's global schemes for his essential claim to remain insightful. (See also note 34 below.)

13. Alvaro visited the Jewish tabernacles in order—so he claimed—to have a good time with the Jews; see Serrano y Sanz, "Noticias biográficas," p. 267. This testimony seems credible: occasional participation in Jewish holiday rites, just like eating Jewish traditional food, had for many conversos the significance of preserving an old identity rather than of a strict observation of a religious law. Compare the case of Pedro de la Caballería, a descendent of a distinguished Jewish family which had converted to Catholicism in the fifteenth century: he had occupied high government posts and had written a polemical book against Judaism, yet was accused by the Inquisition of having frequented the Jews in secret while in the country, enjoying their company and traditional Jewish dishes. (See Y. Baer, *A History of the Jews in Christian Spain*, 2 vols. [Philadelphia: Jewish Publication Society of America, 1961], 2: 276–77, and the references given in the notes there.) The link to Judaism consisted in this case not of religious belief but of a cultural nostalgia, in which food played an important role. A similar nostalgic trait can be found today among Israeli Jews of different origins, and especially among secularized or nonobservant Jews who nevertheless tend to eat traditional dishes on holidays, even using them as a link to tradition and as a kind of substitute for its religious dimension. The role of food as a carrier of cultural continuity is attested, of course, in other ethnic and religious groups as well.

14. See Serrano y Sanz, "Noticias biográficas," p. 262; Gilman, *The Spain*, p. 77. In this case, however, it seems that the Inquisition did not confiscate all of Alvaro's property, for he was able to grant his daughter, Rojas's wife, a handsome dowry.

15. The documents concerning this case were first published by Narciso de Esténaga ("Sobre el Bachiller Hernando de Rojas y otros varones toledanos del mismi apellido," *Boletín de la Real Academia de Bellas Artes y Ciencias Históricas*

de Toledo 4 [1923]: 78–91). A fuller account and analysis is offered in Stephen Gilman and Ramón Gonzálvez, "The Family of Fernando de Rojas," *Romanische Forschungen* 78 (1966): 255–90; see also appendix 3 to Gilman, *The Spain*. See also *The Spain*, pp. 45ff., for fuller quotations and Gilman's defense of the acceptance of the fiscal's statement.

16. Gilman, *The Spain*, pp. 45–46.

17. Ibid., pp. 211–12. The list was published by Francisco Cantera Burgos and P. León Tello, *Judaizantes del arzobispado de Toledo habilitados por la Inquisición en 1495 y 1497* (Madrid: Universidad Complutense, 1969). Gilman adds that *minores* meant "under 25 years."

18. The evidence concerning Rojas's father is extremely vague, and Gilman himself admits that his identity will probably never be decided with certainty. There are two possibilities—either Garcí González Ponce de León, of Puebla de Montalbán, or Hernando de Rojas of Toledo, who was burned by the Inquisition. If we opt for the latter, we run into the difficulty of explaining why the acrostic declared Rojas to be a native of Puebla de Montalbán when his father lived in Toledo. (For similar skepticism see Antonio Marquez, *Literatura e Inquisicion en España 1478–1834* [Madrid: Taurus, 1980], p. 47.) As for Rojas's mother, Gilman's speculation gives her the same name as Rojas's wife, Leonor Alvarez (the daughter of Alvaro de Montalbán), and includes Rojas himself as a minor son. All were supposed to have been condemned and fined by the Inquisition in or around 1497 (see previous note). This brilliant but unfounded speculation would make Rojas condemned by the Holy Office, along with his mother and brothers, shortly before *La Celestina* was published. Would he dare publish it or reveal his true name within a few years? Rojas was by then a student living in Salamanca. Would he appear in an Inquisition list in Toledo—and not by his own name, but still as an unnamed "minor son" of his mother? It hardly stands to reason that the condemned Leonor Alvarez was Rojas's mother; she may have been a complete stranger to him (the name, as Gilman himself admits, was common).

19. Similar cases are known from later periods as well; cf. the clandestine links of Juan de Prado, especially with Baltazar de Orobio, but also with other converso friends (including Juan Piñero), as described in chapter 3 on the basis of Revah's documents.

20. For the hypothesis about reading aloud, see Philip Ward (ed.), *The Oxford Companion to Spanish Literature* (Oxford: Clarendon Press, 1978), p. 112.

21. A partial reconstruction of Salamanca's intellectual and university life is given by Gilman, *The Spain*, chap. 6.

22. The converso ancestry of Miguel de Cervantes, stressed by Americo Castro and others, is not, however, conclusively established. For a good survey of the problem, see William Byron, *Cervantes: A Biography* (New York: Doubleday, 1978), pp. 24–32, whose conclusion tends toward Cervantes' Jewish ancestry but leaves the question unsettled.

23. We may be excused for doubting this statement; *La Celestina*, even the sixteen-act version—even if we accept Rojas's other doubtful statement, that

act 1 (the most daring theologically) has been written by some anonymous hand and only "found" by him—is much too rich, complex, and long to make such a claim plausible. At the same time, there are known cases in which a literary masterpiece was written in one short outburst (Pirandello, for instance, wrote both *Six Characters in Search of an Author* and *Henri IV* in a sequence of a few weeks; Balzac, and, very possibly, Shakespeare worked very fast).

24. EL/BACHJLER/FERNANDO/DE/ROIAS/ACABO/LA/COMEDIA/DE/CALYSTO/Y/MELYVEA/Y/FVE/NASCJDO/EN/LA/PVEVLA/DE/MONTALVAN. (In other editions the spelling is slightly different.)

25. See chapter 2, note 7.

26. Serrano y Sanz, "Noticias biográficas," pp. 251–52; Gilman, *The Spain*, p. 469.

27. Serrano y Sanz, "Noticias biográficas," p. 272; I use Gilman's translations (*The Spain*, pp. 82–83; 88). The original Alvaro quotations read: "*Acá toviese yo bien, que allá no sé si ay nada*"; "*lo de acá vemos, que lo de allá no sabemos qué es.*"

28. There is nothing to indicate that Alvaro went out of his way to point out his family ties with Rojas, as Otis Green suggests in "La Celestina and the Inquisition," *Hispanic Review* 15 (1947): 211–16.

29. Serrano y Sanz, "Noticias biográficas," pp. 263, 269. It seems that the remark about Rojas being a converso is made by the clerk (and not by Alvaro), as a comment on the old man's statement and as an explanation of why "his grace" rejected the request. Having suspected that this is the case, I found corroboration in Antonio Marquez (*Literatura e Inquisición en España 1478–1834*, [Madrid: Taurus, 1980], p. 47), who says that anyone familiar with inquisitorial records of that period will see that the remark is made by the clerk. Marquez, however, goes on to argue that this puts in doubt Rojas's converso status, a conclusion that does not follow. Even if the statement that Rojas was a converso came from the inquisitorial clerk and not from Alvaro (why, indeed, should the old man stress this unfavorable fact?), there is no reason to suppose, as Marquez does, that this was *un rumor posiblemente sin fundamento*. It might well have been an established fact, which the Inquisition took notice of and therefore, indeed, found Rojas "suspect" as a lawyer in cases of heresy. Later (p. 209), when analyzing *La Celestina*, Marquez does not follow through on his doubt.

30. The will was published by Valle Lersundi (see note 11).

31. *A History of the Jews in Christian Spain*, 2: 276–77; 317–18.

32. Serrano y Sanz, "Noticias biográficas," pp. 252–55; Gilman, *The Spain*, pp. 467–68.

33. Serrano y Sanz, "Noticias biográficas," pp. 252–53.

34. Controversies about the meaning of *La Celestina* fall within two major divisions: (1) Should it be taken as a moralizing work, as Rojas pretends in his prefatory comments, or as wearing the masks of equivocation, irony, and so

on? (2) Does it have an important converso-related aspect? On the first issue I shall argue against a moralistic reading of the work and for recognizing the elements of mask and equivocation as essential ingredients in it, indeed as literary and artistic values in themselves. I shall claim that Rojas's equivocal mask applies (and, to the initiated, is meant to be recognized as such) on the meta-level as well, that is, even with regard to his first-order claims in the prefatory verses: they are the *first* to be read equivocally. On the second issue, I shall stress the importance of a converso-related aspect of *La Celestina*, and even make it the theme of this chapter; but I am far from regarding it as *the* central aspect of the work, as a magic clue to its ensemble of meanings, and from Americo Castro's far-reaching historiographic and metaphysical claims about Spain, cultural history, or the semimetaphysical relation between ethnic groups and their "sense of life." As I see it, the converso link of *La Celestina* is only one of its rich and multiple layers, but one that deserves attention and study for itself. I do not share Castro's view of the work as representing the collective consciousness of the conversos as an ethnic group or caste, or as containing the "tragic sense of life" which Castro maintains is essential to the group as such. Nor do I endorse the metaphysics of culture in Castro. Americo Castro was provocative, illuminating, and highly speculative; he was also, I think, too liberal in admitting evidence that seemed to corroborate his theses. But because of the polemic he caused, some of his opponents tended to deny his views wholesale, which is equally unjustified. To a newcomer in the field, unfamiliar with all the emotional and ideological stakes, it sometimes seems that ideas are linked more by association than by logical derivation. There is no logical necessity connecting the statement that *La Celestina*, as one of its significant layers, reflects the experience of Marranism (especially the wavering between two religions and/or the need to play a game of masks and the split between the inner and the outer)—and Americo Castro's metaphysics of culture. Either can be held (or rejected) on independent logical grounds.

A good example of the package approach to this issue is given in Antonio Marquez' critique of Castro's views of *La Celestina*. Most of the critical points are well taken, yet the conclusion is not; for Marquez tends to create an unnecessary dichotomy: either accept Castro wholesale or deny the converso relevance of *La Celestina*. But the converso relevance of *La Celestina* does not reside either in its alleged reflection of the sense of life of the conversos as a caste, or in the actual pressure its author suffered from the Inquisition (this is the theme of Marquez' book, and on this issue his analysis of Rojas is convincing), but in the experience of Marranism, with its two aspects—the confusion of both religions and the play of masks between inner and outer. That this was part of the substance of many conversos' lives, in the milieu from which Rojas sprang, is undeniable; and to investigate its effects in *La Celestina* means neither that it becomes the exclusive clue to this work nor that it must be accompanied by global historiosophic views.

35. Even the decipherable material will have to be represented only in part,

because of space. The full study on which this chapter is based will be published separately.

36. It also recurs in the mouth of Melibea, who explicitly calls Celestina "the mediator of my salvation" (*aquella medianera de mi salud*) (act 10, opening monologue). (The English translator missed the point in rendering this phrase as "my blessed mediator.")

37. See Baer, *History of the Jews*, 2: 280–81. The document was published by H. Pflaum in *Revue des Etudes Juives* 86 (1928): 144–50.

38. Gilman holds that Rojas's allusion in fact has Deza for its target (*The Spain*, p. 274).

39. Matthew 5:10: "Blessed are they which are persecuted for righteousness' sake, for theirs is the kingdom of heaven." The same verse from Matthew, with a similar ironic twist, recurs later in the well-known picaresque novel *Guzman of Alfarache*, where Guzman reports about his origin and about his father, convicted of theft. The author, Mateo Aleman (himself a converso), may have taken this from *La Celestina* or the joke may have become prevalent.

40. The talk about "false witnesses" is made to emphasize another feature of the Inquisition which, beside prosecuting actual Judaizers, also accused innocent people who were the victims of false denunciation.

41. If Rojas's father indeed was burned by the Inquisition, as Gilman supposes—on insufficient evidence—then it would add a particularly dramatic edge to this quote. But even if not, it still is one of the more sincere instances of conversation in the play, even if expressed under the protective shield of "the talk of a prostitute." A similar example is given by Areusa's attack on the Spanish social order and values in act 9. In both cases, once we strip the outer shell of "a prostitute's talk," the text itself becomes direct and sincere, without inner games, irony, equivocation, and the like.

42. This equivocation is so apparent that the English edition (Simpson) had each voice printed in different type.

43. The same hypocritical righteousness recurs in Sempronio in act 9, at Celestina's banquet. The old woman tells how the priests used to worship her, and Sempronio puts on a face of shocked righteousness: "You frighten us with these things . . . they were not all like that!" (Simpson, p. 110, trans. revised).

44. The break to which I am referring here is not between sentences and utterances (the act of saying them), but between ritual and authentic utterances. The unit that becomes a kind of "truth in itself" is the very utterance (also the gesture, the ritual, etc.), not the sentence or the sign by which it is performed. The act of saying the sentence (or performing the gesture) takes on an alienated character. The utterance is inauthentic: it is an imitation of itself (performing an act in an external manner, without subjective involvement and while distancing itself from its meaning) and as such it is being attributed meaning and validity.

45. See S. Serrano Poncela, *El secreto de Melibea* (Madrid: Taurus, 1959); also *The Oxford Companion to Spanish Literature*, p. 112.

46. Here I concur with Brenan who said "there are no signs of Rojas having any religious belief" (*Literature of the Spanish People*, pp. 137–38). With some

modifications, I also accept José Antonio Maravall's talk of the "secularización y mundanización" reigning in the world of *La Celestina* (*El mundo social de "La Celestina"* [Madrid: Editorial Gredos, 1964], p. 132).

47. Sempronio has a recognized status in the play as a knave and rascal. This is not the first time he clowns in this way (cf. the quoted passage from the banquet at Celestina's). This crucial point was missed by Ciriaco Morón Arroyo, a disciple of Otis Green, who tried to give a Christian-moralistic interpretation to *La Celestina* and used Sempronio's clowning words to prove there is a Christian reply in the play to Calisto's heresies (see his *Sentido y forma de La Celestina* [Madrid: Ediciones Catedra, 1974], p. 67).

48. This sentence is possibly an interpolation.

49. At the same time, Celestina's other denomination as "witch" does conform in a sense with Rojas's view of love, for eros, though a natural phenomenon, is seen in *La Celestina* as having a dark, magical side.

50. The dual character of love is referred to also in Celestina's conversation with Melibea in act 10, after Melibea has been more or less seduced. The girl asks: "What do they call this sickness of mine that has so penetrated into every part of my being?" Celestina: "It's called sweet love." Melibea: "Is it so? It makes me happy merely to hear it." Celestina: "Love is a hidden fire . . . a savory poison, a sweet bitterness . . . a joyous torture, a grateful and cruel wound, a gentle death." Melibea: "Alas, poor wretch that I am! If what you say is true, my salvation is doubtful. For because of the contrariness between all these names, what will profit one will cause suffering to the other" (Simpson, p. 118).

51. In this respect, despite the obvious aesthetic differences, there is a similarity between Pleberio's relation to his daughter and Calisto's relation to his lover. For each of them, even if in different modes, the mental relation to this particular figure in the world (Melibea) exhausts the meaning of life and existence at large; this idea in Calisto goes so far as to make him pronounce the heretical words we quoted, and it also expresses itself in Pleberio's final lament. Neither of them has any transcendent substitute for the earthly sense of life, embodied for each of them in Melibea.

52. Otis Green said that the major sin of Calisto and Melibea consists in having broken the codes of courtly love. But they have not thereby arrived at romantic love. Their love is fundamentally a kind of obsessive passion, working like an external constraint. Green's interpretation of *La Celestina* in terms of its relation to courtly love is summed up in *Spain and the Western Tradition* 4 vols. (Madison: University of Wisconsin Press, 1963), 1: 111–19. See also his "The *Celestina* and the Inquisition," *Hispanic Review* 15 (1947): 211–16; and "Fernando de Rojas, *converso* and *hidalgo*, ibid., pp. 384–87.

53. A similar picture of love emerges from a somewhat enigmatic prologue which Rojas later appended to his work. It speaks of love as a war of opposites, an ancient Heraclitean idea which Rojas corroborates by allusions to later writers. The universe is the totality of being; it is a conflict of opposites—a war of all against all—with all the forces being extreme and excessive. "Everything in

nature fights against everything else, and all against us"—thus Rojas paraphrases Petrarch, and explains: "Summer overwhelms us with its excessive heat and winter with its cold and frost; and what are these reversals of climate . . . if not war?" The forces of nature are opposite extremes marked by exaggerated excess, and as such clashing with other excessive forces. This is a Heraclitean war of opposites, yet without the logos and the inherent harmony which governs them in Heraclitus; and the genuine, and most outstanding illustration of that harmony, is the force of love.

54. Gilman, *The Spain*, p. 379.

55. To conclude, let me mention more critics who stress the nonreligious and antimoralistic reading of the text: Ángel del Rio, in *Historia de la Literatura española* (New York: 1963), says that in *La Celestina*, man "seems to be moving in a Godless world." And Frank Casa, in "Pleberius's Lament for Melibeu" (*Zeitschrift für Romanische Philologie* LXXXIV (1968): 19–29 argues against the moralist reading of the text, which is not intended to express Christian morality but to reflect man's tragic existence in conflict with far more potent forces. From both critics, a sense of comic loneliness emerges, which I have linked to the Marrano experience.

CHAPTER 5

1. I use this term in a slightly broader sense than in *Ethics*, pt. 3, prop. 17S, where it is defined as opposition between two contrary emotions. Such opposition—as between love and hatred, joy and sorrow, fear and hope, and their derivatives—is not to be understood as just one emotional state among others, but as the underlying structure of the emotional life of the person of the imagination. As such, the fluctuation of the mind is the most characteristic trait of the multitude, from which most of its other irrational and destructive outbursts derive.

The centrality of this unstable mental state to Spinoza's theory, as the major mental disturbance to be overcome by reason, is also indicated by the opening pages of the *Treatise on the Intellect*, where Spinoza's philosophical program is laid out. (Incidentally, a play by Spinoza's tutor, Frans (Franciscus) Van den Enden, in which Spinoza may even have acted, dealt with the fluctuation of the mind as a theme; I learned this from Mr. Bedjai in Paris, at a meeting of the Association des Amis de Spinoza.)

2. Spinoza did not devote much reflection to the general question of the relation of words to their ideas. He seems to view words as independent designators, which in proper strings and contexts may invoke their designated ideas in precise and adequate ways, and which can moreover be translated from one linguistic system (say, a natural language) into another without losing this function. His declaration that he is interested in the nature of things rather than the meaning of words, may imply a belief that words are neutral vehicles that can be dissociated from their ideas and therefore discounted. Ideas, on the other hand, cannot be dissociated from their objects because the two are on-

tologically the same, and the order and connection of ideas is the same as that of things.

3. There is some understatement in Spinoza's saying that the term he chooses must not "contradict" his new interpretation: this condition should not be construed as sufficient (most words in the dictionary will pass this test) but as an added condition, the first condition being, as stated, that the term has a natural or historical link to the matter under consideration.

4. See chapter 2.

5. That Spinoza succeeds in doing this on the basis of an anti-allegorical method of interpretation is almost a tour de force. Although he is scientific and predominantly literal in his approach to concrete issues in the biblical text, Spinoza reverts to tacit a priori generalizations (motivated by his strategic aims) when declaring that nothing in the Bible contradicts reason or claiming that the Bible teaches nothing except justice and mutual help as practical precepts.

6. It seems surprising that on this occasion Spinoza undercuts his own metaphor by making its rational translation immediately explicit; but at least he gives us here, even if inadvertently or by implication, a statement of his usual rules of the game.

7. Only the seventh principle, that God forgives the sins of the repentent, seems impossible to translate into philosophical language and to reconcile with Spinoza's rejection of guilt and remorse. But we should remember that this rejection applies to the rational person, whereas the "articles of faith" are formulated for the multitude, which should remain affected by guilt no less than by fear and by respect for authority if a semirational pattern is to govern its conduct (and thus benefit or "save" it). Also, Spinoza's "articles of faith" can be translated into philosophical truths only in their general metaphoric outline, not in all the details which accompany them. This is why I spoke above of a "particularly heavy theological idiom."

8. See vol. 2, chap. 6.

9. Spinoza capitalizes here on an equivocation in the concept of "having a right to x." This concept can be construed as meaning that there is no law or norm prohibiting me to do or to possess x. But why is there no such norm? Two totally different reasons can be given: (1) we live in a state of nature where no law exists and hence no norm can have meaning; (2) we live in a legal system which does not prohibit me to do or to possess x. Only the second answer can make Spinozistic sense of the concept of right, which presupposes the existence of a political state and its enforceable legislation. Yet Spinoza uses "right" also in the first context where strictly speaking it cannot yet have any sense. Why? One plausible answer is that Spinoza tries to capitalize on the edifying resonance which the word *right* invokes in his audience (because of the latter's false beliefs) in order to facilitate the ushering in of something very different, indeed, his own naturalistic revolution of the concept of norm. In addition, as the positive halo of the term *right* radiates over the notion of nat-

ural power, nature and all things natural are further highlighted as expressions of the divine. (Here we connect again with the theological context.)

10. I disregard here (without taking a stand on it) the argument known as "the intentional fallacy" because in this case we *do* inquire about the author's relation to his text. Our interest here is historical rather than purely literary.

11. Maimonides had also undergone a Marrano-like experience under the intolerant Almohades, who had forced Jews and Christians to convert to Islam. Maimonides either did so in fact (insincerely) or at least behaved as if he did and let others believe so; see A. L. Ivry in S. Pines and Y. Yovel (eds.), *Maimonides and Philosophy* (Nijhoff, 1986), pp. 139–42.

12. In terms of this book, Strauss (who did not insist on Spinoza's Marrano roots as I do here), overemphasized one Marrano trait in Spinoza, prudential language, while failing to do justice to another, the alternative route to salvation. Yet the latter, as I argue, showed itself even in the use and function of dual language itself. Recognizing Spinoza as a Marrano of Reason will add further dimensions and more restraint to Strauss's thesis without contradicting its core.

Chapter 6

1. The example of the proportion is at best a partial analogy that illustrates the intuitive and synoptic qualities of the third kind of knowledge (its working *uno intuito*—at a single glance) but misses some of the most essential ones. Above all, it is incompatible with the definition of the third kind of knowledge given twice in the *Ethics* (pt. 2, prop. 40, S2; pt. 5, prop. 25 dem.). Knowledge in the example does not "proceed from the essence of some attribute of God" but is gained directly by a particular intuition. Moreover, intuitive knowledge is said to occur spontaneously in Spinoza's early thought, whereas his mature theory insists that it must arise from the second kind of knowledge (pt. 5, prop. 28 & dem.). Furthermore, the rarity and extreme difficulty inherent in the third kind of knowledge is incompatible with the commonplace kind of intuition to which the example refers.

The example illustrates a shortcut scientific cognition which, bypassing deduction, provides a direct grasp analogous to that of axioms. But this in itself does not go beyond the boundaries of *ratio*. A mathematical genius capable of compressing a great many deductive steps into a single intuition will not thereby be in possession of the third kind of knowledge or enjoy a higher moral and metaphysical standpoint than his less talented colleagues, though he will certainly be a far superior scientist.

2. See Jonathan Bennett, *A Study of Spinoza's Ethics* (Cambridge: Cambridge University Press, 1984), pp. 357, 364–75. Bennett dismisses the last section of the *Ethics* in such fierce language (it is an "unmitigated . . . disaster," "nonsense," "rubbish which causes others to write rubbish," and such a scholar as Pollock, who takes it seriously ends up "babbling" and producing "valueless" material), that his dismissal becomes self-refuting: how can so much negative emotion be spent on something that does not matter? It is, however, Bennett's

own book (which otherwise offers interesting and sometimes illuminating microanalyses that comes out the loser; for what it misses is not merely one chapter in Spinoza but a significant perspective from which to understand the whole. This flaw could have been avoided if Spinoza's aims about religion, the transformation of religious language and religious emotions, and ultimately his search for an alternative way to salvation, had been taken into account. Bennett might then have used the argument he elsewhere borrows from Kripke (p. 366) and say that Spinoza (or Christianity, or Judaism, or this and that mystic or theologian) may well be speaking about the same thing, salvation, and participating in a meaningful (and to them, supremely important) discussion, even if some or all of them hold wrong theories about it. In any event, this is a case in which the historical context—Spinoza's Marrano background—could have helped in recognizing the importance which the issue of salvation has taken in Spinoza's systematic work *throughout*.

3. I mean *objectively* interiorized, that is, turned into a representation of what is the thing's internal essence.

4. This picture represents a change from the *Treatise on the Intellect* where external causality is assigned a significantly lesser role. This change, raising the epistemic level of mechanical causation, parallels another: abolishing the immediacy of the third kind of knowledge and making it depend upon the products of *ratio*.

5. Incidentally, the idea that the universe has a "face" or humanlike features, was certainly known to Spinoza from Jewish *Cabbalah*, where the universe is mystically structured on the lines of "primordial man" (*adam kadmon*). In accepting the metaphor Spinoza rejects its anthropomorphic implications: the only "face" the universe has is the network of logical and mechanistic laws, without the slightest shred of teleology or any other humanlike feature.

6. The attributes allow of no interaction, whereas the third kind of knowledge issues from the second as a necessary prerequisite. Also, officially no attribute is superior to the other, yet vertical knowledge through essence is supposed to give a deeper view than the horizontal mechanistic one.

7. Viewing natural laws as God's "immutable decrees" allows us to further develop this metaphor, even beyond Spinoza. To allow for sound natural science which is liable to change, as today we conceive of it, a moderate Spinozist might say that the laws of nature are the fixed divine constitution which each scientific era interprets in its own way, subject to the ruling scientific paradigm; just as in religious tradition, the Bible is considered as God's immutable constitution which later generations are authorized to interpret in their own manner. This is not Spinoza's position, but may be compatible with it.

8. When speaking of a "generative definition," Spinoza gives a technical or constructive example, taken from geometry; but what he is groping for is metaphysical generation. The authentic definition (essence) of a thing is equivalent to, and reached by, the network of causes by which it is generated. I see this intuition accompanying Spinoza from early on to the climax of the *Ethics*. Equally, when he says in the *Treatise on the Intellect* that things are known either

by their essence or by their proximate causes, he creates the disjunction that later will turn into an equivalence.

9. "Being of essence is nothing but that manner in which created things are comprehended in the attributes of God" (*Metaphysical Thoughts*, Eng. 304). (Here the terms are defined to suit both tradition and Spinoza's innovation.) Essences have being "outside the intellect." Every such formal essence has an idea by which it is "contained objectively" (represented) in God's idea. (Later Spinoza will more accurately locate it in God's infinite intellect.) Formal essences exist even if the thing of which they are the essence does not (see *Ethics*, pt. 2, prop. 8: this is because the essence of particulars does not involve existence). They neither exist of themselves nor are created, but "depend on the divine essence alone" (in which everything is contained, including the essences of nonexisting things—*Ethics*, ibid.). "So in this sense," Spinoza adds, "we agree with those who say that the essences of things are eternal."

10. That "which, being given, the thing is necessarily posited and which, being taken away, the thing is necessarily taken away" can be construed both as a logical essence and as a mechanistic process (or set of processes) which, conforming to the laws of nature, is a necessary and sufficient condition for the generation of the specific thing in question.

11. It is interesting to figure out how Spinoza would handle the phenomenon of unsettling philosophical truths. While his system abounds in them, it also states the principle that truth is the source of joy, not of suffering. There must be a moment of suffering in dispelling metaphysical illusion—which also explains the stubborn resistance it provokes. Freud, a disciple of Spinoza in many ways, knew this and accounted for it; so did Nietzsche. Spinoza lacks a theory explaining the mechanism of passage from comforting illusion to (at first) disquieting truth, but his theory, I think, can accommodate one. (In fact, in the opening of the *Treatise on the Intellect*, Spinoza describes such a passage.)

12. See vol. 2, chaps. 2, 5.

13. Given the same body of scientific knowledge, there are three ways of relating to it. First, a positivist, or a scientist uninterested in metaphysics, will try to avoid metaphysical interpretation altogether (though Spinoza will still attribute some metaphysical framework to him or her, possibly derived from the imagination). Second, a philosopher-scientist may interpret the same body of knowledge according to Spinoza's metaphysics but remain on the level of ordinary rationality, with its linear arguments and lawlike explanations, understanding the relation of substance, attribute, mode, law, and the like (or mind and body, emotion and cognition) in the same discursive way that governs empirical science and is expounded in the "geometrical" layout of the *Ethics*. Finally, in the third kind of knowledge the same things acquire a new, or higher interpretation when, through their particular essences, they are grasped as they are in God and God too is grasped only in and through them. This adds new insight and a higher metaphysical interpretation to our knowledge of empirical particulars—and it also forces us to understand Spinoza's own metaphysics differently, since the preceding books of the *Ethics* are now

grasped from the standpoint of book 5. In other words, metaphysical truths, too, are liberated from their linear layout and grasped as the mutual system of ideas in which they actually exist. This new organization, or synthesis, of the same ingredients of knowledge allows a deeper look into the texture of reality and the emotional response corresponding to it.

14. Or in the infinite intellect. Spinoza distinguishes here (pt. 2, prop. 8) between ideas and essences. Essences are immutable entities existing logically and contained in the attribute. Ideas represent these essences and depend upon their state. An essence which has no duration is represented as such, and an essence which does enter duration (or exists in that mode) is also represented as such. It follows that, on the theory implied in pt. 2, prop. 8, essences are immutable but ideas are not.

Since ideas are the same as their objects, they must represent the fact that their object exists in duration or is merely a logical essence. But essences do not represent this difference within themselves. They are indifferent to existence: this is what distinguishes them from ideas.

Yet this theory cannot really work. It breaks down, I think, because it cannot sustain the parallelism between logical and mechanical particularization. If the sum total of transitive causes by which a thing is determined to exist and operate defines its uniqueness in being, and if this is supposed to be equivalent to its essence, then it cannot be that one of the equivalents (the first) includes the parameters of duration and the second (the essence) does not; for in this case they are not equivalents. Spinoza must either include durational parameters in the essence, or omit them from the causal explication, or else abandon the equivalence. He does not want to do the latter and he cannot, by definition, do the second; so it remains for him to include durational parameters in the essence and to do away with the distinction between essence and idea. And although this may raise problems for him elsewhere, I think it would be his most coherent solution.

15. As Spinoza says explicitly in pt. 5, prop. 23, dem. "we do not attribute duration to it [the mind] except while the body endures." But then, his famous sentence, "it is time now to pass to those things which pertain to the mind's *duration* without relation to the body" (pt. 5, prop. 20), is clearly incoherent or intentionally misleading. In Spinoza's thought, the mind has duration while the body endures, and when the mind overcomes its finitude it gains a kind of eternity, not indefinite duration.

16. This is the difference between timelessness (eternity in Spinoza) and immortality. Immortality means indefinite existence *within time*. Moreover, it means indefinite life, since immortality can be attributed only to entities to which mortality, too, is logically attributable. In Spinozistic terms, the semantics of mortality and immortality can only apply to entities in the domain of duration and external causes.

This also distinguishes immortality from sempiternity. The laws of nature (and the infinite mode they depend upon) are sempiternal; belonging to *natura naturata* they determine its everlasting lawlike structure. And like most intermediary stages they occupy a problematic post, for they have (infinite) duration but are not themselves determined by external causes. Given the example of infinite modes, we may conclude that eternal essences are also, in their way, sempiternal, for at any moment in time they can be said to exist—however timelessly. Whatever the solution to this paradox (if it is a paradox), the sempiternal status applies to these essences regardless of whether their objects have entered the actual world of duration and external causality. But once they do, once an existing concrete thing expresses the essence in a definite time and place, it cannot sustain this existence indefinitely but, engendered by external causes which translate the essence horizontally, and resisting, as *conatus*, as long as it can the assault of other external causes, it must eventually, by its ontological mode of being, succumb at a certain point and cease to exist in duration. At that point all that remains—or rather, is—of it is the eternal essence.

17. Of course, a particular essence, because it defines the individual's unique place in being, can and must include its life history or career; but it expresses this from the standpoint of eternity, as a timeless implication of God (and one ontological "spot" in the eternal map of being).

CHAPTER 7

1. Only Hegel returned to it, though he was less radical and confrontational.

2. For a list of Jewish deep structures that persisted in Spinoza's self-image, see below.

3. See chapter 1 of *Theologio-Political Treatise*. In preferring Jesus, Spinoza does not express his own view as a philosopher but what he claims to be the Bible's position. At the same time, attributing to the Bible a preference for Jesus when addressing a Christian audience clearly has a rhetorical purpose.

4. Evidence for this can be found in Spinoza's correspondence with Henry Oldenburg concerning Jesus. Oldenburg (Letter 71 of Nov. 15 1675) quotes some Christian believers who charge that Spinoza conceals his views about Jesus and the incarnation. Oldenburg's letter provoked an energetic response from Spinoza, with an open statement (Letter 73). Of those who say that God had assumed human nature Spinoza says he had already stated that he does not understand what they say, adding that their words are as nonsensical as saying that a circle assumed the nature of a square. He goes on to say that Christians, too, must admit Jesus not in the flesh but metaphorically. The term *God's eternal Son* means God's eternal wisdom, which is present in all things (thus Spinoza equates it with the infinite intellect—as he had already done explicitly in *The Short Treatise*, chapter 9). Jesus in the flesh, the historical figure, was a man only, albeit an exceptional philosopher who discovered rational truth and the man in whom divine wisdom is largely manifest. This is Spinoza's interpretation of the preference given to Jesus by the Scriptures.

5. A similar approach evolved in the Babylonian exile. The experience of a separate Jewish existence in Babylon preceded Rabbi Yokhanan and the destruction of the second temple. The Talmud, too, which contains the results

of these efforts, is known throughout Judaism mostly in its Babylonian version.

6. J. P. Sartre, *Anti-Semite and Jew*, tr. George J. Becker (New York: Schocken, 1974).

7. Y. H. Yerushalmi, "Spinoza's Words on the Survival of the Jewish People," *Proceedings of the Israel Academy of Sciences and Humanities* (Heb.) (Jerusalem, 1984) 6: 176–78.

8. Y. F. Baer, *Galut* (New York: Schocken, 1947), p. 104; see also Yerushalmi, "Spinoza's Words," pp. 181f.

9. Yerushalmi, "Spinoza's Words," p. 182. The purity-of-blood statutes had appeared as early as 1449 (in Toledo, during a riot), but for a long time they had only local effect and were strongly disputed on theological grounds. These statutes became the law of the land only under Philip II over a century later; henceforth they became so important that the Inquisition used them to pry into a person's remote ancestry whenever he became a candidate for important office, to make sure no "impure blood" had penetrated the veins of his grandmother's great-uncle. This custom prevailed not just in Spain but also—perhaps primarily—in Portugal, a fact Spinoza disregards and which made him subject to criticism.

10. In any case even after correcting the picture that Spinoza draws, the following thesis (which also relies on what is known today) deserves to be maintained: the Inquisition and the anticonverso policies not only annihilated many pockets of Judaizing conversos, but at the same time also reinforced their separate existence. This was due to the identification of the conversos not simply as "New Christians" but also directly as "Jews" (especially in Portugal); and by strengthening their inner solidarity as a result of persecutions.

11. This may include Spinoza's implicit explanation of how nations exist in general. According to Spinoza's ontology only individuals are real. "Universals" are unreal abstractions, or mere "names." Yet this nominalism does not prevent the laws of nature (of psychosocial nature, in this case) from producing a network of causes that will make the image, the fate, and the life circumstances of a certain group of individuals change and evolve in a parallel and mutual way, so as to provide a nominalist-naturalistic explanation of the existence of nations. The "nation" as such will not be an actual individual, but using the category of "nation" will be significant and even necessary in explaining an individual's fate and situation.

12. From a linguistic and literary point of view, Spinoza writes as if he were giving actual testimony. Nor does he say "I *heard* of one" but "I knew . . . one" (or "of one"). Associating hearsay with actual knowledge is particularly curious in the case of Spinoza, who had relegated hearsay (*ex auditio*) to a lower kind of knowledge that does not constitute knowledge proper. Also, Spinoza's confusion of "faithful" with "believer" through their Hebrew translations testifies that on this issue his mind was full of conflicting associations and powerful but imprecise connections.

13. Yerushalmi, "Spinoza's Words," pp. 187, 189. Incidentally, Spinoza bor-

rows these factors from Tacitus, who in speaking of the Jews referred both to the "hatred of the nations" and to their "stubborn superstition" which explains their heroic resistance in the siege of Jerusalem. (Spinoza quotes him in the present text.) On Tacitus's influence on Spinoza see Chaim Wirszubski, "Spinoza's Debt to Tacitus," *Scripta Hierosolymitana* (Jerusalem, 1955), 2: 176–86.

14. Therefore, saying that the Jews will "raise up their empire afresh" and that "God may a second time elect them" has precisely the same meaning and their conjunction constitutes a pleonasm.

15. G. Scholem, *Sabbatai Sevi* (Princeton: Princeton University Press, 1973), pp. 518f.

16. This indicates the millennarian atmosphere in England itself, as it prevailed in Oldenburg's circle. Serrarius, who served as go-between carrying messages from Oldenburg to Spinoza, was himself a millennarian believer in the Messiah. If despite these connections Oldenburg turned to Spinoza for information, he must have assumed—not without ground—that Spinoza was well aware of the issue and maintained contacts among Amsterdam Jews.

17. Strictly speaking, Spinoza's ontology does not allow for the concept of possibility, since in itself everything is either necessary or impossible. But ignorance of causes makes us use the notion of possibility as a relative epistemological indication (referring to our state of knowledge rather than to the things' ontic modality). This is a practical necessity for humans, especially in predicting the behavior of others or the turn of historical tides.

18. This is how Spinoza's own words about *historia sacra* are to be understood. Spinoza is speaking rhetorically from the standpoint of his audience, and not in his own name. On Spinoza's abolishing sacred history in general see Shlomo Pines, "Joseph Ibn Kaspi's and Spinoza's Opinion on the Probability of a Restoration of the Jewish State," *Iyyun* 14 (1963/64): 289–317; English abstract pp. 367–69.

19. Heinrich Heine, "Zur Geschichte der Religion und Philosophie in Deutschland," *Sämtliche Werke*, 14 vols. (München: Kindler, 1964), 9: 210.

20. One may even conjecture that Spinoza's philosophical system was seen by him as evolving from the true Jewish tradition. In a letter to Oldenburg he attributes to Paul (and to other ancient thinkers) a pantheistic view according to which God is the immanent cause of nature; all creatures "live and move and exist in God." This view has been abandoned or falsified by later Christian theologians (whom Spinoza calls "New Christians"—perhaps an intended irony). But Spinoza maintains that his immanent philosophy agrees with Paul, perhaps with all the ancient (pagan) philosophers, and, "I dare even say I thereby agree with all (!) the ancient Hebrews" though their traditions have been falsified (by later-day Jews and Christians alike, so he seems to imply). Spinoza's identification with the ancient Hebrews is much more pronounced than with the pagan philosophers—and he has no rhetorical need to evoke the Jews. On the contrary, Spinoza seems to apologize to his Christian audience that he relies here on Jewish ideas. Maybe he mentions them to show that Jew, pagan, and Christian concur in this idea—which is a sign of its universal truth.

Spinoza is writing this letter with some emotional tension—and therefore with less prudence than usual. To Oldenburg's challenge (see note 4) he responds by voicing a much sharper criticism of Christianity than he would normally permit himself. And in this context he sees fit to identify himself strongly with the "ancient Hebrews" and to suggest that his philosophy upholds their message—that is, he, Spinoza, carries on the *true* Jewish message!

21. Alexandre Matheron calls this "the sacralization of the political domain through the politization of the sacred"; see A. Matheron, *Le Christ et le salut des ignorants* (Paris: Aubier-Montaigne, 1971), pp. 14ff.

22. A variant of this position claims that for Judaism to carry a universal "mission" for humanity at large it must, while modernizing, persist eternally in its particular features. This view started in nineteenth-century Germany, and its spread has accompanied the Jewish *Aufklärung*—the *haskala*.

23. The measure in which Prado's challenge to the community defied all accepted categories can be gauged by comparing it to the contemporary position of Father Daniel Rufeisen, a Jew who converted to Catholicism during the Nazi genocide while feeling deep solidarity with his persecuted people. Emigrating to Israel after the war he declared himself a Catholic Jew—Catholic by religion and Jew by nation—and claimed Israeli citizenship based upon the Law of Return (which stipulates that every Jew can become a citizen of Israel). In refusing his demand (he became a citizen by another procedure) the Israeli Supreme Court wisely implied that the strange character of such demands is not absolute but relative to the historical time and conditions (i.e., eventually it may change). Another contemporary case is that of Cardinal Lustiger, also a Jewish convert during the Nazi genocide, who, when he was appointed Archbishop of Paris, declared he had never ceased to be a Jew and was, as a Christian, proud to belong to this ancient people. One must not draw too close an analogy between being a "secular Jew" and a "Christian Jew." Yet the strange character of each idea in its time does suggest a parallelism. No one can predict whether the notion of a "Protestant Jew" or a "Catholic Jew" will some day be as accepted and prevalent as "secular Jew" is today (at least in Israel). Decision in such matters is neither theoretical nor doctrinal but historical; theoretical categories will accompany the real historical situation and the consciousness that rises out of it.

24. Thanks are due to Mr. J. S. Hirsch, the former curator of the Rare Books Collection (which houses the "Spinozaeum") at Haifa University Library, who gave me a photocopy of this letter as well as of other holdings in this collection.

Index